Singapore Comparative Literature Compendium

Balestier Academic
Balestier Press Europe Ltd, Centurion House, London TW18 4AX
www.balestier.com

First published in 2021 by Balestier Academic

A CIP catalogue record for this book is available from the British Library.

ISBN 978 1 913891 30 5

Singapore Comparative Literature Compendium

Edited by

Sim Wai Chew and Yow Cheun Hoe

BALESTIER ACADEMIC
LONDON · SINGAPORE

CONTENTS

Multiculturalism and Minority Concerns

Travel, Regionalism, and Global SG

Genre, Experimental and Speculative Fiction

EDITORS

Sim Wai Chew is an associate professor at Nanyang Technological University. His academic specialisations include comparative literature, postcolonial literature and theory, and translingual literature and theory. His works include *Kazuo Ishiguro* (published by Routledge in 2010), *British-Asian Fiction* (published by Mellen in 2007) and *Island Voices: A Collection of Short Stories from Singapore* (published by Learners in 2007). He also recently published an English translation of Chia Joo Ming's sinophone novel *Exile or Pursuit* (放逐与追逐) (published in 2019 by Balestier Press). His research has appeared in the journals *Textual Practice, Journal of Commonwealth Literature, CLCWeb Comparative Literature and Culture*, and *Sun Yat-sen Journal of Humanities.*

Yow Cheun Hoe is an associate professor at Nanyang Technological University, where he is the head of the Chinese programme, Director of the Chinese Heritage Centre, and Director of the Centre for Chinese Language and Culture. He is a chief editor for *Huaren Yanjiu Guoji Xuebao* (International Journal of Diasporic Chinese Studies) and book review editor for *Journal of Chinese Overseas.* His academic specialisations include Chinese migration and diaspora, qiaoxiang (Overseas Chinese homeland) ties, and diasporic Chinese literature. His books include *Xinjiapo yu Zhongguo xin yimin* (New Chinese Migrants in Singapore: A Question of Citizenship) (published by the City University of Hong Kong Press in 2021); *Yimin guiji he lisan lunshu: Xin Ma huaren zuqun de chongceng mailuo* (Migration Trajectories and Diasporic Discourses: Multiples Contexts of Ethnic Chinese in Singapore and Malaysia) (published by Shanghai Sanlian Shudian in 2014), and *Guangdong and Chinese Diaspora: The Changing Landscape of Qiaoxiang* (published by Routledge in 2013). His articles have appeared in the *Journal of Contemporary China, Modern Asian Studies, Asian Ethnicity, Cross-Cultural Studies, Changjiang Xueshu, and Waiguo Wenxue Yanjiu.*

ACKNOWLEDGEMENTS

The editors would like to thank the following individuals for their assistance in the publication of this compendium. Without their help a publication of this nature would be simply impossible.

We are deeply grateful to Dr Seah Cheng Ta and project officer Winnie Sim Jin Yu for their incredible focus and diligence during the course of the project. Another shout out goes to Hidayah Amin for her help with translation, and to Gerald Teng Yi Shee and Lim Ding Xun for their many many sterling efforts. Thanks are also due to Eunice Lim Ying Ci, Long Chao, Zeng Yajun, Luka Zhang Lei, Koo Wen Hui, Khairul Azri Bin Uthli, Amelia Choo Shu Xian, Li Meiyin, Lim Xin Hwee, Nursarah Binte Safari, Raja Syazana Khairunnas Binte Raja Emran, Dhanya Lingesh, Nur Sorfina Binte Ibrahim, Nurul Asyikin Binte Yusoff, Nur Izzati Binte Mohamed, Freda Peh, Ina Isabela Venegas Esteban, and other student and staff assistants who contributed to our project and its associated activities including the series of talks that we organised in 2021 under the "Singapore Comparative Literature Lecture Series" rubric. We would also like to thank Balestier Press for believing in our project and for working with us.

Lastly, we would also like to express our deep gratitude to Ms Joyce Tan Wee Ngar of the research office who always offered excellent advice and patiently guided us whenever we needed help with various amendment and variation requests.

This research/project is supported by the Ministry of Education, Singapore, under its Academic Research Fund Tier 1 (RG74/17(NS)).

NOTES FROM THE EDITORS

By Sim Wai Chew and Yow Cheun Hoe

Code-switching and code-mixing are unremarkable aspects of everyday life in Singapore. Among the reasons for its prevalence, the republic pursues an "English Plus" bilingualism policy (Caravallo and Ng), with English operating as the main medium of instruction in schools and supplementary instruction given in a second language dubbed the "mother tongue," one that, according to commonly accepted doxa, provides cultural ballast and moral direction. Remarkably however—or perhaps because of such a fact-value distinction—cultural discussion in Singapore tends to take place in separate language-denominated silos with critics focusing on works in their "own" tongue even as English translations of vernacular works have proliferated in recent years. Within each silo, the intrication of consensus and dissensus that gives rise to disciplinary knowledge appears lively and vibrant. Nevertheless, dialogue or discussion across the different language divides is limited and arguably wanting; the dominant view seems to be that the republic's languages are engaged in a "zero-sum game where increased knowledge or use of one…. [will come] at the expense of some other" (L. Wee 205).[1] In the short run, such insularity may not be impactful, but over time, we believe, the living of, so to speak, "parallel lives" by intellectuals and opinion-makers will enervate public discourse in any formation.

The present compendium is meant to redress this lacuna, to encourage inter-ethnic, inter-lingual, and inter-cultural transfer through the established methodology of comparative literature, a discipline that studies cultural expression across language and cultural divides. While its Eurocentric ambit has elicited finger-wagging in recent times (Spivak), the modes of discovery of comparative literature are arguably pertinent to the nuances and complexities of the Singapore experience, given that it has "an ideology of inclusion of the Other" (Tötösy de Zepetnek 13). As stated on the home page of the *American*

1 Exceptions include Bernards (2016), Sim (2013, 2017, 2020), and Zhang (2020). Bernards compares works by Suchen Christine Lim and Chia Joo Ming. Sim compares works by Goh Poh Seng and Yeng Pway Ngon (2013), Claire Tham and Xi Dan (2017), and Vyvyane Loh and Chia Joo Ming (2020). Zhang compares the works of Tan Kok Seng, Chong Han, and Md Sharif Uddin.

Comparative Literature Association, comparative literature is concerned in the largest sense with "promot[ing] the study of intercultural relations that cross national boundaries, multicultural relations within a particular society, and the interactions between literature and other forms of human activity including the arts, the sciences, philosophy, and cultural artifacts of all kinds." The authors of the present volume certainly hope that it will encourage analysis and debate, that it will help to break down the mentioned barriers and foster the development of new directions in Singapore studies.

To give one example of how a comparative approach can be illuminating, the "education and language policy" section of the compendium (one of eight) itemize a range of aesthetic responses to the seminal development of the seventies and eighties when vernacular schools were incorporated into a national system. Among its entries is *A Man Like Me* (一个像我这样的男人) (Yige Xiang Wo Zheyang de Nanren), a novella by Yeng Pway Ngon, the doyen of Singapore Sinophone writing. Published in 1987 and now acknowledged as a local classic, *A Man Like Me* spotlights the difficulties encountered by individuals educated in the Chinese-medium schools that flourished prior to the mentioned historical shift. Other writers who explore this trope include Teoh Hee La and Zhang Hui (both featured in the section), and indeed, linguistic-cultural displacement is one of the major foci of Sinophone writing in Singapore. While some may see this emphasis as parochial and isolationist (as the mainstream narrative has it), comparison of these works with another novel featured in the section, namely Mohamed Latiff Mohamed's *Confrontation* (original title: *Batas Langit*) immediately gives pause to the notion, for one also finds in the last an implied author engaging in what Freud calls the work of mourning. Among its concerns, *Confrontation / Batas Langit* laments the enfeeblement of Sino-Malay hybrid ("peranakan") culture in Singapore following its ejection from Malaysia in 1965. This riff is symbolised in the text by an adopted child of Chinese parentage who is fiercely loved by her adoptive Malay mother even though she is developmentally challenged. Taken together, then, these works may not be so much adamantine espousals of particularism as perhaps a critique of the (re)invention of particularism to serve narrow statist objectives, to promote an ideology of hyper-developmentalism operating under the guise of "Asian" values (C. Wee). If so, this would dovetail with the critique of philistinism that we can find running like a thread through all of Yeng's writing (Sim 2013).

Apart from "education and language policy," the compendium features the following seven sections: politics and history; gender, sexuality, and patriarchy; growing up, ageing, mortality; new migrants; multiculturalism and minority concerns; regionalism, travel and global SG, and lastly, genre, experimental and speculative fiction. It should be stressed that this arrangement is not meant to be exhaustive or critically authoritative. We merely aim to engage some burning social issues of the day, and address specifically *aesthetic* concerns in the case of the last category. Organized like this, the compendium no doubt invites comparison between works put into the same category, as the above illustrative example suggests, but other organizational rubrics are of course feasible and to be encouraged.

In the area of working-class writing, for instance, a juxtaposition of Tan Kok Seng, an acknowledged pioneer of anglophone writing in Singapore, and the relatively unknown sinophone writer Chong Han is arguably illuminating. In a recent article doing just that, Zhang (2020) is able to draw a line of descent between these two authors and recent migrant-worker writing, in particular that of Md Sharif Uddin, whose works, originally composed in Bengali and published in English, have received a warm welcome in the republic. This concatenation can arguably be extended to include writers (e.g., Jiu Dan) who delineate the experiences of individuals caught up in Singapore's demi-monde world. Apart from Md Sharif, the other mentioned authors are all featured in the compendium, but in different categories. The entry on Tan Kok Seng's *Son of Singapore* states that its subtitle is "The Autobiography of a Coolie." The entry on Chong Han's work, *Pulau Tekong Love*, details the experiences of outer islanders who practice agricultural and plantation lifeways; it mentions protagonists who move to mainland Singapore to enter apprenticeship arrangements, and others having to do "multiple jobs" to get by. On its part, the entry on Jiu Dan's work, *Crows*, tells us that it delineates, among other things, the experiences of sex workers. While the entries are slotted into the above-named areas, we are hopeful that their individual perusal will generate new constellations, insights, and points of entry into the cultural archive.

For each entry, we provide some basic publication information, a separate note on characterization, and also one on "significance and remarks." We also provide a brief synopsis and give some suggestions for comparative analysis work. We draw mainly on contemporary literature, with a focus on novels, novellas, short stories, and documentary fiction, the one exception being *Growing Up Perempuan*, a collection of testimonies and essays published in association with the Association of Women for Action and Research. The entries appear in both English and Chinese. Our original intention was to publish in English, Chinese, and Malay. Some work was done on the last but for funding and practicality reasons, we eventually decided to publish in a two-language format. Readers who wish to consult an (in-progress) Malay-language version of the compendium should contact the authors.

The working languages of the compendium project are English, Chinese, and Malay—so in the case of the one work that originally appeared in Tamil and then in English translation, viz., Singai Ma Elangkannan's *Flowers at Dawn*, we relied solely on the English translation. For entries on works originally composed in Chinese and Malay, we relied mainly on the original-language editions. Among the vernacular writing entries, several of the sinophone works and one work composed in Malay, viz., Isa Kamari's *Selendang Sukma*, have not been translated into other languages. Hampered as we are by our range of working languages, we were not able to cover works appearing in all *four* of Singapore's official languages. This limitation will hopefully be tackled by future research and collaboration.

As can be readily perceived, the compendium is not comprehensive in its coverage of literary genres. And rather than strive for an all-embracing list of "must know" writers, we chose notable ones as well as some lesser-known writers, example being, Chong Han, as mentioned earlier. Even within the ambit of prose fiction, other selection criteria, weightage, and parameters can obviously be deployed. But the point is that we make no claim to comprehensiveness. What merits repeating is our wish to encourage movement beyond the ascriptive parameters that organise cultural discussion in Singapore, some of which, it should be noted, have a century-long colonial provenance (Chua). If this compendium helps to alter entrenched orientations and habitus, then we will feel that we have done our job.

绪论

沈伟赳、游俊豪

语码转换与语码混用，是新加坡日常生活的常见现象。其在诸多方面盛行的原因，是基于新加坡共和国奉行“英语+”的双语政策 (Caravallo & Ng)，即英语作为学校的主要教学媒介，而被称为“母语”的第二语言作为补充教学。一般观点认为，第二语文的作用是提供文化基石与道德指导。值得注意的是，也许因为这样的事实与价值的区分 (fact-value distinction)，新加坡的文化讨论往往在各别语言体系中进行。即使近年来英译本不断增加，评论家大多专注于他们“自己”语言的作品。在每个单独系统内，学科知识产生的共识与异议，可说错综复杂，生动并具有活力。然而，跨越不同语言鸿沟的对话或讨论非常有限，甚至是匮乏的。主流观点似乎是，新加坡的语言正在进行一场 “零和博弈，掌握或使用一种语言知识……将以牺牲其他语言为代价”(L. Wee 205)。[2] 这种隔绝，短期内可能不会产生影响，但随着时间的推移，我们相信，知识分子和舆论引导者的所谓“平行生活”(parallel lives)，会使得公共话语的发展失去活力。

为了填补这方面的不足，本汇编通过比较文学的研究方法，跨越语言和文化鸿沟，尝试克服文化表达的既定方法，鼓励种族之间、语言之间、文化之间的交流。尽管它的欧洲中心意识最近在学界遭受指责 (Spivak)，但比较文学的探索模式适用于新加坡人经验的细微与复杂性，因为它有“包容他者的意识形态”(Tötösy de Zepetnek 13)。正如美国比较文学协会的主页所说，比较文学的最大意义在于“促进跨越国界的文化间关系、特定社会中的多元文化关系、文学与其他形式的人类活动 (包括艺术、科学、哲学与各种文化艺术品) 之间的互动的研究”。本书的主编希望它能鼓励更多研究和讨论，打破上文提到的阻碍，促进新加坡研究往新方向发展。

在此，举例说明比较研究如何具有启发性。本汇编中，“教育和语言政策”部分 (八大部分之一) 的作品对70年代和80年代各种中文源流学校被纳入国家体系的开创性发展，作出了回应。其中一项条目，是新加坡华语写作大师英培安的长篇小说《一个像我这样的男人》。此小说在1987年出

2 当然也有例外，包括Bernards (2016), Sim (2013, 2017, 2020), and Zhang (2020). Bernards 对Suchen Christine Lim 与谢裕民进行了比较研究。Sim 对 Goh Poh Seng 与英培安 (2013), Claire Tham 与 喜蛋 (2017), Vyvyane Loh 和谢裕民 (2020) 做了比较研究. Zhang 对Tan Kok Seng, 崇汉, Md Sharif Uddin 进行了比较研究。

版，现被公认为本土经典之作。故事聚焦于在那些在1980年代之前繁荣的华文学校中接受教育的人们，揭示他们在教育政策转变后所经历的种种困难。探讨同一命题的作家还有张曦娜和张挥（两人都列在这一部分）。事实上，语言与文化的迁徙(linguistic-cultural displacement) 是新加坡华语写作的主要焦点之一。虽然评论者可能把它视为个狭隘与孤立的比较(正如主流叙述所述)，但如果与本部分中其他语文的小说，即Mohamed Latiff Mohamed的*Confrontation*（对抗）(原名*Batas Langit*) 进行对比，上述看法很快就会改变。在“对抗”的结尾里，读者会发现作者隐含弗洛伊德的“哀悼”(mourning) 概念。在其关注的问题当中，“对抗”哀叹1965年新加坡被逐出马来西亚后，土生华人文化在衰落。这篇小说讲述了一个具有象征性意义的被收养的华族小孩。她虽然有发育障碍，但她的马来养母还是对她深爱有加。综合来看，这些不同语系的作品可能不是特殊主义的坚决拥护，而是批判狭隘的国家主义目标，在“亚洲 ”价值观下的发展主义所作出的（再）发明（C. Wee）。与此类似，我们也可以发现英培安所有作品贯穿了对庸俗主义的批判（Sim 2013）。

除了“教育和语言政策”之外，本汇编还有七个部分，即“政治与历史”、“性别、性向、父权制”、“成长、年龄歧视、死亡”、“新移民”、“多元文化与少数族群问题”、“区域主义”、“旅行与全球SG”、“实验与推想小说”。应强调的是，此安排并不详尽无遗，也不意味是最具批判性的权威。我们的目的只是为了解决当今一些紧迫的社会问题，以及在最后一部分“实验与推想小说”里进行美学讨论。这样的编排方式就像上面举例所表明的那样，试图促进同一类别的作品之间的比较。当然，其他的组织编排方法也可行，并值得鼓励。

例如，在工人阶级文学领域，将新加坡英语写作先驱 Tan Kok Seng（陈国盛），对比不知名的华语作家崇汉，可以带来启发作用。在最近的一篇论文中，Zhang Lei (2020) 把这两位作家和近期的外来劳工写作联系起来。例如， Md Sharif Uddin的作品以孟加拉语创作，后来以英语出版，在新加坡受到了热烈欢迎。这种联系具有扩展潜能，包括那些描述新加坡风月场经历的作家（例如：九丹）。除了Md Sharif Uddin，该文还提到的其他作家都被收录在本汇编不同的类别中。陈国盛的 ***Son of Singapore***（新加坡仔）的条目，副标题是 “The Autobiography of a Coolie” 《一个苦力的自传》。崇汉的作品揭示有关农人的生活、新加坡外岛人的经历，也呈现了迁移到新加坡做学徒的主人公，以及其他不得不做“多种工作 ”维持生计的人。九丹的作品的条目，还描述了性工作者的经历。我们希望通过对这些作品的逐一阅读，为文化档案提供新的联系、见解，与切入点。

在每个作品条目中，我们提供一些基本的出版信息、作品特征与“意义和评论”的阐述。我们还提供简明的梗概，给出一些比较分析研究的建议。我们主要取材于当代文学作品，重点是长篇小说、中短篇小说、纪实小说。唯一的例外是 ***Growing Up Perempuan*** (女性成长)，这是一本与妇女行动与研究协会 (Association of Women for Action and Research) 联合出版的个人陈述和散文集。所有条目皆中英双语列出。我们最初的打算是以英文、华文、马来文出版，但在做出一番努力后，由于资金和操作性的原因最终决定先以两种语言的形式出版。读者若想查阅此汇编里面的马来语版本(正在进展中)，请与其中一位主编联系。

此汇编项目的工作语言是英语、华语和马来语。因此，对于最初以泰米尔语出版，后以英语翻译的一部作品，即 Singai Ma Elangkannan 的 ***Flowers at Dawn*** (黎明之花)，我们不得不依靠英语翻本。对于最初用华语和马来语创作的作品，我们主要依靠原文版本。有几部华语作品和一部马来文作品，即Isa Kamari的***Selendang Sukma***，目前还未被翻译成其他语言。由于我们的工作语言范围有限，我们无法涵盖以新加坡四种官方语言的作品。希望未来的研究和合作可以解决这一局限。

我们可以看出这汇编对文学体裁的覆盖并不全面。然而，我们并不追求创造一个"必知"作家的全面名单，我们既选择了一些著名的作家，也包括了一些不太知名的作家，例如前文提到的崇汉。即使在小说的范围内，显然也可以使用其他选择标准、权重和尺度。我们并不声称该汇编是全面的。要重复强调的是，我们希望鼓励超越新加坡文化讨论的既有范围，其中包括长达一个世纪的殖民地渊源 (Chua) 。如果这个汇编有助于改变根深蒂固的倾向与状态，我们的工作就已经达到目的。

参考文献
Works cited

American Comparative Literature Association, www.acla.org/. Assessed 20 Aug. 2021.

Bernards, Brian. *Writing the South Seas: Imagining the Nanyang in Chinese and Southeast Asian Postcolonial Literature*. NUS Press, 2016.

Cavallaro, Francesco, and Ng Bee Chin. "Language in Singapore: From Multilingualism to English Plus." *Challenging the Monolingual Mindset*. Eds. John Hajek and Yvette Slaughter. Multilingual Matters, 2014. 33–48.

Chua, Mui Hoong. "Categorising Singaporeans by Race: The CMIO System is 100 years old and Needs an Update." *The Straits Times* [Singapore], 16 July

2021, www.straitstimes.com/opinion/the-cmio-system-is-100-years-old-and-needs-an-update/. Assessed 20 Aug. 2021.

Sim, Wai Chew. "Becoming Other: Literary Multilingualism in the Chinese Badlands." *Textual Practice* 34.2 (2020): 235–53.

——. "Super-Diversity and Its Implications in Two Singapore Texts." *Singapore Literature and Culture: Current Directions in Local and Global Contexts*. Eds. Angelia Poon and Angus Whitehead. New York: Routledge, 2017. 181–197.

——."尼采存在主义与英培安和吴宝星的作品" ["Nietzschean Existentialism in the Work of Yeng Pway Ngon and Goh Poh Seng."] 尼采与华文文学论文集 [Nietzsche and Chinese Literature]. Ed. Chiu-yee Cheung. Singapore: World Scientific, 2013. 33–48.

Spivak, Gayatri Chakravorty. *Death of a Discipline*. Columbia UP, 2005.

Tötösy de Zepetnek, Steven. *Comparative Literature: Theory, Method, Application*. Studies in Comparative Literature, volume 18. Rodopi, 1998.

Wee, C.J.W.-L. "Capitalism and Ethnicity: Creating 'Local' Culture in Singapore." *Inter-Asia Cultural Studies* 1.1 (2000): 129–43.

Wee, Lionel. "Language Policy Mistakes in Singapore: Governance, Expertise, and the Deliberation of Language Ideologies." *International Journal of Applied Linguistics* 21.2 (2011): 202–21.

Zhang Lei, L. "Red Scare to Capitalist Showcase: Working-Class Literature from Singapore." *Working Class Literature(s): Historical and International Perspectives*, volume 2. Ed. John Lennon and Magnus Nilsson. Stockholm UP, 2020. 139–164.

POLITICS AND HISTORY

骚动 UNREST

Primay Language: Mandarin
Secondary Language: No
Translation Available: Unrest
Number of Pages: 295
Author: Yeng Pway Ngon
Year of Publication: 2002
Publisher: Elite Books
Characterisation Notes:

The characters in *Unrest* can be divided into two groups:

1. **Zi Qin and Da Ming**

Zi Qin is married to Da Ming. In his secondary school years, Da Ming is considered a "little teacher" who studies and discusses current affairs and philosophy with his classmates. Zi Qin is one of the many girls who swoon over Da Ming's talents. Both Zi Qin and Da Ming are politically active and participated in anti-colonial protests and the Hock Lee bus riots.

As a student leader, Da Ming attracted the attention of the Internal Security Agency. To evade capture, he flees to Hong Kong after telling his friends in Singapore that he intends to return to his motherland (China). Zi Qin lies to her parents that she has had sexual intercourse with Da Ming and follows the latter to Hong Kong. In Hong Kong, Da Ming founds a publishing house, and begins to print pornographic magazines due to their high profit margins. He then branches into real estate and becomes immensely wealthy. Da Ming's obsession with money alienates Zi Qin, and they part ways as strangers.

2. **Wei Kang and Guo Liang**

Wei Kang emigrates to Singapore to study at the age of 15 and is Guo Liang's classmate. In addition to their friendship, the two are lovers (Wei Kang sexually initiates Guo Liang). The two heed calls to participate in the protests and riots of the 1950s and 1960s and are eventually expelled by their school. They hide in a temple, where they shared intimate physical contact. After the political turmoil has died down, Wei Kang returns but is immediately arrested. After his release, Wei Kang returns to China, only to be embroiled in the much more terrifying and insidious cultural revolution.

Text Synopsis:

The novel begins in the 1950s. Da Ming, Zi Qin, Guo Liang, and Wei Kang are all passionate and politically active youths. They fight against colonialism and participate in protests such as the May 13 incident and the 1955 Hock Lee bus riots.

In 1956, the colonial government in Singapore exercises the Internal Security Act and arrests more than 200 political and student leaders. To evade capture, Da Ming tells his friends that he intends to return to China to further his studies. He convinces Zi Qin to leave her family behind and travel with him. The couple never returned to China and instead goes to Hong Kong where they continue to fight colonialism as "leftists."

The protests increase in violence and the extremists begin to employ explosives (some even mailed an explosive to Jin Yong, the editor of the newspaper Ming Bao). Da Ming falters and decides to preserve his life and leave the revolutionary cause. He starts a successful publishing business and soon becomes wealthy. He cheats on Zi Qin and their marriage starts to fall apart.

Wei Kang also attempts to avoid the government crackdown. He hides in a temple, where he meets Guo Liang. They grow close during their time spent copying sutras and discussing philosophy. Wei Kang decides to leave the temple and return to China a month later but is immediately arrested and detained for half a year. After his release, Wei Kang proceeds to return to China, only to find himself embroiled in the Cultural Revolution. Guo Liang remains in the temple for two months and evades capture. He eventually finds a job and starts a family.

30 years later, Guo Liang takes a commercial flight to Guangzhou to visit Wei Kang. Wei Kang passes him Zi Qin's contact, and Guo Liang meets with the latter in Hong Kong, where they have a one-night stand. At the end of the novel, Da Ming and his son moves to Vancouver, and Zi Qin reignites the theme of "unrest" by inviting Guo Liang to live with her in Hong Kong.

Significance and Remarks:

Unrest is the first Singaporean Mandarin metafiction that employs metanarration[3] that calls into question the novel's own artificiality. In addition, the narrative is non-linear and dismembered. It is only possible to understand the entire story through careful and patient reading.

The author employs numerous audacious and explicit depictions of sex in the novel (through the experiences of the four protagonists) to drive home the point that sexuality is inseparable from and intimately connected to politics. To Zi Qin and Da Ming, "sex" is instrumental to their rebellion against the control of their parents through emigration overseas. Zi Qin's parents heavily favoured her brother over her, and her hatred of her parents deepens with each passing day. Zi Qin, deprived of familial love, finds solace in Da Ming; unknown to Zi Qin, however, Da Ming wishes to merely possess Zi Qin's body. He exploits Zi Qin's love for him and her hatred for her misogynistic family to convince her to leave her family in Singapore.

30 years later, a divorced Zi Qin meets Guo Liang in Hong Kong. Guo Liang discovers that he still has feelings for Zi Qin and finds in her the love and satisfaction which denied him during his adolescence. Guo Liang does not resist Zi Qin's seduction and they have sex. The experience leaves Zi Qin conflicted and frustrated. Nevertheless, sex is also emancipatory for Zi Qin: through "sex," Zi Qin can exercise her agency to obtain pleasure, transcends the strictures of traditional marriage and morality, and exact revenge upon her husband for his infidelity. For Wei Kang, his experience of "sex" reflects the psychological trauma of his political life. Upon returning from the self-imposed exile at the temple, he immediately seeks out his girlfriend Shu Mei for sex to release his pent-up desires, stresses, and fears. Later, during his long and isolated confinement, Wei Kang sexualizes a banana: he imagines the banana skin as a woman's clothes, and slowly peels the skin off to devour the flesh within. His thirst for freedom and companionship is quenched through the sexualization of quotidian life.

Unrest is not strictly a political novel,[4] despite its intimate connection with the 1950s anti-colonialist movement in Singapore and the Chinese

3 Lin Gao, "Gudu liaowang: Ying Pei'an xiao shuo shi jie," [Vision in solitude: the literary world of Yeng Pway Ngon] (Singapore: Global Publishing, 2019), 148.

4 Ibid, p.141.

Cultural Revolution. In an interview with *Lianhe Zaobao*, Yeng Pway Ngon expresses that the actual political events of the novel are to be treated as mere backdrops that foreground the "existence of people under such political circumstances— their mind and thoughts, their hopes and dreams, desires, and disenchantment."[5]

The author draws upon the philosophical works of Martin Heidegger and Karl Jaspers to remind the reader to ponder the meaning and value of life as they read about the experiences of the novel's four protagonists. Heidegger and Jaspers are leading figures of existentialism: Heidegger proposes that human life is Being-towards-death, whereas Jaspers stresses the existential condition of social relationality for the individual. In its adolescence, "unrest" is political and external to the individual. The four young protagonists fight passionately against the colonial government to demand benefits for other students and workers. They naïvely believe that their mere existence can revolutionize society. None of the novel's four protagonists retain their original revolutionary passion in the face of their indignance towards an uncompromising reality. In reading *Unrest*, the reader must consider the following questions about existence: Have the characters actualized themselves? Have they found out the meaning of life? If we exist as being-towards-death, what can we ever actualize through our existence?

Potential areas of comparative analysis:

Political History, Sex and Sexuality, Metafiction, Philosophy, Existentialism, Feminism, Master-Slave Dialectic, Patriarchal Society, Meaning of Life

5 Zhang Xina, "Zouguo fanhua shengkai de wenxue shidai, fang bendi zuojia Ying Pei An, Sun Ai Ling yu Xie Qing," [A Walk Through the Flouring Literature Era, an interview with Yeng Pway Ngon, Soon Ai Ling and Xie Qing], *Lianhe Zaobao*, May 14, 2018.

骚动 UNREST

主要语言： 中文
次要语言： -
翻译版本： Unrest
页数： 295
作者： 英培安
出版年份： 2002
出版社： 尔雅出版社

人物简介：

《骚动》的主要人物分为以下两组：

1、子勤和达明

子勤和达明是一对夫妻。中学时期，达明帮大家温习功课、兼教哲学，为大家分析时事，是公认的"小老师"。和大部分女同学一样，子勤崇拜他的学问和才华。他们积极参与反英国殖民地的抗争游行，其中包括1955年的福利巴士工潮。身为学生领袖，达明很快就被内安局盯上。为躲避追捕，他声称将回到祖国（中国）深造，子勤为追随达明向父母谎称和他发生关系。但他们实则去了香港，达明在香港成立印务馆，高调出版盈利丰润的黄色刊物，并进军房地产。 致富后，他流连于纸醉金迷的世界，夫妻感情变质，形同陌路。

2、伟康和国良

伟康15岁时离乡背井到新加坡念书，是国良的同校同学。两人积极响应号召，参与50年代与60年代的游行工潮，后被学校开除，躲进寺庙。国良的性启蒙来自伟康，他在伟康身上找到安慰，两人有肌肤之亲，关系暧昧，既是朋友也像恋人。伟康待风平浪静后回到家乡，却被逮捕。他被释放后回到祖国（中国），却卷入更暗潮汹涌的文革斗争中。

文本概要：

上世纪五零年代，达明、子勤、国良和伟康是充满激情的少年。他们积极参与反英帝国殖民地斗争，包括向英国政府请愿免除兵役的五一三事件和1955年的福利巴士工潮。1956年，新加坡英殖民地政府援引内安法令，展开搜捕行动，一连两天逮捕了职工和学生领袖等两百余人。达明是活跃分子，为躲避内安部特务的追捕，他借口逃回祖国(中国)，并怂恿子勤抛下家人一同前往。

他们没有踏上中国一步，反而到了香港，继续以“左仔”的身份参与反殖民抗争。抗议游行愈演愈烈，激进分子四处置放炸弹，甚至将炸弹邮包寄送给《明报》社长金庸。眼看骚乱持续升级，达明心生怯意，决定明哲保身、置身事外。达明的生意蒸蒸日上，他在致富后出轨，与子勤的感情开始生变，渐行渐远。

伟康在寺庙避风头时结识了国良；两人抄经书、讨论哲学，关系愈加亲密。一个月后，伟康决定离开新加坡返回家乡，却被特务逮捕在拘留所关了半年。释放后，他决定回到祖国(中国)，却深陷中国文化革命的政治迫害之中。国良隐匿在庙里两个月，逃过一劫，在书摊找打一份工作，后娶妻生子。30年后，国良为寻找商机来到广州，并探望伟康；伟康把子勤的联系方式给了他，国良后与子勤在香港重逢，两人发生一夜情，再次燃起骚动的心。

重点与备注：

《骚动》的叙事策略和文本结构新颖独特，是新华文坛的第一部后设小说。作者采用元叙述（Metanarration）[6] 的写作方式，揭露其虚构性的叙事创作，提醒读者小说是虚构的产物。小说的呈现方式破碎，时空交错、篇幅凌乱，读者须耐心阅读，前后对照，才能将碎片化的事件拼凑，组合成完整的画面。

大胆露骨的“性”和“性欲”描绘充斥文本，透过四人的遭遇。读者可以从中理解政治和情欲的相互纠缠和关联。

对子勤和达明而言，“性”是摆脱长辈操控的工具。子勤的父母重男轻女，日复一日，子勤对父母的积怨越来越深。子勤在达明身上找到爱，但达明把子勤当作自己的工具，他利用子勤对她的爱占有她的身体，目的是从子勤母亲身边抢走她。子勤谎称已和达明发生男女

6 林高:《孤独瞭望：英培安小说世界》(新加坡：八方文化创作室，2019年), 页148。

关系，决意跟达明一起离开新加坡，展现出其反抗父母的意志。30年后，婚姻失败的子勤和国良重逢，国良对子勤的爱慕依旧，在她身上找到久违的甜蜜恋爱滋味，他无法抗拒子勤的挑逗，两人发生关系，尽管事后她为此感到纠结，但她通过“性”逃出了传统婚姻价值观的樊笼，找回主导权，也从中报复丈夫对她的不忠。伟康的情欲折射搜捕行动对他造成了心理创伤。当他回到家乡时，便急着找女朋友淑玫，透过“性”排解他高度压抑、充满恐惧的内心。他被关押在拘留所时，也把香蕉外皮想象成女人的衣服，慢慢地剥下，一口口咀嚼，希望借由它填满内心的枯寂。

虽然《骚动》描绘上世纪50年代新加坡的反殖民斗争，但它不是一部关于政治运动的小说。[7] 英培安在一次《联合早报》的采访中表示，虽然《骚动》的政治背景是真的，但只把它当作小说的时间背景，他想要写的是：“在这政治环境下人的存在；他们的思想意识、内心世界，他们的理想、欲望与幻灭。”[8]

作者引用哲学家海德格尔和雅斯培的思想，提醒读者思考生命的价值和意义。海德格和雅斯培是存在主义哲学的代表人物——前者强调，人的存在，即是趋向死亡的存在。后者则主张：人只有在与其他人有交往关系的时候，才能实现自己。 年少时，“骚动”是动荡的时局和外在的抗争。他们带着满腔热血参与反殖民抗争，为学生、工友争取福利权益。他们认为他们的存在，能推动改革、改变社会。30年后，当年的一腔热血已不复存在，只剩下看清生活本质后的无奈。他们是否实现了自我？他们是否找到了生命的意义？如果死亡是客观且必然存在的终点，那他们存在的意义是为了实现什么？

潜在的比较文学分析：

政治史、性和情欲、后设小说、哲学、存在主义、女性主义、主导/从属、父权社会、生命意义

7 同上注，页141。
8 张曦娜：《走过繁花盛开的文学时代 访本地作家英培安、孙爱玲与谢清》，《联合早报》，2018年5月14日。

FLOWERS AT DAWN

Primary Language: English
Secondary Language: No
Translation Available: Flowers at Dawn
Number of Pages: 178
Author: Singai Ma Elangkannan (pseudonym of M. Balakrishnan)
Year of Publication: 2012
Publisher: Epigram Books

Characterisation Notes:

The protagonist, Anbarasan, emigrates to Singapore from India in the 1940s. He intends to make enough money to get married with his cousin, Manimekalai, and to support his family back home. However, his plans are thwarted by the Japanese invasion of Singapore. After listening to a speech by the Indian nationalist Subhas Chandra Bose, both Anbarasan and Manimekalai decide to join the Indian National Army and fight alongside the Japanese. The war brings out their bravery, loyalty, and perseverance, and the couple emerge stronger and more willing to fight for their dreams and desires.

Text Synopsis:

Set in the years just before Singapore fell to the Japanese, *Flowers at Dawn* begins with the protagonist, Anbarasan's, boat journey to Singapore. He travels from India in the 1940s, with the intention of making his fortune and marrying his cousin, Manimekalai.

Anbarasan and his travel companion, Muthiah, are rudely introduced to racial segregation upon their arrival in Singapore. They realise that third-class passengers on the ship are required to serve a two-day quarantine on a separate island while white, upper class passengers have the liberty to disembark immediately.

Reunited with his extended family, Anbarasan soon finds himself a job with the help of his uncle, Thangavelu, and aunt, Valliammai, at Nee Soon

Camp. Anbarasan, however, constantly feels as though he is "a slave in another country" forced to bend to the will of his white masters. The author foreshadows the imminent anti-colonial revolt: Anbarasan recalls a public meeting that he had witnessed in Chennai, where Gandhi spoke of the need to drive away the colonial government who are exploiting them.

Complications arise within Anbarasan's private life as well, as Manimekalai's childhood playmate and neighbour, Nalliah, begins to show his interest in Manimekalai. A gentle woman, Manimekalai finds it challenging to reject the aggressive Nalliah. Secretly, Nalliah makes anonymous reports to the police and denounces Anbarasan as a "communist sympathiser" in a bid to remove his competition for Manimekalai's hand.

Toward the middle of the novel, the Japanese arrive in Singapore. They drop bombs, thus forcing the locals to take refuge in trenches. Food also becomes scarce. Anbarasan's family soon resorts to eating rice gruel and tapioca. After the collapse of the British regime, the Japanese assigns Anbarasan to run their warehouse, and he slowly wins their respect. Nevertheless, Anbarasan's hatred for British colonial exploitation never ceases.

Along with Manimekalai, Anbarasan and many locals join the Indian National Army after listening to a speech given by Indian National Army leader, Subhas Chandra Bose. Together with the Japanese, they fight against the British in Southeast Asia. Anbarasan saves Nalliah's life by shooting a tiger and the two man made amends. After the Japanese Occupation, Anbarasan and Manimekalai return from the war with stronger personalities. In a final bid to win Manimekalai's hand, Nalliah molests her, but the latter fights back ferociously and shouts: "Trying to threaten me! I'm not the old Manimekalai but a veteran of many battles!" (171) Anbarasan returns at this moment and teaches Nalliah a final lesson. In the end, the happy couple is married and set their sights on the future.

Significance and Remarks:

Singai Ma Elangkannan is the pseudonym of M. Balakrishnan, the first Tamil writer to receive the S.E.A. Write Award in 1982. In addition, he was also conferred the prestigious Singapore's Cultural Medallion in 2005 for his contributions to literature. *Flowers at Dawn* is his first novel to be translated into English.

Flowers at Dawn attempts to showcase the experiences of an Indian immigrant family in Singapore during the years before its fight for independence. The novel gives readers the chance to explore the everyday realities of immigrants who were forced to serve—first the British, and later the Japanese. Most notably, the narrative highlights a relatively unknown perspective on Singapore's history: that of the Indians who join the Indian National Army to fight against the British in the jungles of Southeast Asia.

Potential areas of comparative analysis:

Historical fiction, Gender, Marriage, Sexuality, Traditional Values, Social Commentary, Politics, Religion, Culture, Colonialism, War, Family

FLOWERS AT DAWN

主要语言： 英文
次要语言： -
翻译版本： Flowers at Dawn
页数： 178
作者： Singai Ma Elangkannan
出版年份： 2012
出版社： Epigram Books

人物简介：

1940年代，男主人翁安巴拉桑（Anbarasan）从印度漂洋过海到新加坡谋生。他希望早日赚到足够的钱接家人，以及和心上人曼尼麦卡莱（Manimekalai）结婚，然而，随着日军侵入，他的计划也被迫搁置。在偶然的机缘下，安巴拉桑和曼尼麦卡莱苏听了印度民族主义者、政治人物苏巴斯·钱德拉·鲍斯（Subhas Chandra Bose）的演讲。他们深受感召，决定加入印度国民军（Indian National Army），和日军联手对抗英殖民地政府，解放印度。战争的洗礼带出两人勇敢、忠诚和坚韧毅力的一面，也使他们更坚强，更勇于为理想和未来奋斗。

文本概要：

二战前夕，安巴拉桑从印度漂洋过海来到新加坡工作，期盼自己早日致富，早日成家立业。船靠岸后，安巴拉桑和他的同乡穆提雅（Muthiah）即面对粗暴、无礼的待遇。船上三等舱，来自印度的乘客必须在外岛隔离两天，但在上等舱的白人乘客却能在船只靠岸后，直接从港口前往市区。

安巴拉桑在坦格维鲁（Thangavelu）和婶婶瓦利阿梅（Valliammai）的帮助下，迅速地在英军军营找到工作，然他始终认为自己是“在异乡工作的奴隶”，只能屈从于英殖民政府。安巴拉桑回忆起他在印度听的一场演讲，当时民族解放运动著名领导人甘地（Gandhi）强调，印度必须推翻剥削他们的殖民地政府。

安巴拉桑在感情方面遇到了强劲的对手。曼尼麦卡莱的邻居兼童年玩伴纳里亚（Nalliah）对她有好感，但处处咄咄逼人，柔弱的曼尼麦卡莱不知如何拒绝纳里亚强强势的态度。为了从安巴拉桑手中夺走曼尼麦卡莱，纳里亚暗地里向警方匿名举报，污蔑安巴拉桑，说他是名“共产主义的同情者”（communist sympathiser）。

日军侵入后，他们从高空投掷炸弹，使居民躲进战壕避难。食物稀缺，安巴拉桑和家人以米粥（gruel）和木薯充饥。安巴拉桑被日军委派负责管理仓库，他出色的表现渐渐赢得日军的尊重。然而，安巴拉桑始终不耻英殖民政府的剥削行为，因此当他和曼尼麦卡莱听了苏巴斯的喊话后，决定加入印度国民军，和日军联手深入东南亚的森林对抗英军。安巴拉桑在过程中从老虎口中救了纳里亚一命。纳里亚感到内疚与惭愧，向安巴拉桑道歉。

日军投降后，安巴拉桑和曼尼麦卡莱带着更强悍的性格从战争中归来。面对为迎娶她过门而企图非礼她的纳里亚，曼尼麦卡莱勇敢反抗：“想威胁我！我已经不是当年的曼尼卖卡莱了，我现在是名沙场老将！”安巴拉桑也乘机教训了纳里亚一顿。小说尾声，幸福的两人步入婚姻，把目光投向未来。

重点与备注：

M. Balakrishnan（笔名：Singai Ma Elangkannan）于1982年荣获东南亚文学奖（S.E.A. Write Award），是首位获颁此殊荣的淡米尔文作家。为表彰他在文坛的卓越贡献，他也于2005年获颁新加坡文化奖（Cultural Medallion）。*Flowers at Dawn* 是他第一部译成英文的小说。*Flowers at Dawn* 试图刻画安巴拉桑身为印度移民在新加坡争取独立以前的故事：不论是英殖民时期抑或二战期间，身为移民，他们必须对掌权者（先是英殖民政府，后是侵入的日军）俯首称臣——这是他们每天都得面对的现实。最值得注意的是，作者描述安巴拉桑等人加入印度国民军，和日军一同深入东南亚的丛林对抗英军的故事——这是一段相对鲜为人知的新加坡历史。因此，作者亦可说是给读者提供了一个全新的视角。

潜在的比较文学分析：

历史小说、性与性别、婚姻、传统价值观、社会评论、政治、宗教、文化、殖民主义、战争、家庭

STATE OF EMERGENCY

Primary Language: English
Secondary Language: A few Mandarin and Chinese dialect words
Translation Available: No
Number of Pages: 245
Author: Jeremy Tiang
Year of Publication: 2017
Publisher: Epigram Books

Characterisation Notes:

The overarching narrative is told in the perspectives of six main characters whose timelines and lives intersect, sometimes obliquely.

Jason is an ailing civil servant, who revisits his life through fragmented memories on his deathbed. He is lucid, hyper-aware and filled with regret. He interacts with his daughter, Janet, who is characterized as cold and unfeeling; she stays with Jason because it is the socially appropriate thing to do. Janet is an archetypical high-flying civil servant—dedicated and meticulous, but mechanical and unfeeling.

Jason's wife, Siew Li, is pictured to be decisive and rational, but motivated by naïve idealism. In the novel, a newly married Siew Li struggles with her newfound responsibilities of a mother and her calling as a member of the Malayan Communist Party. Nam Teck, Siew Li's next partner, is a mechanic in Kuala Lumpur. He dwells under the spectre of his father, a Communist executed by the British, and the torments of his childhood spent in a British "new village", even as his life turns for the better in the city. Nam Teck questions his dull comforts and his lost sense of purpose in this chapter.

Revathi, a Singaporean-born Indian who works as a journalist for a British newspaper, digs into the history that is forgotten. She is deeply introspective and naively humanistic as she works to expose and right injustices.

Jason's niece, Stella, characterizes a descent into meek conformity. She is detained for suspicion of involvement in Communism under the Internal Security Act. Tiang depicts a painful degeneration of Stella's will as she is forced to confess despite her innocence. Stella's interrogators systematically dismantle her defenses, and force her attitude from indignance to total and utter compliance.

Jason's son, Henry, is a gay professor teaching History in England. A complex character, Henry's narrative invokes nostalgia, regret, curiosity and intense sadness as he re-examines his past after his father's death.

Text Synopsis:

Jason, on his deathbed, considers why his relationship with his two children has broken down—his daughter Janet visits but is curt and reticent, and his son Henry seldom returns. He misses his wife, Siew Li, and recalls the seemingly impossible and brief romance they had. She had mysteriously left soon after their wedding, leaving him to take care of their two children. Jason recalls his sister, Mollie, who cares for his children in his stead, but who was killed in the Macdonald house bombings. He ponders and hallucinates, in the backdrop of a cold, unfeeling modernity. Jason eventually dies, filled with sadness and regret.

The narrative flashes back to Siew Li, then a student in a Chinese school. Her good grades caught the eye of a Communist Party member, and she finds herself introduced and then drawn into Communist ideology. At the same time, she meets Jason, an English educated student from an affluent background. They fall in love and marry, to the dismay of her comrades. Soon after, she bore two children, Henry and Janet. Siew Li's family life is disrupted as she is forced to leave abruptly to evade the Singaporean crackdown (Operation Coldstore). She eventually joins the resistance in the Malayan jungle and never sees her family again. However, her figure looms over them—an irresponsible mother and wife, but also as a naïve idealist.

In the Malayan jungle, Siew Li meets Nam Teck, a mechanic from Kuala Lumpur. Nam Teck grew up in a "new village" where he spent his childhood in the years of the Malayan "Emergency". Life was difficult but Nam Teck and his mother got by. At the end of the "Emergency", he left for the city Kuala Lumpur in search of greener pastures. He becomes well to do, but gradually feels that life has become devoid of meaning. Once, by chance, he is exposed to Communist rhetoric in a party. Nam Teck discovers his affinity with the ideology, and feels connected with his father, who had died in the insurgency against the British earlier. He joined the Communist Party, and lived with

Siew Li until her death years later.

Back in the present, a Singaporean-Indian journalist based in Britain, Revathi clinches the job of a lifetime to pursue a lead in a story concerning British war crimes in Malaya. She visits, and confirming her suspicions, publishes an article about the atrocities. The article secures her career, but fails to indict anyone or precipitate any political action. Revathi becomes disillusioned with Britain, and eagerly takes the chance to return to Singapore later.

In Singapore, Siew Li's niece, Stella, a schoolteacher, continues to bear the brunt of Singapore's crackdown on Communism. Active in humanitarian work and advocacy of migrant workers' rights, Stella is suspected of involvement in Communism and detained under the Internal Security act. Despite being innocent, she is coerced to confess to radicalization and is released, jaded and distrustful.

Upon hearing of Jason's death, Jason's son, Henry, who is an acquaintance of Revathi, returns with her for Jason's funeral. He meets Stella and is shocked by her nonchalance and reticence. Soon after, he discovers letters written by Siew Li years ago when she just left, and Revathi convinces him to journey to find his mother. He travels to the Malaysian-Thailand border, upon which he meets an ailing Nam Teck, who shared that Siew Li has passed away, leaving their daughter, who is introduced to Henry as the novel ends.

Significance and Remarks:

Drawing from real historical events, Jeremy Tiang constructs a narrative that spans every major milestone in the region's struggle against Communism. This novel is especially significant not just for its historical accuracy, but for its refreshing take on the genre of the Singaporean political novel.

Tiang's greatest achievement is his construction of the human face of ideology. By characterizing individuals like Siew Li, as well as minor characters such as Lay Kuan (a Communist politician reminiscent of the former left-wing MP Loh Miaw Gong), Tiang paints a human face to formerly faceless Communist mass. He highlights their motivations, and above all, reveals their humanity. He shows that Communists are no different from you and I—we can be naively idealistic like Siew Li, or looking for a cause to follow just like Nam Teck. Instead of monsters and terrorists, we see mothers who believed in making a difference, and mundane labourers who saw the appeal of Communist ideology amidst the shortfalls of Capitalism.

Tiang highlights their insecurities, their passion, and their sacrifices to give ample voice to their indignance and hatred towards the British and governments that followed. In this light, Tiang constructs an alternative paradigm to view history, one that is sympathetic to the perspectives of the ones that are demonized in mainstream discourse.

In a similar vein, Tiang gives a face to Singapore's modern civil service and legal institutions. Paradoxically, this dehumanizes the bureaucracy. In Stella's case, the officers are self-righteous to a point of delusion, and outright racist and xenophobic. Separately, Jason himself led an unremarkable career as a civil servant, whereas his daughter Janet and her minister husband do well, presumably due to their mechanical fastidiousness and high regard for appearances. In this narrative, we see a Kafkaesque bureaucracy which actively strips its workers of identity. Although it runs like clockwork, the bureaucracy is piloted by unfeeling beings, gray and cold in contrast to the colourful lives of the Communists of the past.

In *Emergency*, Tiang reminds us that history is written by the victor. We need to hear the stories of certain individuals airbrushed from history to be fully conscious of the historicity of the present. Only then, can we understand that the State of Emergency may still be in full force today.

Potential Areas of Comparative Analysis:

Postmodernism, Political History, Historiography, Rural vs Urban, Traditional vs Modern Values, Rich-Poor Divide, Emigration, Journalism, Feminism, Elderly in Singapore, Social Commentary

STATE OF EMERGENCY

主要语言： 英文
次要语言： -
翻译版本： -
页数： 245
作者： 程异（Jeremy Tiang）
出版年份： 2017
出版社： Epigram Books

人物概要：

《紧急状态》(*State of Emergency*)从6名主要人物的角度出发，讲述他们相互交错的生命际遇。

公务员杰森 (Jason) 在临终之际，透过零碎的片段回忆他的人生：他头脑清晰、意识清楚，充满悔恨。他的女儿珍妮特 (Janet) 是典型出色的公务员。她敬业、细致，但也机械化般冷漠。她到医院探访父亲，不过是为了符合他人的道德标准，而非出于真正的孝心。

杰森的妻子秀丽 (Siew Li) 性格果断、理性，是名天真的理想主义者。她新婚不久，是两名孩子的母亲，同时也是马来亚共产党 (Malayan Communist Party, 俗称"马共") 的成员，要同时履行身为人母的义务。完成身为马共成员的使命对她而言是个巨大的挑战。

南德 (Nam Teck) 是秀丽的第二任丈夫。南德年幼时，他的父亲因涉嫌参与共产党武装斗争，惨遭英殖民政府枪杀。他和母亲随后搬迁至士毛月新村 (Seminyih New Village)，在那里度过童年时光。他成年后到吉隆坡谋生，在汽车维修行行担任技师，尽管生活改善不少，但父亲的遭遇始终使他活在童年的阴影和恐惧中。面对眼前舒适但枯燥的生活，他感到迷茫，开始失去方向。

旅居英国的雷瓦蒂 (Revathi) 是名新加坡籍印度裔记者。她善于自省，秉持人本主义的精神，开始挖掘被遗忘的历史、以揭露真相，伸张正义。

杰森的外甥女史黛拉（Stella）本性温顺，安分守己，但却因涉嫌参与共产主义活动，而在内部安全法令（Internal Security Act）下遭拘捕审问。她愤慨地推翻所有指控，但在一连串精心计划的疲劳轰炸和盘问后，她的意志力逐渐开始瓦解，脆弱的防线已无法支撑她，无辜的她不得不"承认"罪行。

杰森的儿子亨利（Henry）是名男同性恋，他长居伦敦，在大学任教。他性格复杂，在接获父亲的死讯后，他重新审视过去，唤起对昨日的怀念、好奇、懊悔以及强烈的悲伤情绪。

文本简介：

临终之际，杰森在病榻上沉思他和子女感情破裂的原因。他的女儿珍妮特前来探访他，但态度草率、不愿多谈；而儿子则在国外，鲜少回国。他始终惦记着妻子秀丽，以及当年看似不可能发生的短暂恋情。婚后不久，秀丽神秘失踪，留下杰森照顾年幼的孩子。杰森的妹妹茉莉（Mollie）代哥哥照顾小孩，但不幸在1965年的麦唐纳大厦（MacDonald House）爆炸案罹难。医院的氛围冰凉冷漠，他沉思、甚至产生幻觉，最终带着悲伤和遗憾离开人世。

作者以倒叙的手法，将视线切换到华校生秀丽身上。她优异的成绩引起另一名共产党员丽娜（Lina）的注意，在后者的介绍下，她开始接触、并发现自己被共产主义的思想体系（ideology）所吸引。同时，她认识了家境优渥的英校生杰森，两人坠入爱河，不久后结婚，生下了珍妮特和亨利，令秀丽的战友大失所望。

一家四口的幸福生活并不长久。为躲避冷藏行动（Operation Coldstore），她抛夫弃子，逃亡到马来西亚，参与反殖民斗争，至此没再见过家人。尽管如此，秀丽的身影依然不断、若隐若现地笼罩着他们——对杰森和孩子而言，她不仅是个不负责任的妻子和母亲，亦是个天真的理性主义者。

南德小时候和母亲住在新村，童年时光在马来亚紧急状态（Malayan Emergency）度过。生活艰辛，但他和母亲还是熬过来了。紧急状态结束后，他前往吉隆坡，在汽车维修行担任技师。尽管生活条件改善了，但他渐渐觉得人生缺乏意义。在偶然的机缘下，他在一场文娱晚会上认识了秀丽，并接触到共产主义的宣言。他深深被共产理念所吸引，也感受到了和早年因反殖民斗争而身亡的父亲的连结，因此决定离开母亲，追随秀丽加入马共，投身反殖民抗争。两人一起生活，直到秀丽过世为止。

长居英国的记者雷瓦蒂来到马来西亚，追踪英殖民政府的战争罪行的真相。这是她职业生涯的代表作——她在采访过程中证实了她的怀疑，随后刊登了关于英军暴行的报道。尽管引起广泛讨论（英国政府也在议会中要求重启调查）但依然不足以进入审判程序，或使政府采取政治行动。雷瓦蒂感到失望，急切地抓住返回新加坡的机会。

秀丽的外甥女史黛拉也难逃一劫，成为新加坡政府镇压共产主义的牺牲品。史黛拉是名老师，她积极投身人道主义工作，致力于维护外籍劳工的权益和福祉，但也因此引起当局怀疑，被指控参与共产主义行动，在国家内安法令下被拘留。尽管她是清白的，但面对高压盘问，她被迫承认参与激进活动，她被释放后对生活感到厌倦，产生怀疑。

听闻杰森的死讯后，亨利和雷瓦蒂一同回到新加坡奔丧。亨利再次见到史黛拉时，被她冷淡、沉默不语的态度所震慑。亨利在整理父亲的遗物时发现当年秀丽失踪不久后，寄回家中的信件和照片。雷瓦蒂说服亨利寻找母亲的下落，两人来到马泰边境，遇见南德（现改名雄民）。雄民告诉他们，秀丽已过世，留下他和女儿。小说结尾，南德将女儿介绍给亨利。

重点与备注：

取材自历史事件，作者在《紧急状态》中诠释横跨新马地区、反共产主义斗争的每一个重要的里程碑。小说的重要性并不仅在于它的历史写实性（historical accuracy），也在于作者从全新的视角创作新加坡的政治题材小说，令人耳目一新。

程异（Jeremy Tiang）描绘在意识形态面前，人物人性化的一面——这也是他最成功的一点。透过刻画秀丽、甚至像丽娟（Lay Kuan，一个让人联想到前左派国会议员卢妙萍的共产党政治人物）等配角，作者突出左翼成员色彩鲜明的人物性格，他不仅强调了他们的动机，也描述了他们人性化的一面。作者告诉我们，共产党员和你我并无不同——我们可以像秀丽一样是个天真的理想主义者，也可以和南德一般找寻生命的意义。我们看到的不是妖魔鬼怪或恐怖分子，而是一个相信能改革社会的母亲，以及看见共产主义的吸引力和资本主义的缺陷的劳动者。

作者强调他们的不安、他们的激情以及他们的牺牲奉献，充分表达他们对英殖民政府的愤懑和恨意。有鉴于此，作者建构了一个主流观点之外的替代论述（alternate paradigm），它以一个更具同理心的立场，包容和接纳一直以来被“妖魔化”（demonized）的视角和声音。

同样的，作者也刻画新加坡公务部门以及法律机构的轮廓。矛盾的是，他的描述反而使政府机关失去人性化的一面。以史黛拉的案件为例，审讯者的自以为是彻底暴露出对外籍劳工的歧视和厌恶。另一边厢，同为政府官员，杰森平淡如水的公务员生涯和女儿、部长女婿的亮眼的成绩单显得黯然失色。这或许能归结于后者机械式般、一丝不苟的严谨态度，以及对外在表现形式的高度重视。在整体的论述中，我们看到一个卡夫卡式的官僚制度（Kafkaesque Bureaucracy）——它由一名高冷的总指挥领导着，像钟表般无时无刻运转，剥夺劳动者鲜明的身份特征。它们的灰暗和冷漠，和过去共产党员丰富多彩的生活形成强烈对比。

在《紧急状态》中, 作者提醒读者, 唯有胜利者才能书写历史。我们有必要倾听完全从官方历史记载中被抹去的故事和声音, 才能充分意识"当下的历史性"(historicity of the present)；只有这样, 我们才能明白, 直至今时今日, 我们仍可能处在"紧急状态"之中。

潜在的比较文学分析：

后现代主义、政治史、史学、偏乡与城市、传统与现代价值观、贫富分化、移民、新闻学、女性主义、新加坡年长人士、社会评论

A CANDLE OR THE SUN

Primary Language: English
Secondary Language: No
Translation Available: No
Number of Pages: 196
Author: Gopal Baratham
Year of Publication: 1991
Publisher: Serpent's Tail

Characterisation Notes:

Hernando Perera runs the furniture department at Benson's, the oldest department store in Singapore. Hernando is also an aspiring writer—he would jot down ideas or sequences of words for his upcoming stories. Su-May, Hernando's lover, is a member of "Children of the Book", an unorthodox Christian sect that hopes to overthrow the oppressive incumbent government through the publication of clandestine street papers. When Hernando's job is threatened by a supposed joint-venture between Benson's and another company, his childhood friend Samson promises him a role in a government-run publication in exchange for insider information of the sect. Hernando vacillates between Samson's proposal and staying true to his conscience.

Text Synopsis:

Hernando works a daily job at Benson's. In his free time, he works on his short stories and has extramarital affairs with Su-May. Su-May is a member of the Christian sect "Children of the Book." She works with the sect's leader Peter Yu to publish and distribute a clandestine street paper that aims to bring anti-government sentiments to the boil.

Hernando's seemingly comfortable life comes to a halt when his father is diagnosed with terminal cancer and his position is threatened by a planned merger between Benson and Teng's (another departmental store). He decides to resign and rings up Samson Alagaratnam, his childhood friend and a high-ranked civil servant in the Ministry of Culture. Samson offers Hernando a job in the ministry and the possibility of an adjunct job as a professor in creative writing. He even promises Hernando recognition from the Singapore Guild of Writers. However, Samson has one condition—Hernando must prove his loyalty and trustworthiness by betraying the Christian sect.

Naively believing that Su-May and the sect would only be fined or imposed with "minor deterrent sentences" (155), Hernando decides to betray them. He fills Samson in with his knowledge of the sect, including Peter's intention to encourage "displays of defiance" (151). To his horror, Hernando learns from Samson's assistant, Anuita, that the government will delineate the religious group as a "massive conspiracy" (155) between various parties including the Communists.

Spurred on by his fictional writings, Hernando decides to help Su-May and Peter escape; they manage to flee the country before the authorities close in on them. Hernando is subsequently arrested. In the interrogation room, he visualizes an idyllic image: a pregnant Su-May and Peter working in a hospital in Tanzania, vaccinating new-borns and teaching a paralyzed man how to walk again.

Significance and Remarks:

Widely regarded as Baratham's most successful novel, *A Candle or the Sun* was shortlisted for the Commonwealth Writers' Prize in 1992. The novel is especially notable for its construction of an alternative Singaporean political history and for the considerable controversy the novel aroused.

Baratham's novel had been rejected by Singaporean publishing firms[9] for its uncanny resemblance to the 1987 "Marxist conspiracy" known as "Operation Spectrum." In that incident, Singaporean authorities detained more than 20 people (some of whom were affiliated to a Catholic Church) without trial under the Internal Security Act. However, Baratham had completed the novel at the end of 1985,[10] more than 2 years before the operation.

The internationally acclaimed political thriller explores the theme of betrayal in both the narrative and the short fictions which are interpenetrated

9 Klein, R. D. (Ed.). (2001). *Interlogue: Studies in Singapore literature* (Vol. 4). Singapore: Ethos Books, p. 95.

10 Philip Holden (2006) WRITING CONSPIRACY, *Journal of Postcolonial Writing*, 42:01, 58-70, DOI: 10.1080/17449850600595665

within.[11] The three short stories—*Kissful of Tears, Double Exposure* and *Dutch Courage*—have previously appeared in Baratham's earlier collection titled *People Make You Cry and Other Stories* (1988).[12] In *A Candle or the Sun*, the short stories are presented as stories authored by Hernando, when he found himself in a catch-22 situation. As much as Hernando needs another employment, he is certain that accepting Samson's proposal is synonymous to betrayal.

In the beginning of the novel, Hernando indulges in writing fiction to enter "an inaccessible world in the only way possible" (82). At the end of the novel, he has to "prostitute" his love for words, which are more than "a part of the body (he) could put up for hire" (85;86). Hernando is distressed by "this loss of self-respect" (85) but convinces himself to compartmentalize his life—to separate personal life from political work such that "the contents of one compartment (do) not leak into another" (86). Eventually, to earn a livelihood, Hernando brings *Double Exposure* to Samson's apartment, only to realize the latter's intention to "dictate and censor"[13] his writings. Here, the theme of betrayal and fiction writing become entangled.

Besieged by guilt, Hernando pens the third short story *Dutch Courage*. He finds great fortitude in the protagonist, Captain Cornelius Vandermeer. Cornelius is a Dutch Javanese who arrived in Singapore during the 1930s. When World War Two broke out, Cornelius joined the Singapore Volunteer Corps and fought as an "effective guerilla force" (119) in the jungles of Malaya. Cornelius was said to have been ambushed by his erstwhile comrades after the war.

Hernando is inspired and emboldened by Cornelius' insight in his final days that "concern for the well-being of others is the only defence we have against terror and death" (158). Hernando ultimately redeems himself by planning Su-May's and Peter's escape route to Bangkok, where they can take a flight to Tanzania.

The title *A Candle or the Sun* references the song "The First of My Lovers" by English songwriter and folk musician Sydney Bertram Carter. The song is

11 Puthucheary, R. (2009). 'A Candle or the Sun', in *Different Voices: The Singaporean / Malaysian Novel*. Singapore: ISEAS Publishing, p. 99

12 Koh, T. A. (2008). *Singapore literature in English : an annotated bibliography* / Koh Tai Ann, compiler and editor. National Library Board and Centre for Liberal Arts and Social Sciences, Nanyang Technological University, p. 70

13 Puthucheary, R. (2009). 'A Candle or the Sun', in *Different Voices : The Singaporean / Malaysian Novel*. Singapore: ISEAS Publishing, p. 109

also sung by Su-May at a gathering in the novel. It features the lines: 'For the same light can shine in / A candle or the sun'. Read in tandem with the closing passages of the novel, the song is a poignant reminder of Hernando's guilt towards Su-May and his struggle en route to self-atonement.

Potential areas of comparative analysis:

Political History, Historiography, Free Speech, Censorship, Nationalism, Social Commentary, Dictatorship

A CANDLE OR THE SUN

主要语言： 英文
次要语言： -
翻译版本： -
页数： 196
作者： Gopal Baratham
出版年份： 1991
出版社： London: Serpent's Tail

人物简介：

赫尔南德 · 佩雷拉（Hernando Perera）是新加坡最古老百货中心班森(Benson's)家具部门的负责人。工作之外，他渴望成为一名作家，习惯随手记下创作灵感和点子。赫尔南德的情妇淑梅（Su-May）是极端宗教组织“书童”（Children of the Book）的成员，她和组织的其他成员企图暗中出版街头密报，以推翻高压、强势的当权者。赫尔南德因企业合并而面临失业危机，他的童年好友、政府官员山姆森（Samson）向他伸出橄榄枝（在隶属政府的出版刊物部门担任要职），但条件是他必须向政府提供关于“书童”的情报，赫尔南德在接受山姆森的提议和忠于自己的良心之间感到进退维谷。

文本概要：

赫尔南德平日是一般上班族，是班森百货中心家具部门的负责人。闲暇时，他爱创作短篇小说，和淑梅发生婚外情。淑梅和“书童”的领袖余彼得（Peter Yu）合作出版，发行一份旨在让“反政府情绪沸腾”的街头密报。

随着父亲被诊断为癌症末期、工作因合并计划而受到威胁，赫尔南德看似舒适的生活嘎然而止。他决定辞职，并联系山姆森。后者告诉赫尔南德，他不仅可以在公务部门为他安插一份工作，也可以帮他获得在大学兼差、教授创意写作的职位，甚至助他得到作家协会的赏识。然，山姆森有一个条件：赫尔南德必须背叛淑梅以及“书童”以证明自己的忠诚。天真的赫尔南德认为淑梅和组织的其他成员只会收到轻微的处分，于是决定背叛他们，因此他向山姆森全盘托出他所知道的、关于组织的一切，包括余彼得企图煽动叛乱的不良意图。然而，让他惶恐的是，他从山姆森的秘书阿努伊塔（Anuita）口中得知，政府认定“书童”和其他共产主义组织等正在筹划一个“大规模的阴谋”（massive conspiracy），计划把他们缉拿归案。

受到短篇小说创作的鼓舞，赫尔南德决定帮助淑梅和余彼得逃离新加坡，两人成功逃过一劫，前往坦桑尼亚；赫尔南德随后被捕，在审讯室里，他幻想着一幅田园诗般、恬静的画面：淑梅已怀有身孕，和彼得在一家医院工作，他们一起帮新生儿接种疫苗，并教一名瘫痪病人重新站起来。

重点与备注：

A Candle or The Sun 被广泛认为是作者最成功的小说，于1992年入围英联邦作家奖 (Commonwealth Writers' Prize)。尤其值得注意的是，小说就新加坡历史建构了另一替代叙述所引发的争议。作者早在1985年便完成小说手稿，[14]但新加坡的出版社却以小说情节和1987年的“光谱行动” (Spectrum Operation) 极其相似为由，拒绝出版此小说。[15] “光谱行动”又称“马克思主义者阴谋” (Marxist Conspiracy)，1987年，新加坡当局援引内部安全法令 (Internal Security Act) 逮捕并拘留超过20人 (部分隶属天主教会)，过程中并未接受审判。

这部享誉国际的政治惊悚小说 (political thriller) 穿插作者早期收录在作品集People Make You Cry and Other Stories (1988) 的3篇短文：Kissful of Tears、Double Exposure以及 Dutch Courage；[16] 连同小说本身带领读者探讨“背叛”这个主题。[17]

在小说中，这3篇故事是赫尔南德闲暇时的短篇创作，他认为写作是进入“一个难以接近、到达的世界”的唯一途径；然，在他急需下一份工作时，他拿着Double Exposure的手稿到山姆森的家中，却发现后者有意“支配和

14 Philip Holden (2006) WRITING CONSPIRACY, *Journal of Postcolonial Writing*, 42:01, 58-70, DOI: 10.1080/17449850600595665

15 Klein, R. D. (Ed.). (2001). *Interlogue: Studies in Singapore literature (Vol. 4)*. Singapore: Ethos Books, p. 95.

16 Koh, T. A. (2008). *Singapore literature in English : an annotated bibliography* / Koh Tai Ann, compiler and editor. National Library Board and Centre for Liberal Arts and Social Sciences, Nanyang Technological University, p. 70

17 Puthucheary, R. (2009). *'A Candle or the Sun', in Different Voices : The Singaporean / Malaysian Novel*. Singapore: ISEAS Publishing, p. 99

审查”[18] 他的作品。对赫尔南德而言，文字比他“身上任何一个可以出租的地方”来得更珍贵。因此，接受山姆森的提议就等同于背叛，背叛他对文字的热爱以及他创作的才华。在这里，“背叛”和“虚构小说创作”这两个主题纠缠在了一起。深感失去自尊的赫尔南德感到烦躁焦虑，他尝试说服自己精细地划分生活和工作，以公私分明。

挥之不去的内疚感缠绕着赫尔南德。他开始创作了第三篇短篇故事Dutch Courage，他在主人翁科尔尼里斯·范德美 (Cornelius Vandemeer) 身上找到了勇气。科尔尼里斯拥有荷兰和印尼爪哇血统，1930年代抵达新加坡；第二次世界大战爆发后，他加入新加坡志愿军 (Singapore Volunteer Corps)，以游击队员的身份，在马来亚丛林作战。据说，在二战过后，科尔尼里斯遭昔日战友伏击身亡。科尔尼里斯认为，关心他人的福祉是对抗恐怖和死亡的唯一防线。赫尔南德深受启发，策划淑梅和余彼得的逃亡路线，先将他们送到曼谷，让他们从那前往坦桑尼亚，终于为自己赎罪。

小说名称*A Candle or The Sun*是英国作曲家、民谣音乐人西德尼·伯特伦·卡特 (Sydney Bertram Carter) 的歌曲《我最初的情人》(The First of My Lovers) 中的其中一句歌词。淑梅曾在一次聚会上诠释这首歌曲：“For the same light can shine in/A candle or the sun”(因为同样的阳光可以照亮/一根蜡烛或太阳)；结合小说结局，这首歌是个凄美的提醒，提醒我们赫尔南德对淑梅的愧疚，以及在自我救赎的路上、内心的煎熬和挣扎。

潜在的比较文学分析：

政治历史、历史学、言论自由、审查制度、民族主义、社会评述、独裁统治

18 Puthucheary, R. (2009). *'A Candle or the Sun', in Different Voices : The Singaporean / Malaysian Novel*. Singapore: ISEAS Publishing, p. 109

DUKA TUAN BERTAKHTA

Primary Language: Malay
Secondary Language: No
Translation Available: 《悲君统治》, *1819*
Number of Pages: 563
Author: Isa Kamari
Year of Publication: 2011
Publisher: Al Ameen Serve Holdings Sdn Bhd

Characterisation Notes:

Duka Tuan Bertakhta narrates the history of Singapore in the 19th century from three main perspectives: that of the British colonial masters, Sultan Hussein, and the Islamic holy man Habib Nuh. Tengku Hussein, the Malayan crown prince, absent from his father's funeral, is unable to ascend the throne. Nevertheless, with the help of Stamford Raffles, he successfully becomes the sultan of Singapore. However, Tengku Hussein lacked political agency and becomes a mere puppet of the British. In all, the British are depicted as greedy, cunning and ambitious, and the Sultan as inebriated and inept. The novel also brings up other eminent figures of the time: Wak Cantuk, Munsyi Abdullah, William Farquhar and John Crawfurd, who add colour to the novel by giving readers an insight of the then socio-political and economic development of the Malay Community.

Text Synopsis:

The novel opens as Stamford Raffles and his fleet land in Singapore in search for a new trading post. He first installed Tengku Hussein as the Sultan of Singapore before signing a treaty with him and the Temenggong, permitting the British to set up a new trading hub on the island. The agreement also surrenders part of the island's administration to the British colonial masters. Raffles appoints William Farquhar as the first Resident of Singapore to develop its landscape. Contemporaneously, the Islamic sage Habib Nuh arrives from Penang and finds himself at odds with the British.

Significance and Remarks:

Duka Tuan Bertakhta is a full-length novel divided into many small narratives; together, the cacophony of voices illustrates the four-sided power tussle among the British, the local Sultan, Habib Nuh and Temenggung Abdul Rahman soon after Raffles' landing in 1819.

Mainstream discourse largely lionizes Raffles as the Founder of Singapore and glorifies his contributions thereafter. More often than not, his intervention in Royal politics—how he first crowns Tengku Hussein as the Sultan of Singapore, and later dupes him and Temenggong to sign a treaty allowing the British to establish a trading centre, redeveloping the urban landscape of Singapore—are completely excluded from general discussions. The author deviates from mainstream views in his cynical depiction of Raffles' 1819 landing in Singapore—he focuses on the political jostling between the Malayan Sultan, the Temmengong, and Habib Nuh, inviting further examination on Singapore's history in its depiction of the role that Raffles played.

The author is harsh in his evaluation of the British colonialists. To that end, Raffles is deeply unscrupulous and manipulative: he bribes the Sultan and Temenggong with wealth and opium to achieve his political objectives (to set up Singapore as the commercial hub of the East India Company). It is also indisputable that Raffles is intimidated by the increasing influence that Islam has on the Island upon the arrival of Habib Nuh, and hence he gives John Crawfurd, the Resident, a mandate to curb the growth of religious impact and eliminate all who opposes the British.

Under the administration of John Crawfurd, Singapore was ceded fully to the British following the signing of the Anglo-Dutch Treaty of London and the Treaty of Friendship and Alliance. In return, the Sultan and Temenggong receive a lump sum of 33,200 and 26,800 Spanish Dollars, and a monthly allowance of 1300 and 700 Spanish Dollars respectively.[19]

Munsyi Abdullah, the erudite writer and a master of language, represents a rational and objective voice which succinctly charts the declining relevance and power of the Royal Sultanates. The Sultan declines Raffles' offer to educate their sons in Bengal. Abdullah is pained by the short-sightedness that refuses knowledge; this proves brutal as Malay children grows up illiterate and unable

---

19 Isa Kamari, et al. Bei jun tong zhi / zuo zhe, Yisha Kamali zhu ; yi zhe, Chen Miaohua, Wen Chang. (Singapore: Singapore Literature Society, 2018), p.172.

to break free from penury. As Abdullah emphasizes, the Malay community needs a strong leadership, but neither Wak Cantuk nor Habib Nuh possess the qualities of a commander, thrusting the Malay community into a future of uncertainty. The depiction of the weakness of the Malay society serves as an important lesson for the contemporary Malay community of Singapore. Raffles is obsessed with his legacy as the "founder" of Singapore. The author dedicates one chapter to Raffles' letter to Crawford in order to double down on his point on the unchecked ruthlessness of the British. However, according to the novel, Raffles only lived on the island for an accumulative 296 days before he departs for the UK in 1824; whereas William Farquhar takes charge of the island for 58 months (almost 5 years).[20] Thus, Raffles' significance in transforming Singapore into a thriving port remains largely debatable.

Potential areas of comparative analysis:

Islamic Faith, Colonization, Race, Royal Politics, Singapore History, Historical Awareness

20 Ibid, p.160.

悲君统治 DUKA TUAN BERTAKHTA

主要语言： 马来文

次要语言： -

翻译版本： 《悲君统治》以及1819

页数： 563

作者： 伊沙 · 卡马里（Isa Kamari）

出版年份： 2011

出版社： Al Ameen Serve Holdings Sdn Bhd

人物简介：

《悲君统治》主要从以莱佛士（Raffles）为首的英殖民政府、苏丹胡先（Sultan Hussein）以及伊斯兰教圣人哈比诺（Habib Nuh）这三组人物的视角叙述新加坡于19世纪开埠之初的故事。胡先原为柔佛苏丹王储继承人，由于没见到父亲最后一面，失去继承皇位的权利；在莱佛士的帮助下，他成为新加坡的苏丹——一个有名无实的政治傀儡。英殖民政府野心勃勃、阴险狡猾，苏丹胡先则沉迷鸦片、平庸无能；参与这段历史的还包括马来武术老师瓦张铎（Wak Cantuk）、史官蒙西阿都拉（Munsyi Abdullah）、驻扎官法夸尔（William Farquhar）和哥罗福（John Crawfurd）等人，他们为小说增添多一层色彩，让我们一窥当时马来社群的社会、经济和政治发展。

文本概要：

1819年1月，为寻找新的贸易据点，莱佛士率领的舰队登陆新加坡。他先拥立东姑胡先（Tengku Hussein）为新加坡的苏丹，之后连同他和天猛公阿都拉曼（Temenggung Abdul Rahman）签订条约，让东印度公司在新加坡设立贸易站。莱佛士从两人手中取得部分的新加坡行政管制权，并委派法夸尔出任驻扎官和总指挥，重新规划新加坡的城市版图。此时，伊斯兰教圣人哈比诺也从槟城抵达新加坡，与英殖民政府形成对立局面，关系一触即发。

重点与备注：

《悲君统治》是一部回溯19世纪加坡开埠之初的长篇小说。故事分小节，以多元的视角描绘殖民政府、哈比诺、天猛公阿都拉曼以及马来王室的四角政权斗争。

一般主流论述提到莱佛士时，总不乏赞美他的丰功伟业，赞誉他为新加坡开埠的功臣元勋；但关于他插手干预马来宫廷政治，拥立东姑胡先为新的苏丹，后又是如何贿赂、利诱他和天猛公，签订建立贸易战的条约，重新形塑新加坡的城市面貌之过程完全被排除在主流观点之外。因此，小说的核心在于作者对莱佛士登陆新加坡做出有异于官方历史的替代表述，引导读者重新审视新加坡的开埠以及思考莱佛士扮演的角色。

作者毫不留情地揭示莱佛士权欲熏心、手段粗暴的真面目：他先利用财富和鸦片将苏丹胡先与天猛公玩弄于鼓掌之中，让他们签署合约，同意东印度公司在新加坡插旗，设立新的贸易据点；后因畏惧宗教势力在新加坡扩张，罢免和马来社群过于亲密的法夸尔，并下令新任驻扎官哥罗福瓦解所有对英殖民政权有威胁的外部力量。

1824年，哥罗福和天猛公、苏丹胡先签订新的条约：根据协议，新加坡将永久割让给英国东印度公司，苏丹胡先和天猛公除了分别获得33200和26800西班牙元的一次性丰厚报酬外，也能终身享有1300元和700元的月俸。[21] 随着条约的签订，新加坡进入新的殖民时期，马来王室主权也正式告终。

学识渊博、精通五种语言的蒙西阿都拉是一把理性且客观的声音，他精准地分析了马来王权走向衰败的过程：苏丹胡先不思进取,染上鸦片瘾，拒绝莱佛士让小孩求学的邀请.同样的，其马来族小孩终日游手好闲，目不识丁、身无一技之长的他们因此摆脱不了穷籍。当年的马来社群需要一个强而有力的领军人物，但无论是哈比诺或瓦张铎，都不具备和法夸尔或莱佛士同样的领导能力，马来族群的命运又蒙上了一层厚厚的未知。从这点来看，作者有意提醒马来社群借鉴历史，勿重蹈覆辙。

莱佛士希望后人视他为发现新加坡的第一位人。作者用完整一章，写莱佛士给驻扎官哥罗福的信，彻底揭露他居高临下的虚伪、无知与傲慢。然而，莱佛士于1824年启程回英国前，前后在新加坡居住了296

---

21 《悲君统治》。作者，伊沙 · 卡马里著；译者，陈妙华，温昌。（新加坡：新加坡文艺协会，2018年），页172。

天。相反的，法夸尔驻守管理新加坡58个月（接近5年之久）。[22] 如此一来，莱佛士发展新加坡的贡献仍有待商榷。

潜在的比较文学研究分析：

伊斯兰教信仰、殖民统治、种族、皇室政权斗争、新加坡历史

22 同上，页160

可口的饥饿 (DELICIOUS HUNGER)

Primary Language: Mandarin

Secondary Language: some Malay

Translation Available: No

Number of Pages: 274

Author: Hai Fan

Year of Publication: 2017

Publisher: Got One Publisher Sdn Bhd

Characterisation Notes:

In 1976, the author Ang Tiam Huat joins the Malayan National Liberation Army. He will fight for the Malayan Communist Party (MCP) and live in the Malaysian rainforest for the next 13 years (up till the 1989 Hat Yai Peace Agreement between Thailand and Malaysia). In 1989, Ang leaves the forest and emigrates to Singapore. The text *Ke Kou De Ji E* (*Delicious hunger*) draws from Ang's experience as a soldier and a guerilla fighter and features characters inspired by real historical figures.

Text Synopsis:

Ke Kou De Ji E (*Delicious Hunger*) is a collection of 11 short compositions by the author. Many of these are inspired by the author's real experiences. For instance, the author likens fighting in the Malayan rainforest to treading on thin ice—one must evade the torrent of enemy bullets and also mines and other dangerous animals of the forest. The author also shares some of the small pleasures of daily life: the camaraderie among the soldiers, the tragically beautiful romances, and the intelligent attempts at hunting. The author masterfully depicts the difficult and isolated conditions faced by the MCP in the Malayan rainforest through his moving depictions of the richness of quotidian life.

Significance and Remarks:

Hai Fan was born in 1953 in Singapore. He participated in left-wing politics since young and gained the attention of the Singaporean government. Hai Fan narrowly escaped a political purge when he was not home and fled to Malaya with the help of a friend. He then joined the armed forces of the MCP.

Ke Kou De Ji E (*Delicious Hunger*) is Hai Fan's second work. The book is both a work of literature, and a valuable first-hand source for the history of the MCP. In fact, Hai Fan is granted admission to the group "writings of Malayan Communists" (a group that specializes in literary creations inspired by the histories and characters of the MCP) as an ex-member of the MCP itself. For its authentic representation of daily life and the zeitgeist of the 1980s, the novel was nominated as the 2017's Top 10 Chinese Novels by Asia Weekly.

The collection is named after an eponymous short story within the collection. In the Malayan forest, food shortages are common, and the soldiers can only rely on wild tapiocas most of the time. One of the author's (protagonist's) comrades possessed the enviable ability to treat all foods as if they are delicacies, thus earning his nickname "delicious." His appetite was enormous, and he once ate more than 80 rambutans whole during a hunger spell and became terribly constipated. To the author, hunger was a despair worse than their military isolation: the author opens the novel by emphasizing the many soldiers that perished due to malnutrition; in the story "*Ye Mang Guo*" (Wild Mangoes), a female soldier contracts scurvy due to a lack of vitamin C and turns deathly pale; the author also mentions that, in hard times, all every soldier can get for dinner was two teaspoons of sugar.

The author's portrayal of life in the rainforest is not one that is completely without reward. Despite the difficulties, life was resilient and vibrant. In the short stories "*Lie Wu*" (Hunting) and "*Zhou Yu*" (Spell), the author discusses the varies methods the soldiers employed to set traps, or to identify the locations frequented by deers, bears and wild boars. The author even illustrates some of the daily items (such as water bottles/packs, metal buckets to hide food, ropes for hunting, etc.) himself to deepen the reader's impression of daily life in the rainforest.

Potential areas of comparative analysis:

Malayan Communist Party, Communism, Malaysian Politics, Guerrilla Warfare, Historiography, Writings of Malayan Communists

可口的饥饿

主要语言：中文
次要语言：零星马来文
翻译版本：-
页数：274
作者：海凡（本名：洪添发）
出版年份：2017
出版社：有人出版社

人物简介：

1976年，作者海凡加入马来亚民族解放军（Malayan National Liberation Army，后更名为马来亚人民军），参与马来亚共产党（简称"马共"）领导的武装斗争，并在雨林作战、生活13年。1989年12月2日，随着马共与泰国及马来西亚政府签订"合艾和平协议"，军队卸下武器、解散士兵，他也走出丛林，重返新加坡定居。《可口的饥饿》的人物原型源自上述历史，作者以此为背景书写部队的游击生活。

文本概要：

《可口的饥饿》共收录11篇、依据作者亲身经历展开的创作，取材多元：在深林中作战的日子可谓如履薄冰，除了令人胆战心惊的枪林弹雨，还必须提防凶险的地雷和毒蛇猛兽，更别说长期的营养匮乏是部队的日常。但在腥风血雨之外，还有同袍间的战友情、唯美的军中爱情和机智的狩猎行动，透过丰富多元且生活化的题材，作者生动地叙述马共游击队在森林作战的艰苦无援的生活。

重点与备注：

海凡1953年生于新加坡，年少时曾参加左翼文化组织的活动，引起政府的高度关注。当局某晚展开围剿行动，作者因不在家中幸运逃过一劫，后在朋友的通知和协助下逃亡到马来西亚，后辗转加入马共所领导的武装部队。

《可口的饥饿》是作者的第二本创作，它既是文学作品，也可视为研究马共历史不可多得的一手史料: 在马华文学的发展历程中, 海凡以前马共武装部队成员的身份参与"马共书写" (围绕马共和相关人物或历史为题材展开的创作), 反映时代的生活和精神面貌。小说也因此在2017年入选亚洲周刊十大中文小说。

书名《可口的饥饿》取自小说的同名压轴作品。军中生活条件严峻, 部队成员常以野薯果腹, 面对严重的粮食短缺, 作者的其中一名战友却总能将不易获得的食物吃出个美味与可口, 因此在部队里得"可口"这可爱的绰号。"可口"的食量比一般人大, 一次饥饿难耐, 居然连核带肉吞下超过80颗红毛丹, 造成下腹严重不适, 引发严重便秘。和四面楚歌的窘境比起来, "饥饿"才是武装部队无法摆脱的绝望: 作者在小说开篇描述, 士兵因营养不足而牺牲。在〈野芒果〉中, 女士兵患上缺乏维生素C的症状, 脸色苍白。情况更严峻时, 他们晚餐只能分得两汤匙的糖。

雨林生活固然充满艰辛, 但海凡也不忘将充满生命力的生态风景融入小说。在〈猎物〉和〈咒语〉两篇短文中, 作者描述军队如何透过猎物足迹以决定设置陷阱、猎捕黄麂、黑熊和野猪等动物的地点。小说穿插插图, 附录之一也呈现作者手绘的生活用品, 例如: 行军水袋、藏粮使用的铁桶以及扑杀动物所使用的装吊器具等, 丛林生活瞬间跃然纸上, 显得更加栩栩如生。

潜在的比较文学分析:

马来亚共产党、共产主义、马来西亚政治、游击战争、史学、马共书写

GENDER, SEXUALITY, AND PATRIARCHY

戏服 COSTUME

Primary Language: Mandarin
Secondary Language: Cantonese
Translation Available: Costume
Number of Pages: 319
Author: Yeng Pway Ngon
Year of Publication: 2015
Publisher: Tonsan Publications Inc.

Characterisation Notes:

Costume's major characters can be grouped into three sets based on their narrative plotlines:

1. Liang Bing Hong, De Zai, and Ah Yu:

Liang Bing Hong is the protagonist's (Liang Ru Xiu's) grandfather. Liang emigrated from Guangdong to Singapore with De Zai when they were 15 years old. Both fancied Ah Yu, who eventually married Liang.

2. Liang Ru Xiu, Shao Hua, Jia An:

Liang Ru Xiu, the protagonist, is initially engaged to Jia An. She breaks up with him due to his repeated infidelity. Liang then meets Shao Hua while learning Cantonese songs at a community centre. Overcoming all odds, they marry.

3. Liang Jian Qiu, Lin Meng Xiong, Zhang Li Li.

Liang Jian Qiu (梁建秋), stage name Liang Jian Qiu (梁剑[23]秋), is the protagonist's elder brother. Zhang Li Li and Liang Jian Qiu are co-stars in a Cantonese opera troupe. Lin Meng Xiong is a close friend of Liang's. Lin

23 "剑" (Sword) as a substitute for "建" (to build)

marries Zhang and emigrates to Canada. It is revealed, at the end of the novel, that Lin and Liang had been homosexual lovers.

Text Synopsis:

The novel depicts Liang Bing Hong and De Zai as they leave Guangdong for Singapore. It was the 1930s, and Cantonese Opera was immensely popular in Singapore. De Zai impresses an opera troupe leader and is accepted as a disciple. Liang, despite his interest in Cantonese Opera, is not willing to endure hardship, had no such opportunity, and thus starts to work for the coffee shop "Yong Fang Tea House" which he eventually inherits. Both Liang and De Zai fancied Ah Yu, who took a liking to De Zai. However, as De Zai leaves Singapore with his troupe, Liang decides not to reveal De Zai's love to Ah Yu and proposes to her himself instead. They marry and give birth to two sons, Guan Wen and Guan Wu. Years into the marriage, Liang remains conflicted over his deception, and his temper would flare whenever Ah Yu mentions De Zai.

At the beginning of the novel, an old Liang Bing Hong sits on a wheelchair reminiscing about the past (despite his failing memory). Liang regrets his inability to pursue a career in Cantonese opera. He projects his adolescent dreams onto his grandson, Jian Qiu, hoping that he would succeed in that regard. Jian Qiu becomes obsessed over Cantonese opera and quits secondary school to join an opera troupe. Jian Qiu attains a brief renown as a performer before Cantonese opera falls out of trend in the early 1960s. A disappointed Jian Qiu then leaves home, and his whereabouts thereafter become unknown.

Years pass and Liang Bing Hong dies. Ru Xiu, Bing Hong's granddaughter, in an occasional conversation with her second brother (after Jian Qiu), Jian Ming, learns of Jian Qiu's whereabouts—he had been living in poverty working as a plate-cleaner at a hawker centre. At the end of the novel, Ru Xiu, together with Zhang Li Li, meets with Jian Qiu, who reveals that he had been Meng Xiong's homosexual lover.

Significance and Remarks:

The novel has a deep relationship with Cantonese opera and songs: the novel is sprinkled with conversations that employ operatic or lyrical elements; a few of these songs even serve as a melodic background that foregrounds the main narrative. The narrative itself employs verses of Cantonese in dialogues between characters—while this employment of Chinese dialects is historically authentic, it may hamper the reader if he/she does not know Cantonese.

The novel spans 80 years (1930s to present) and presents many different images of Singapore across time. Its narrative focuses on thick descriptions of its characters' inner emotional lives rather than events. The narrative is also polyphonous: the tale is narrated both by an invisible narrator and the characters themselves (mainly Ru Xiu and Liang Bing Hong, but also other minor characters). The narrative weaves back and forth between reality and memory of the three generations of characters: characters appear, disappear, and then reappear again as the story unfolds.

The novel also broaches the topic of sexuality. The author describes the sex between Liang Bing Hong and Ah Yu: "he turns and mounts her, furiously stripping her of her clothes; he torments her for the entire night." Liang expresses his agency, authority and disdain for De Zai through sexual violence towards Ah Yu; their sex scene brings to mind a war zone. The novel clearly delineates lines of power between characters: certain characters maintain their social positions and respectability even as they act upon their vengeful sexual urges. For Jia An and Ru Xiu, the former views sex as a conquering of Ru Xiu's person: "he mumbles, nibbling her earlobe; he kisses her frantically and searches her body. She resists at first, but eventually relents and sidles up close to his body, tears flowing freely." From these instances, it is clear that the novel's depictions of sex cannot be separated from the discourse of gendered power dynamics.

The novel also broaches homosexual relations in addition to the heterosexual ones already mentioned. Indirectly, the author paints Liang Jian Qiu and Lin Meng Xiong as homosexual lovers. In the novel, Jian Qiu is not "given" in person to the reader—instead, he is pieced together by the recollections and conversations of other characters. This "imagined" Jian Qiu does not correspond to the "real" Jian Qiu. In the beginning of the novel, the reader is led to believe (along with the other characters) that Lin Meng Xiong had betrayed Liang Jian Qiu in his getting engaged with Zhang Li Li, for it is assumed that Liang fancied Zhang.

As the novel progresses, the author drops "clues" that slowly surfaces the suggestion that Jian Qiu might have been homosexual. Here, the novel also links its exploration of sexuality with gender presentation. For instance, Ru Xiu notices that Jian Qiu has thin slender hands and that her "elder brother could feasibly star as opera's female protagonist." This depicts Jian Qiu's femininity and hints that he may transgress traditional expectations of gender and sexuality. Further, the line "why don't we try again from the start" of the comradely film *Happy Together* watched by Liang and Lin gestures at the clandestine romance between the two. At the end of the novel, the author affirms the relation between Liang and Lin, writing that they had "intimate skin-to-skin" contact (but does not describe in detail).

In all, the three groups of characters in the novel depict different types of romantic relationships. Ru Xiu is betrayed by Jia An, but finds love with Shao Hua; Liang Bing Hong marries Ah Yu but has an unhappy marriage due to his guilt and disdain for De Zai; Lin Meng Xiong attempts to conceal his homosexual past from his wife Zhang Li Li to no avail. Viewed in totality, the novel reveals highly gendered power differences, and the tragedy of "comradely" love.

Potential areas of comparative analysis:

Historical Memories, Traditional Culture (Cantonese opera), Family History, Conflicts over Love, Presentation of Human Sexuality, Gender & Sexual Orientation

戏服 COSTUME

主要语言： 繁体中文
次要语言： 粤语
翻译版本： Costume
页数： 319
作者： 英培安
出版年份： 2015
出版社： 唐山出版社

人物简介：

《戏服》的主要角色依照人物的故事线可分为三组：

1. 梁炳洪、德仔、阿玉

梁炳洪是女主角梁如秀的爷爷。他和德仔十五岁时一起离开广东来到新加坡谋生。两人在新加坡认识、并同时爱上阿玉，但阿玉最后嫁给了梁炳洪。

2. 梁如秀、劭华、家安

如秀和家安本是情侣关系，发现家安出轨后，如秀断然与他分手。之后，如秀在联络所认识了一起学唱粤曲的劭华。两人历经各种困难后，终成眷属。

3. 梁剑秋、林孟雄、张荔丽

梁剑秋本名梁建秋，是梁如秀的大哥，而张荔丽是剧团花旦，是梁剑秋的搭档。林孟雄则是梁剑秋的好友，三人关系十分密切。林孟雄后与张荔丽结婚，移居加拿大。作者在小说结尾揭露梁剑秋和孟雄曾是同性恋关系。

文本概要：

小说描述梁炳洪与德仔15岁时一起从广东向下漂洋过海到新加坡谋生。30年代的新加坡，粤剧非常兴盛与蓬勃。德仔因得到一名粤剧老倌的赏识收为徒弟，加入戏班。梁炳洪虽然对粤剧感兴趣，但因为吃不起苦而没加入戏班，他转而在永芳茶室当“咖啡仔”，并继承了茶室。两人都爱慕阿玉，但阿玉和德仔比较亲近，德仔随剧团离开新加坡后，梁炳洪非但没有向阿玉代为转达德仔的心意，反而趁虚而入。梁炳洪和阿玉结婚，并生下冠文与冠武两个儿子。德仔一直是梁炳洪心中的芥蒂，只要提起德仔，梁炳洪就对阿玉发脾气。

小说开始，年迈的梁炳洪坐在轮椅上，记忆虽然逐渐衰退，却常常想起过去种种经历。梁炳洪始终对无法加入戏班而感到遗憾，因此将希望寄托在孙子剑秋身上，将他培养成戏子。剑秋沉迷粤剧无心读书，中学未毕业即加入戏班，并在剧坛崭露头角，但到了六十年代中，粤剧开始没落，剑秋因无法施展抱负郁郁不得志，选择离家出走，不知去向。

多年后，梁炳洪去世，梁如秀联络上二哥建明，并找到大哥剑秋。此时剑秋在熟食中心收拾碗碟，生活落魄潦倒。梁如秀带张荔丽和剑秋见面，揭露剑秋和孟雄多年来隐瞒的同性恋关系。

重点与备注：

《戏服》与粤剧（广东大戏）密不可分，穿插小说的粤剧曲目和台词作为背景旋律，能引起粤语读者的强烈共鸣。在叙事语言方面，作者因应人物的出身，设计粤语对白，这虽然使小说更贴近新加坡华人当时的真实生活，但对不谙懂粤语的读者来说，或许造成阅读上的障碍，得依靠小说结尾的粤语对照表有限度地理解内容的情节发展。

故事从上世纪三十年代开始说起，直到现在，呈现新加坡八十余年来的社会风貌。相较事件本身，作者更聚焦各种复杂的情感。作者采用复调的叙事技巧，除了隐形的叙述者，也包含主要的叙述者（梁炳洪和如秀）和其他次要的叙述者；由于情节发展在现实与回忆之间交错、切换，人物也不断出现、消失，然后再现。

小说有不少对身体情欲的描绘。梁炳洪“一个翻身爬到她（阿玉）身上，愤怒地剥她的衣服，折腾了她一晚”。(99) 床上的肉搏犹如行军打仗的场景，他借由性暴力宣示主权，发泄对德仔的厌恶，报复性地掌握着支配地位，维持着他的威严和体面，形象化带出权力关系的存在。又如家安欲以性征服如秀，“他喃喃地说，轻咬她的耳垂，激动地吻她，搜索她的身体。开始的时候她仍有点抗拒，然后她渐渐软化了，她贴紧他的身体，眼泪簌簌地流”。(182) 由此可见，性描写与男女权利有着密不可分的联系。

除了异性间的情感，作者也间接揭露梁炳洪和林孟雄之间的同性之情。在《戏服》中，剑秋在人物的回忆与对话中渐渐现形：如秀忆起林孟雄与张荔丽结婚，众人皆认为林孟雄横刀夺爱，让读者误以为剑秋喜欢的是张荔丽; 然而, 这个靠褪色的记忆所拼凑出来的剑秋和"真正"的他相差甚远。

作者随着故事的发展透露出蛛丝马迹, 暗示梁炳洪德为同性恋的事实。在这里, 小说将情欲的探索和性别的呈现 (gender presentation) 联系在一起: 如秀注意到剑秋纤细、修长地手指, 脑子闪过"大哥其实是可以演花旦的" (310) 。这描写剑秋的女性气质和女性化的一面, 也暗示了他有违社会对性别和性向的传统期待。另外, 作者轻描淡写点出剑秋和孟雄之间的肌肤之亲, 两人在香港一起观看经典的同性爱情电影《春光乍泄》后, 孟雄激动地对剑秋说: "不如我哋由头嚟过" (粤语, 中译: 不如我们从头来过) , 两人不可告人的同性关系浮出台面。

三组人物分别展现不同的情感关系: 梁如秀虽然遭到家安的背叛, 却遇到真爱劭华, 有情人终成眷属。梁炳洪虽然娶了阿玉, 却因良心的折磨以及对德仔的介怀, 导致夫妻关系破裂。至于林孟雄, 他试图隐藏对剑秋的同性情欲, 与张荔丽结婚, 殊不知妻子早已之情。整体来看, 作者的情欲书写, 除了揭露男女之间的权力关系, 也点出同志的爱情悲剧。

潜在的比较文学分析:

历史记忆、传统文化 (粤剧) 、家族历史、爱情纠纷、性别呈现、性别与性向

PECULIAR CHRIS

Primary Language: English
Secondary Language: No
Translation Available: Chris
Number of Pages: 228
Author: Johann S. Lee
Year of Publication: 1992
Publisher: Singapore: Cannon International

Characterisation Notes:

A coming-of age story in Singapore, the protagonist Chris "outs" his sexuality and same-sex relationships (from his relationships in Junior College till his departure for London after completing National Service). Chris also loses his alcoholic father to cancer. The novel features six other gay characters—Kenneth, Nicholas, Jack, Samuel, Paul and Dominic. The characters Nicholas, Dominic and Samuel had been sexually abused by older male figures in their childhoods.

Text Synopsis:

The novel opens with Chris' diary entry on Samuel's death. The narrative then flashes back to Chris' days in Junior College when he meets and falls in love with Kenneth, a scholar from Indonesia. While Chris has the courage to embrace his sexual orientation, Kenneth grapples with his homosexual identity. Kenneth eventually deserts the relationship in favor of an arranged marriage with his prospective wife back in Jakarta.

Chris then encounters his second partner Jack in Sydney, while on vacation from National Service. They had met for a one-night affair, which unexpectedly blossomed into a long-distance relationship.

The couple exchange correspondence until Chris falls in love with his superior in the army, Lieutenant Samuel Lye. Chris' third relationship ends in tragedy when Samuel dies of AIDS, contracted via a blood transfusion gone awry. As the novel closes, Chris leaves for London to read Law.

Significance and Remarks:

Born in 1971, Johann S. Lee was 21 when he authored *Peculiar Chris*. The novel subjected Lee to an onslaught of public scrutiny and criticism in conservative Singapore. We can understand the novel's controversy in light of the fact that homosexuality remains a taboo in (and is virtually non-existent in the public discourses of) most Asian countries. In violation of the taboo, Lee's Bildungsroman featured a homosexual protagonist and detailed the pain and the prejudices experienced by the gay community. Most importantly, the novel crashes through conventions to give voice to the voiceless and forgotten margins of the conservative Asian society. *Peculiar Chris* serves as an emotional catharsis for Lee and many other homosexual males who faced "growing-up gay" blues.

Peculiar Chris is notable for its portrayal of the differential treatment of a soldier that has "come out." During his medical check prior to military service, Chris confesses his sexual preference. He is then subjected, along with all other homosexuals, to repetitive blood tests and monotonous administrative tasks in military logistics and is prohibited from staying overnight on military compounds. In addition, the novel reveals that male homosexuals are also denied prospects of scholarships and employment opportunities in the civil service.

In the epilogue, the character Kuang Ming makes a brief appearance. The Chinese characters of his name signifies a bright, promising future—a metaphor that symbolizes Lee's hopes that all can grow up without agonizing over their sexual identities.

Peculiar Chris is the debut of Lee's queer triptych. The sequels—To Know *Where I'm Coming From* (2007) and *Quiet Time* (2008)—continue to capture the incessant tension and conflicts which remain part and parcel of the lives of the oppressed (in Singapore, homosexual activities remain criminalized under the state's penal code). The novels are a plea for all of us to put aside prejudices to be more gracious and accepting in hopes of building a society that supports a spectrum of sexual identities.

Undoubtedly the pioneer of gay fiction writing in Singapore, Lee opens the floodgates for the Singaporean queer literature scene by documenting the encounters and experiences of the gay community of Singapore. Ultimately, queer literature is all about love—we all yearn for the deepest interpersonal affection, without fear, and regardless of our sexual affiliations.

Potential areas of comparative analysis:

LGBTQ, Homosexuality, Homosexual Bildungsroman, Homophobia, Sexual Identity, Sexual Orientation, Gender, Coming-of-Age, Queer Literature, Queer Theory, Gay/Lesbian Studies, Growing Up in Singapore, Cultural Taboo, Gay Fiction

PECULIAR CHRIS

主要语言： 英文
次要语言： -
翻译版本： Chris
页数： 228
作者： Johann S. Lee
出版年份： 1992
出版社： Singapore: Cannon International

人物简介：

Peculiar Chris 是一部描述男同性恋克里斯（Chris）成长过程（coming-of-age）的小说，记录着他确认性取向，以及从初级学院至服完兵役后、远赴伦敦留学前的三段同性恋情。克里斯的童年并不愉快，他的父亲酗酒，在他10岁时因癌症逝世。除了克里斯，小说还有另6名男同性恋——肯尼斯（Kenneth）、尼可拉斯（Nicholas）、杰克（Jack）、塞缪尔（Samuel）、多米尼克（Dominic）以及保罗（Paul）。其中尼可拉斯、塞缪尔以及多米尼克幼年时曾被男性长辈性侵犯，留下不可磨灭的童年阴影。

文本概要：

小说从塞缪尔的死开始。克里斯先在一篇日记中描绘塞缪尔临终之际被病魔折磨的煎熬，后以倒叙的手法将视线拉回克里斯的高中生活。当时，克里斯和来自印度尼西亚的奖学金得主肯尼斯相遇相爱；然而，与克里斯不同的是，肯尼斯还未完全接受自己身为同性恋的身份，他最后选择舍弃这段感情，听从父母之命，返回雅加达相亲。在服兵役期间，克里斯在雪梨（Sydney）遇见杰克，和他发生一夜情；两人都没预料到这短暂的邂逅会发展成一段长距离恋情。他们开始以书信往来，一直到克里斯爱上他在军队中的上司塞缪尔。可惜的是，克里斯的第三段感情也以悲剧告终——塞缪尔因一次输血事故不幸感染艾滋病，撒手人寰。小说最后，克里斯远赴伦敦修读法律。

重点与备注：

Peculiar Chris 是本地首部以同性恋为题材的小说，于1992年出版后争

议不断，使当时年仅21岁的作者承受社会大众严厉的审视和强烈的指责。在保守的新加坡（和其他亚洲社会），同性恋是个禁忌话题，然作者打破沉默、冲破传统，以男同性恋克里斯的成长过程为主线，刻画在传统亚洲社会、被边缘化的同性恋社会群体所饱受的痛苦和偏见，同时也赋予他们话语权。因此，不论是对作者、克里斯还是其他男同性恋者而言，创作和阅读是一种情感上的宣泄（emotional catharsis）。

格外值得注意的是，作者对已“出柜”（即承认自己同性恋身份）的军人所遭受到的差别待遇的描写。入伍前，克里斯坦在体检时坦白了性取向。随后，他和其他男同性恋者一样，在军营的后勤部门负责单调的行政工作。他们不能在军中过夜，也必须定期接受抽血检查。不仅如此，“出柜”也意味着葬送仕途——一旦坦诚身份，便失去领取奖学金以及在公务部门服务的机会。

在小说的结尾（epilogue）部分，克里斯在班机上认识了光明（Kwang Ming）。这短暂出现的人物是个隐喻，蕴含着作者对同性恋社群的期许，希望他们在成长过程中不因性倾向而感到苦恼，迎接光明的未来。

Peculiar Chris是作者酷儿文学 (Queer Literature) 三部曲的第一部作品，续集To Know Where I'm Coming From (2007) 以及Quiet Time (2008) 延续Peculiar Chris的基调，继续捕捉同性恋群体长期面对的紧张关系和无可避免的冲突。根据新加坡刑事法典第377A节条文，男性同性性行为属犯罪行为。因此，在社会层面上，作者透过这三部曲恳请大众放下成见、以更慈悲、更包容的心，共同营造一个性别友善的环境。

毋庸置疑，作者Johann S. Lee是新加坡同性恋小说写作 (Gay Fiction) 的先锋人物。通过记录同性恋社群的遭遇和经历，他开创了本地酷儿文学（Queer Literature) 书写的先河。酷儿文学是聚焦于爱的故事——我们都渴望人与人之间最深层的情感连结，我们都不应被性向所及，任何人都应该能毫不畏惧地去爱人，以及被爱。

潜在的比较文学分析：

LGBTQ、同性恋、同性恋题材小说、恐同症、性取向（性倾向）、性别、青少年成长小说、同性恋文学、同性恋小说、同性恋理论研究、文化禁忌、新加坡成长故事

DELAYED RAYS OF A STAR

Primary Language: English

Secondary Language: Some Chinese, French and German

Translation Available: No

Number of Pages: 383

Author: Amanda Lee Koe

Year of Publication: 2019

Publisher: Bloomsbury Publishing

Characterisation Notes:

The narrative primarily revolves around three legendary 20th-century cinema figures: Marlene Dietrich, Anna May Wong, and Leni Riefenstahl. The trio first meet at a Berlin soirée in 1928.

Of the three women, Marlene Dietrich is a bisexual German American actress and one of the highest-paid Hollywood stars of her time. Dietrich is portrayed as having a provocative allure as a result of her eccentricity and complete disregard for conventions. In her twilight years, Dietrich is depicted as a cantankerous recluse.

Anna May Wong, or Wong Liu Tsong, is the first Chinese American actress to grace the silver screen and achieve international recognition. She is a second-generation immigrant with little knowledge of her ancestral heritage. As such, her character is shaped by both her experience as a racial minority, and a cultural traitor.

Leni Riefenstahl is introduced against the backdrop of a rising Nazi regime, wherein she is a director and actress of her own movie, *Tiefland*. She would later be known as the director and producer the Nazi propaganda film, *Triumph of the Will.*

The novel also features side characters who orbits the female protagonists: Hans Haas, a homosexual member of a German film crew who had lost his lover Schmitz in a battle; and Josef von Sternberg, an Austrian-American filmmaker who worked with Hollywood movie stars. We are also introduced to Bébé, an illegal Chinese immigrant, who had been unknowingly sex-trafficked to Marseille after she boarded a boat in search of a better life. She escapes and makes her way to Paris, where she avoids deportation by lying that she was seeking asylum in the wake of the Tiananmen Square massacre.

Text Synopsis:

Delayed Rays of a Star opens at a Soirée in Berlin in 1928, which features three up-and-coming actresses: Marlene Dietrich, Anna May Wong and Leni Riefenstahl. The novel traces the career and life trajectories of the three actresses.

As the novel unfolds, Anna May Wong waits eagerly for her first breakthrough as a lead actress in a Hollywood film despite her father's skepticism about her career choice—till that point, limited in roles by her ethnicity, Wong had played only minor characters. At the same time, Marlene Dietrich wins the role of Lola Lola in Josef von Sternberg's *The Blue Angel* and immediately attains international fame.

The narrative then moves on to Leni Riefenstahl, who had lost the role of Lola Lola to Dietrich. Riefenstahl meets Adolf Hitler at one of his rallies and the pair acknowledge their mutual admiration for ambition and drive. Hitler then extends Riefenstahl a job offer as a filmmaker for the Nazi party, which she accepts. Riefenstahl is heavily criticized for her support of the atrocities of the Nazi regime and is even alleged to be Hitler's lover. However, Riefenstahl denies all allegations and claims that she had been motivated by art and not politics; instead, she believes that she should be remembered as a trailblazer for feminism and female empowerment in the film industry.

The narrative concludes with Dietrich, who lives out her final days closed off from the world in an apartment in Paris. She is taken care of by Bébé, a Chinese immigrant who visits every Sunday. However, tragedy strikes as Bébé falls in love with Ibrahim Max Müller, a rebellious student of German-Turkish descent, despite their language barriers. Müller is expelled from university for damaging public property and eventually shot for trespassing into East Germany, and Bébé is deported back to China. Dietrich becomes livid that the only person with whom she had a genuine connection with in her life had disappeared. The novel closes with a monumental historical moment: Dietrich watches as the Berlin Wall falls on television.

Significance and Remarks:

Delayed Rays of a Star is a refreshing departure from the common themes of local politics and national identity that permeate most of Singaporean literature. The novel plunges the reader into the lives of three legendary actresses of varying racial and national backgrounds, Marlene Dietrich, Anna May Wong, and Leni Riefenstahl, and engages the reader in a rich discussion of the interplay between personal identity, history and memory.

The author, Amanda Lee Koe, does not hold back in her intimate and portrayals of the protagonists' lives and career. Her prose accentuates Dietrich's charisma, Wong's stubbornness, and Riefenstahl's ambition, thereby enabling the reader to empathize with the protagonists' attitudes towards life and its challenges.

Koe presents a controversial—painful yet comforting—notion of identity: that identity is only partly externally constituted, and hence not even a lifetime's dedication and individual effort suffices to change one's identity. The novel features three protagonists with larger-than- life personalities as actresses and performers active in golden age Hollywood. They strive to create and inhabit their desired identities but ultimately remain within the externally constituted strictures that define their identities. While they act for a living, their identities are not defined by acting alone. Dietrich is a German, and an American; she is white, bisexual, and eventually, old. Wong is an outsider: she is an ethnic Chinese in a society of white people, and an American in her homeland of China. Riefenstahl is a politician and a social activist: she had capitalized on politics and gender discourse to advance her career. Thus, to Koe, identity is a concatenation of sociality and politics, and not merely the product of individual agency.

The reader can appreciate the evolution of society and culture over time through the personal and social challenges to the protagonists' identities. Each of these women had been a pioneer in their time: Dietrich was an openly genderbending bisexual, Wong the first Chinese American woman on the silver screen, and Riefenstahl one of the few high-profile female directors. In their respective roles, the women faced discrimination and injustices we may consider unthinkable and even ludicrous today. As such, the reader is made aware of the privileges and the historicity of the present: that modern society and culture is shaped by the actions and sacrifices of historical agents.

Lastly, *Delayed Rays of a Star* explores the immortality of art in conjunction with memory and history. The novel was inspired by a photograph of the three women, Dietrich, Wong, and Riefenstahl, at a party in Berlin nearly a century ago. The moment depicted in the photograph has long passed and can never be repeated or recreated to perfection; however, the photograph seems to have immortalized the moment—the photograph ensures that the legacies and the memories of the women continue to inspire artists today. Hence, art creates history due its reproducibility in time; art is one of the few ways that we can leave an immortal mark on the world.

Potential Areas of Comparative Analysis:

Postmodernism, Film History, Historiography, Traditional vs Modern Values, Emigration, Feminism, Social Commentary, Race, Women, Politics, Art vs Politics, Intersectionality, Art, Memory, History

DELAYED RAYS OF A STAR

主要语言：英文

次要语言：些许中文、德文和法文

翻译版本：-

页数：383

作者：Amanda Lee Koe

出版年份：2019

出版社：Bloomsbury Publishing

人物简介：

故事围绕三位20世纪的传奇电影人物展开，她们分别是：玛琳·黛德丽（Marlene Dietrich）、黄柳霜（Anna May Wong）以及莱妮·里芬斯塔尔（Leni Riefenstahl）。1928年，三人在德国柏林的一场晚宴上第一次见面。

在她们三人当中，玛琳是一名德裔美籍的双性恋女演员，也是当时收入最高的好莱坞电影明星之一。她性格古怪，天生反骨，离经叛道的人物形象使她浑身上下散发出具挑衅意味的吸引力，充满诱惑。到了晚年，上了年纪的她过着独居生活，平时爱争吵、抱怨不断。

黄柳霜是首位登上大银幕，并获得国际认可的美籍华裔女巨星。她是第二代移民，对祖籍的文化遗产知之甚少；因此，她在美国是少数民族（racial minority），也是个文化叛徒（cultural traitor），这两种身份一同塑造她的人物性格。

莱妮是纳粹政权崛起的年代的导演兼演员，除了自编自导自演电影《低地》（Tiefland），也是政治宣传片《意志的胜利》（Triumph of the Will）的导演和制片人。

小说也带出围绕在三位女主角身边的配角的故事。汉斯·哈斯（Hans Haas）是德国剧组的成员之一，不久前在战争中失去同性伴侣施米茨（Schmitz）。曾和多名好莱坞电影巨星合作的奥地利裔美国导演约瑟夫·冯·斯登堡（Josef von Sternberg），以及来自中国的非法移民贝贝（Bébé）。为追求更好的生活，贝贝误上贼船，惨遭人口贩子拐卖到法国马赛（Marseilles）卖淫。她逃到巴黎后，谎称刚参与天安门事件，正在寻求政治庇护，逃过被遣送回国的命运。

文本概要：

1928年，柏林：玛琳、黄柳霜以及莱妮这三名刚崭露头角的女演员在一场晚宴上第一次遇见彼此，小说由此开始，追溯三人的演艺事业和生命轨迹。

黄柳霜美籍华人的身份极度限制了她能接演的角色，因此她的父亲始终对女儿的职业选择有所保留，尽管如此，她依然急切地争取好莱坞电影女主角的角色，期盼在演艺生涯获得突破。与此同时，玛琳凭借着在约瑟夫 · 冯 · 斯登堡的电影《蓝天使》（The Blue Angel）中的罗拉（Lola）一角赢得满堂彩，一举成名。

没能获得罗拉一角的莱妮在群众大会上遇见希特勒（Hitler），两人认可彼此的野心和魄力，希特勒随后向莱妮提出工作要约，希望她担任纳粹党的电影制作人。她接受了希特勒的邀请，但在接下来的日子里，她也因支持纳粹政权的暴行而遭到严厉批评，甚至被指控是希特勒的情人。她矢口否认，并强调艺术、而非政治才是自己的推动力；相反的，她希望世人能记得，她是电影界女性主义和女性赋权运动（female empowerment）的开拓者。

玛琳晚年在巴黎过着与世隔绝的日子，由贝贝每逢周日上门照料。此时，悲剧发生了。尽管两人之间存有语言障碍，贝贝还是爱上了因破坏公物而被大学开出的德国土耳其裔的叛逆男子伊布拉欣 · 穆勒（Ibrahim Max Müller）。一次，穆勒擅自闯入东德境内，当场被击毙，而贝贝也因这次事件被遣返回中国，玛琳为失去生命中唯一真挚的联系而感到愤怒。小说以一个重大的历史事件收尾：玛琳坐在电视机前见证柏林围墙倒下。

重点与备注：

大部分的新加坡文学作品以本地政治或国家认同为题，*Delayed Rays Of A Star* 则另辟蹊径，呈现电影史上三名来自不同国籍背景的传奇女星的一生，并和读者就身份认同、记忆以及历史的相互作用展开丰富的讨论，令人耳目一新。

文本强调了三人的特点——玛琳的魅力、黄柳霜的固执和强硬，以及莱妮的野心勃勃，作者极尽能事地描述她们在生活中以及事业上，亲昵和人性化的一面，使读者能感同身受三人面对生活各种挑战时的人生态度。

作者提出一个具争议(即痛苦但又欣慰)的身份概念(notion of identity)：虽然外部因素有助于建构身份认同，但这只是部分的，因此即使倾其一生的奉献和力量都不足以改变一个人的身份。不论是玛琳、黄柳霜还是莱妮，她们个性鲜明、光鲜亮丽，是非同凡响的女演员和表演者；她们活跃于好莱坞的黄金时代，靠演技谋生，努力活成想要的样子，但始终无法从外界的定义和束缚中挣脱出来，因为世人不仅用演员这份职业定义三人。

玛琳是德国人、是美国人、是白人，同时也是个双性恋者，最终也会年华老去；黄柳霜除了是名演员，也是个局外人——她在白人眼中是华裔，回到中国却成了他们眼中的美国人；莱妮是个政治人物，也积极推动社会运动，她曾利用政治与性别论述来推动她的事业发展。因此，对作者而言，身份的建构绝不是个体能动性（personal agency）的产物，她们和社会、政治运动之间的互动也共同的形塑她们的身份。

读者可从三人面对的个人以及社会层面的挑战感受社会和文化随着时间的演变。她们是属于那个年代的先行者：玛琳公开承认自己是名双性恋者，黄柳霜是首位登上好莱坞大银幕的美籍华裔女性，而莱妮是当年少数的知名女导演。她们在各自的角色中饱受今日难以想象、甚至觉得可笑的不公义和歧视现象，使读者意识：上一代人的牺牲和付出，换来了现代、文明社会的生活，以及我们能享有的权利，这就是历史的真实性。

小说结合记忆和历史，探索艺术不朽的特质。作品的灵感源自于近百年前，三人在柏林的一个晚宴上的一张合影。按下快门的那一瞬间已经远去，永远无法复制或完美重现，但那张照片上似乎将那一瞬间定格、化为不朽。这张照片确保三人所留下的精神遗产继续激励着今天的艺术家们，而艺术也因其可复制性(reproducibility)的特点能在历史上留下光辉一页，成为我们在世界上留下不朽印记的少数方式之一。

潜在的比较文学分析：

后现代主义、电影史、史学、传统与现代价值观、移民、女性主义、社会评论、种族、女性、政治、艺术与政治、交织性（交叉性）、艺术、记忆、历史

绿绿杨柳风 (THE SWAYING GREEN WILLOWS)

Primary Language: Mandarin
Secondary Language: No
Translation Available: No
Number of Pages: 127
Author: Soon Ai Ling
Year of Publication: 1988
Publisher: Grassroots Book Room

Characterisation Notes:

The Swaying Green Willows is a collection of four short stories told from the perspective of four women: the young widow Qin Qin, the Chinese-educated graduate Ke Xin, Chen Mei Di, a woman who had just entered society, and the single mother Tang Xuan Ru. The author analyzes the ideological superstructures that guide the character's thoughts and reflects upon the concept of female identity.

Text Synopsis:

After her husband's death, the protagonist Qin Qin emigrates to Hong Kong with her daughter Xiao Ying to further her studies. While taking classes at a university. Qin Qin meets an Indonesian professor named Han Yi Wen who has a daughter with his French ex-wife. Qin and Han find that they have much in common and a romance blossoms between the two. Qin Qin's parents and in-laws are in support of Qin and Han's marriage, but Han's daughter cannot and does not accept Qin. In the end, Qin voluntarily steps out of the romance with Han to focus on her daughter.

Fang Ke Xin hails from a Chinese-educated background. Despite her three years of English studies in the United Kingdom, Fang is spurned by many employers. By sheer chance, Fang meets the civil servant Song Qi Wen, and the couple decides to marry. Before the marriage, Fang meets with her former classmate Ma Guo Ping at their alma mater to reminisce about their past.

Ma dies in a road accident that day when his car collides with an army truck. Unfortunately for Fang, the news media described Fang and Ma as a couple tragically separated because Ma had forgotten to put his seatbelts on. Song breaks up with Fang and cancels their wedding, and the latter moves out and begins life anew.

Chen Mei Di had originally intended to move to Singapore after completing her university degree but decided to stay in Muar to work as an accountant and care for her ailing mother. Chen meets her superior Chen Li Wei and the couple soon falls in love. The two move to Kuala Lumpur, where the latter proposes that they live together before marriage. Chen Mei Di rejects him, applies for a transfer and returns to her hometown.

Tang Xuan Ru's seemingly ideal marriage with Wu Yi Jie starts to fall apart after the birth of their daughter Xiao Qin. Wu divorces Tang and abandons her to raise their daughter by herself. Tang struggles against discrimination and an uncaring world. Her cousin Xun Ru advices her to teach Xiao Qin basic life skills to alleviate Tang's burden. A few years later, Xiao Qin tragically passes away due to a heart condition. Tang is inspired to open a center for children with learning disabilities with Xun Ru.

Significance and Remarks:

Narrative point of view

The Swaying Green Willows narrates the lives of women from their own perspectives and thus empowers women with a voice and the agency to define modern femininity. For instance, Qin Qin narrates her own experiences in the first person. She has to overcome sorrows and trepidation that follows her husband's demise and rise to become an independent and rational modern woman (by leaving her past behind and by furthering her studies in Hong Kong). From such a perspective, we can apprehend Qin's fortitude and courage in life.

The images of women: in tradition and in modernity

The author also frames a conflict between traditional and modern images of women to emphasize the importance of female agency: in the novel, the women struggle to overcome the strictures of patriarchy in both the traditional and modern contexts.

Qin Qin fails to shake her label as a widow. She feels indignant that she cannot change her reality as a "widow"—in a patriarchal society, women are traditionally expected to remain chaste and not remarry after their husband's deaths. Hence, Qin's romance with Yi Wen is doomed by the gossip and judgement of society.

On the other hand, Fang Ke Xin's mother is an archetypically traditional mother. Her dogmatism is evident in her interactions with her three daughters: her life philosophy is that it is only appopriate that women find and marry and give up on their careers to become stay-at-home mothers. Fang's mother resolutely believes that all women belong at home to care for their children. In contrast to her dogmatism, Fang's sister Ke Ming can be seen as an archetypically progressive modern female. She rejects her mother's moral systems and denies her mother control over her life. Ke Ming proclaims that she wishes to be a strong and independent woman and enjoy a life of sophistication without worry about marriage and children, against her mother's severe rebukes.

From conformity to the transcendence of patriarchy: the awakening of modern feminism

Fang Ke Xin originally intends to subordinate herself to a man in her life. Upon meeting the civil servant Song Qi Wen, Fang surrenders herself to the patriarchal norm of womanhood. She believes that she is willing to marry him despite their differences because she wishes to rely on him for the rest of her life. An accident before Fang's marriage shocks her out of her ideals. She cancels her marriage because she finds that she has lost herself: she shouts "come back to me, my spirit for the East is not for you..." as if she wishes to find her lost self. Fang moves out and decides not to rely on her family or other men. At that moment, Fang overcomes the bonds of tradition, and adopts an independent attitude characteristic of modern women.

The protagonist Chen Mei Di also perfectly embodies the characteristics of a modern woman: an independent character and financial freedom. Chen's ancestors had been servants of a plantation in Maur for generations. After obtaining her degree, Chen works as an accountant at a bank and is promoted to a post at the bank's headquarters in Kuala Lumpur. Chen affirms her self-value and most importantly, she is able to make a living for herself and shake off the century-old strictures that plagued her family.

Wisdom for modern women

In the last story of the collection, the protagonist expresses: "survival depends on one's own ability and vitality. All life— be it animal or plant—survive only because they fight" (118). This is the novel's inspiring message for modern women.

The author Soon Ai Ling analyses the existential conditions for womanhood. She finds that womanhood is solely dependent upon humanhood—the social conditions of marriage and divorce or the derogatory labels of the "widow" and "divorced wife" are merely incidental to the condition of womanhood. As such, the external situations do not impede the transcendence of women; on the contrary, the challenges posed by women's situations enable them to be more resilient and adaptable than men.

The author Soon Ai Ling focuses the attention of the novel on the core theme of womanhood. Her female characters are highly educated and financially able—they are no longer objectified nor presented as traditional women attached to men. Despite the characters' diverse situations, they are united in their rejection of the traditional expectations of women, and they believe that they can exercise their agency through hard work and self-mastery.

Potential areas of comparative analysis:

Traditional Femininity, Modern Feminism, Women's Image, Women's Perspective, Patriarchy, Control/Subordination, Post-colonial Language Environment, Chinese vs English Educated Students in Singapore

绿绿杨柳风

主要语言：中文
次要语言：-
翻译版本：-
页数：127
作者：孙爱玲
出版年份：1988
出版社：草根书室

人物简介：

《绿绿杨柳风》由四篇短篇小说组成。作者以四名女性的视角：育有一女的年轻寡妇秦勤、华校毕业生方可欣、社会新鲜人陈美娣以及婚姻破裂、独自照顾智钝女儿的汤瑄如，叙述她们面对的意识形态和其对女性身份的反思。

文本概要：

丈夫意外过世后，秦勤带着女儿小颖到香港深造，认识了大学教授韩逸文。来自印尼的他和法国籍前妻育有一名女儿。两人志趣相投，关系愈加亲密，尽管秦勤的父母和家翁家婆都不反对她再嫁，但眼看逸文的女儿无法接受他再娶，秦勤自愿退出，把重心放在小颖身上。

即使在英国修读英文三年，华校生方可欣在求职路上依旧处处碰壁。迷茫的她偶然结识了公务员宋启文，两人论及婚嫁。婚前，她和老同学马国平回母校叙旧，途中发生车祸，马国平意外身亡。车祸隔天，报章误报两人是情侣关系，两人因此取消婚礼，可欣离开家庭在外租房，展开新生活。

陈美娣计划在大学毕业后到新加坡求职，但因母亲身体状况不佳，选择在麻坡一间银行担任会计员。她和上司陈立威谈起恋爱，不久后，两人被调到吉隆坡银行总行。立威提出婚前同居试婚的建议，但被否决，美娣选择调职返回麻坡，重返故乡的怀抱。

汤瑄如和丈夫吴义杰原是令人称羡的一对，但女儿小芹出生后，两人的感情逐渐被消耗殆尽。义杰对女儿感到不耐烦，和瑄如提出离婚，抛家弃女，留下瑄如一人扛起养育小芹的重责。面对外界异样的眼光与不谅解，瑄如被折磨得身心俱疲。她听从当护士的堂姐珣如的话，放手训练小芹，让她具备基础的生活自理能力，减轻她的精神负担。小芹几年后因心脏出现问题离世。此时，珣如邀请她一起经营一间专为迟钝儿童开设的幼稚园。

重点与备注：

《绿绿杨柳风》围绕女性的生命遭遇展开，作者以女性为中心的叙事观点，充分赋予她们话语权，从中构建现代女性的自主意识。秦勤以第一人称"我"的叙事形态告诉读者，丈夫过世后，她沉浸在伤痛和彷徨当中，但身为一个受过教育的现代女性，她得走出丧夫之痛，因此，她到香港深造。从她的视角里，不难洞悉她内心的坚毅与生存下去的勇气。

女性形象：传统VS现代

与此同时，作者刻画传统和现代女性的冲突，强化女性自主的重要性。不论时代如何变迁，小说的女性依然摆脱不了封建社会的桎梏。

寡妇的身份是秦勤永远都摆脱不了的枷锁。她非常排斥"寡妇"这个标签，但她无法改她的确是个寡妇的这个事实。在父权社会中，女性在丈夫死后若不改嫁，便是符合封建社会对女性的道德要求。这也是为什么，当她和逸文来往时，依旧躲不过"人言可畏"这一道坎。

方可欣的母亲是典型的传统女性，在和三个女儿的谈话与互动中，她根深蒂固的传统价值观可见一斑。她主张，女人应该和一个老实人结婚，并放弃事业、在家相夫教子。可见，她认为女人最后的归属只能是家庭和孩子。如果说方可欣母亲的依附性正好就是传统女性意识的体现，那方可欣的妹妹方可明则是现代女性主义的代表人物。可明非常抗拒她母亲的那番论调，更不愿意母亲操控她的人生。她强调自己要当女强人，享受高尚的生活，而结婚生子不在计划之内，却被母亲严厉斥责。

从屈就到跨越父权的樊笼：现代女性主义的苏醒

方可欣也曾动过依附男性的念头。在遇到公共服务部门高层主管宋启文后，她掉进了传统女性价值观的陷阱。她心想：不论启文在思想和生活上和她有多不同，她都愿意嫁给他，期盼下半辈子可以依赖宋启文过日子。她的觉醒来自于婚前的车祸。决定取消婚礼后，她惊觉她早已失去自我，呐喊“魂兮归来，东方不可以托些……”（《楚辞·招魂篇》），仿佛在召唤在外游荡的魂魄，希望早日找回失去的自我。她决定搬出去住，不再依附家人或依靠男人。从这一刻起，她挣脱了传统价值观的束缚，追求自由自主的生活，建立了现代女性所拥有的独立人格。

陈美娣也完美体现了现代女性所具备的特质：人格独立和财务自由。陈美娣的祖辈多年来是麻坡一片种植园的员工，她痛恨这主仆关系。大学毕业后，她在银行担任会计员，受到上司赏识，调往吉隆坡总行。一纸文凭赋予了她摆脱余家的筹码，找到自己的价值，最重要的是，她能和母亲一起摆脱整百年来的桎梏。

《绿绿杨柳风》给予现代女性的启示

在小说的最后一个故事，汤珣如说：“生存是靠自己的能力，靠自己的生命力。生命这样东西，无论动物、植物都是靠自己奋斗而生存的。”（118）这是《绿绿杨柳风》给现代女性最重要的启示。不管是未婚、已婚或是离婚，女性的婚姻状况从来都不是孙爱玲塑造女性形象的重点。先是一个人，才是一个女人，因此寡妇或离婚妇女等带有贬义的标签并不会成为女性实现自我的绊脚石，反之，这恰恰展现比起男性，女性在逆境中较强的生存意志和适应能力。孙爱玲关注女性议题，她把女性推向中心，让她们成为《绿绿杨柳风》的焦点。她笔下的女性受过高等教育、性格独立、财富自由，不再是附庸品，完全颠覆了传统女性依附于男性的形象。她们的际遇各不相同，但肯定的是，她们不愿符合传统社会对女性的期待，透过努力掌握人生的主导权。

潜在的比较文学分析：

传统女性意识、现代女性主义、女性形象、女性视角、父权社、从属/掌控、后殖民语境、华校生VS英校生

他乡女子 (WOMEN FROM A FOREIGN LAND)

Primary Language: Mandarin
Secondary Language: No
Translation Available: No
Number of Pages: 228
Author: Effie Lo
Year of Publication: 2020
Publisher: Global Publishing

Characterisation Notes:

《他乡女子》(*Ta Xiang Nü Zi*), is a collection of five short stories. Central to these stories is the theme of love: the first three stories adopt a modern woman's perspective on the value of love, family, and marriage; the latter two stories discuss the theme of familial love from the perspective of children.

Text Synopsis:

1. "*Ta Xiang Nü Zi*," (*Woman from a foreign land*)

The protagonist Zheng Xun Xun meets and falls in love with the wealthy Huang Shicheng. They get married and move to Singapore, where she will spend ten years of her life. Zheng's character conforms to an archetypal woman who is "successful in career, but a failure in love." Zheng is confident and achieves great success in her advertising career; in contrast, Zheng's marriage ends in failure as she is unable to stand her husband's conservative disposition and constant deference to his mother's wishes. Zheng takes her husband to court over custody of their son. However, upon learning of her foreign lover Shidan's childhood tribulations arising from his parents' custody battle for him, Zheng relents and drops her case against Huang. Zheng also ultimately relinquishes a future with Shidan abroad in choosing to stay in Singapore to be close to her son.

2. "*Wang Qing Ji*," (*The story of frustrated love*)

The story is split into two narratives. The first narrative explores the failing marriage of the wealthy Yu Weite and his wife Lisa. Yu Weite had been unable to sexually satisfy Lisa, and the marriage is further complicated by his infatuation with his colleague He Shu Ting. The second narrative concerns He Shu Ting's romance with Xiao. The couple is deeply in love but Xiao refuses to leave his wife for He. Eventually, Xiao's wife divorces Xiao and frees him to pursue a relationship with He.

3. "*Chun Meng Wu Hen*," (*The dream of romance leaves no trace*)

The protagonist Zhang Kangni hails from an English-educated background. She is strongly prejudiced against Chinese culture and language and takes great pride in her views. In the story, Zhang meets and becomes infatuated with her colleague Ban Jieming. Zhang reverses her earlier Sinophobic position to work on her Mandarin in hopes of impressing Ban, who is passionate about Chinese culture. However, Zhang's idyllic dreams of a life with Ban evaporates as she soon learns that Ban is already attached to a partner who shares his love of Chinese culture. Like a dream that leaves no trace, the story ends on a woeful note.

4. "*Mu Nan Ri*," (*The day of mother's suffering—one's birthday*)

Ailin is a vain, hedonistic, and uncaring woman. She abandons her daughter Hanhan a year after her husband passes away in favour of her plans to leave the country with another man. The plan never materializes, but Ailin never once returned to her daughter. Without parental love, Hanhan is quiet, has low self-esteem and almost goes astray. In her mother's absence, Hanhan remains desiring of care and affection from a maternal figure, and so continues to pine for Ailin. Fortunately, Hanhan is saved from a path of ruin by her aunt Jingfen. Jingfen educates Hanhan and even encourages communication between Ailin and Hanhan, thus holding the family together.

5. "*Fu Yu Zi*" (*Father and son*)

Lin Changwang is a Chinese immigrant to Singapore. He remains loyal to his friends, only to be plagued with disabilities. Lin's temper worsens with his economic situation and his wife and children soon leave him. Lin's son Leimeng even sees his father as a useless parasite who gambles and drinks his life away. Lin spends his last years alone and in the hospital for a terminal illness. Despite his hatred towards his father, Leimeng visits him upon learning of his illness. The story ends as Leimeng learns of his father's past and forgives him.

Significance and Remarks:

The first three stories of the collection discuss the themes of romance, marriage, and familial values from the perspectives of white-collared women.

The women Zheng Xunxun, He Shu Ting and Zhang Kangni are highly educated women who achieve great success in their careers. However, all three women do not find similar success in their relationships—they remain alone after their divorces or breakups. For instance, the protagonist of "*Ta Xiang Nü Zi*" Zheng Xunxun is especially sceptical of marriage. Zheng is an independent woman who looks down on her spineless husband to the detriment of their marriage. She eventually divorces him to relieve herself of a marriage that had become insufferable for her. However, Zheng could not forfeit motherhood as easily as marriage. At the end of the story, Zheng chooses to stay in Singapore for biweekly visits of her son over a marriage with Shidan in Canada.

Moving on, the next two stories center on the theme of familial love. The author depicts parental love through the perspectives of Hanhan and Leimeng. Hanhan never experienced motherly love, despite the best efforts of her aunt Jingfen to fill the maternal void in Hanhan's life. On Hanhan's 21st birthday, she expresses her gratitude to both her biological mother and her aunt for their roles in her life. In so doing, Hanhan forgives her mother for leaving her at birth. In "*Fu Yu Zi*," the author discusses the strong bonds of kinship, this time through the relationship between father and son. Leimeng discovers that he has a red mole in the exact same position as his estranged father. Leimeng realizes the closeness and indelibility of blood ties and decides to make peace with his father.

In addition to the themes of sexuality, family and relationships, the novel also discusses the diasporic experiences of the Chinese immigrant communities. In "*Wang Qing Ji*," the protagonist He Shu Ting, who is studying in America, excitedly participates in a protest in New York. In "*Ta Xiang Nü Zi*," the protagonist Zheng Xunxun takes part in a movement to "protect the Diaoyu islands" along with many other international students of Chinese descent. Zheng's position and experience recall increasing Chinese ethnonationalist sentiments: in the author's depiction of a historical event, she invokes a "shared memory" amongst all Chinese emigrants in the world, and thereby foregrounds the core themes of "emigration," "Chinese diaspora," and "identity."

"*Ta Xiang Nü Zi*" also makes two telling observations about the Singaporean Chinese: their non-identification with Chinese culture and their commitment towards utilitarian principles.

Zhang Kangni is a classic example of a pragmatist: she revels in her dismissal of Mandarin as impractical and is not embarrassed by her inability to converse with her mother and elder sister. From such a perspective, her reaffiliation with Chinese culture is an ironic one—Zhang is motivated by impulses of love and guilt, and not by authentic self-discovery. "*Ta Xiang Nü Zi*" also engages with Singaporean pragmatism. Huang Shicheng and his wife initially intended for their child to go through traditional Chinese education. As time passes, however, Huang abruptly changes his position, believing that his child must attend a renowned "English" school to avoid the stigma attached to the Chinese educated within an anglophilic society. Similarly, in "*Wang Qing Ji*," Yu Weite's mother insisted that her children undergo "English" education despite her own love for Chinese culture because "one can only find a job and succeed in life with an English education."

The author Luo Yifei is an experienced writer. Born in Hunan and educated in the United States, she now lives with her husband in Singapore. Informed by her transnational experiences, Luo observes the changes in Singaporean society through the lens of a foreigner and the thematic focus of love and other relationships. Luo's fictional works are sophisticated and multi-layered—especially in their depiction of urban love as transcending generations, sex, nationality and race. This collection of stories, *Ta Xiang Nü Zi*, was published in the Singaporean Chinese flagship daily *Lianhe Zaobao* from 1986 to April 1994. The republication of the stories as a collection systematizes a rich source of material for academic research and thus the book can be considered a significant contribution to the domain of Singapore Sinophone literature.

Potential areas of comparative analysis:

Diaspora Literature, Sexuality, Post-Colonialiam, Familial Ethics, Emigrant Chinese, Post-Colonial Language Environment, Singapore's Language Policy, Cultural Identity, Nationalism, Feminism

他乡女子

主要语言： 中文
次要语言： -
翻译版本： -
页数： 196
作者： 罗伊菲
出版年份： 2020
出版社： 八方文化创作室

人物简介：

《他乡女子》共收录〈他乡女子〉、〈惘情记〉、〈春梦无痕〉、〈母难日〉以及〈父与子〉五篇短文，各篇核心可用"爱"一字概括：前三篇从现代女性的角度探讨她们对爱情、家庭和婚姻的价值观；后两篇则从子女的视角，聚焦于亲情之爱。

文本概要：

1. 〈他乡女子〉

郑恂恂在留美期间与富家子弟黄士诚萌生爱意，婚后随他移民到新加坡生活十年。她是典型的事业得意、爱情失意的女子：在职场上，她自信坚强、驰骋广告界。但在情场，面对思想保守、唯母命是从的丈夫，她决定离婚，摆脱婚姻的束缚。为争取儿子的抚养权，郑恂恂不惜一切和前夫对簿公堂。然而，当她得知异国情人史丹童年时期也曾因父母离异而陷入抚养权的纷争时，他放弃法律诉讼，不再争夺孩子的监护权；而为了陪在儿子身边，她最后放弃和史丹到国外展开新生活的机会。

2. 〈惘情记〉

〈惘情记〉有两条故事线：因无法满足妻子丽沙的性需求，富家子弟余维特与太太婚姻触礁，不想在职场上再度遇见何淑婷，为之倾倒。另外，何淑婷真正的意中人是使君有妇的萧，虽两情相悦，但萧重情重义，难以割舍婚姻，两人纠结痛楚，后萧的妻子主动提出离婚，恢复自由身的萧希望和何淑婷再续前缘。

3.〈春梦无痕〉

张康妮自小接受英文教育，不谙中文，言谈间流露出对中文及其文化的无感与偏见，甚至为此自鸣得意。自从她在办公室和热爱中华文化的白人男子班杰明不期而遇后，她扭转先前排斥中文的立场，开始恶补这门语言，希望给班杰明留下深刻的印象，并和他步入婚姻。然而，康妮却发现班杰明早已心有所属，其另一半也同样醉心于东方文化，康妮如梦方醒，结局令人惆怅。

4.〈母难日〉

艾琳贪图享乐、天性凉薄，她在丈夫周年忌日后不久抛下女儿涵涵，计划和另一男子远走他乡，然她的计划并未实现。她和小孩住在同一座城市，但从未探望孩子、尽母亲的责任。面对缺席的父母之爱，涵涵自小性格乖僻、自暴自弃，险些误入歧途。缺乏母爱的涵涵终究渴望母亲的关怀和呵护，因此一直盼望艾琳的归来。涵涵的姑姑静芬在破裂的家庭中扮演重要的角色：她斡旋于艾琳、母亲和涵涵之间，尝试化解她们之间的矛盾，并帮助母亲教育涵涵，阻止涵涵走上歪路。

5.〈父与子〉

林长旺年轻时候从中国来到新加坡谋生，为人要强讲义气，不想弄得身残，以致脾气暴躁、妻离子散，成为孩子眼中只会烂赌和酗酒的寄生虫。他晚景凄凉，垂暮之年孤身一人住进医院，儿子雷蒙虽极其痛恨父亲，然听闻父亲不久于人世后依然前去探望，并从父亲老友得知父亲不为人知的过往，最终主动化解与父亲的矛盾。

重点与备注：

小说集的前三篇短文（〈他乡女子〉、〈惘情记〉和〈春梦无痕〉）从现代白领丽人面对的情感纠葛出发，探讨她们对两性关系、婚姻和家庭的价值观。

郑恂恂、何淑婷和张康妮均受过高等教育，在职场上叱咤风云，但她们在情场总是失意者，或离婚或失恋，最后孑然一身。以〈他乡女子〉为例，郑恂恂展现出独立女性对婚姻生活的质疑，她鄙视懦弱、毫无个人主见的丈夫，夫妻矛盾加剧，最后决定以离婚摆脱婚姻带来的折磨，还复自由身。然而，骨肉至亲无法割舍，在儿子和恋人史丹之间，她毅然选择前者，先是退出儿子监护权的争夺，后放弃与史丹奔赴加拿大结婚的幸福生活，只为每个月能见儿子两次。

〈母难日〉和〈父与子〉则聚焦于亲情，从涵涵和雷蒙的视角诠释和解读父母之爱。以前者为例，尽管姑姑静芬试着填补艾琳的空缺，但涵涵始终从未感受过母爱。在涵涵21岁生日会上，她借母难日感谢祖母的养育之情和母亲的生育之恩，某种程度上原谅当初抛弃自己的母亲。〈父与子〉处理父子之间无法割舍的血缘关系：雷蒙在帮父亲洗澡时看见父亲身上有和自己一模一样的红痣，深感血缘之亲，决定和父亲和解。

在探讨性别、家庭和亲情之外，小说也涉及海外华人及其离散经验。〈惘情记〉中的何淑婷负笈美国时在纽约参与游行示威，心中满腔热血。〈他乡女子〉的郑恂恂70年代在美国参与"保卫钓鱼台"运动，来自各界的华裔学子因这场抗议而团结起来。郑恂恂的立场、经验，透过作者对这段历史事件的描述勾勒海外华人的共同记忆，再现离散华人的民族主义情操（Ethnonationalist Sentiments），于是"移民"、"海外华人"和"身份认同"等构成了小说另一个核心主题。

《他乡女子》也揭示新加坡华人薄弱的文化认同和对功利主义的追从。

张康妮是经典的实用主义论者，她无法用中文和母亲、姐姐沟通，但她不为此感到惭愧，反而沾沾自喜认为华文不实用。受班杰明的启发，她对华文和华族文化产生兴趣，但这是具讽刺意味的——她重新接触中华文化的动力并非来自自我意识的觉醒，而是源自洋人的指责和爱情的推动作用。在〈他乡女子〉中，黄士诚和妻子希望孩子能接受传统的华校教育，但时过境迁，他一反常态坚持要儿子进入知名英校。他辩称：新加坡已是英语挂帅的社会，若反其道而行，儿子将受歧视。同样的，在〈惘情记〉中，余维特的母亲虽然热爱中华文化，喜欢阅读古典诗词，但因现实考量，坚持将余维特和其弟妹转入英校就读，理由是：把英文学好才能找到好工作，出人头地。

罗伊菲是资深作家，她生于湖南、负笈美国深造，最后和丈夫落脚新加坡。从她的跨国经验中得到启发，罗伊菲从异乡人的视角观察新加坡的社会变迁，描绘跨越世代、性别、国籍和种族等的都市情感，提升了小说的维度和层次。《他乡女子》中的小说均于1986年至1994年4月间刊登于联合早报上，如今重新出版，为文学研究提供丰富的题材，可视为对新华文学的重大贡献。

潜在的比较文学分析:

离散文学、性和性欲、后殖民社会、家庭伦理、海外华人、后殖民语境、新加坡语言政策、文化认同、民族主义、女性主义

瑰丽的旋涡 (THE SPELLBINDING VORTEX)

Primary Language: Mandarin

Secondary Language: No

Translation Available: No

Number of Pages: 225

Author: You Jin (Pseudonym of Tham Yew Chin)

Year of Publication: 1995

Publisher: EPB Publishers Pte Ltd

Characterisation Notes:

Alienated by their domestic situations, three students find solace—the satisfaction of the longing to be heard, felt, and understood—in each other. All three protagonists are students in the Normal Academic Stream.

18-year-old Ji Hong Quan grew up under an abusive father, unable to defend himself and his mother from his father's physical blows. In his youth, Ji subconsciously emulates his father's violence through self-righteous acts of social justice in school. After his mother's death from gastric cancer, Ji leaves home as his father grows increasingly violent and engages in extramarital affairs. Ji also quits school after he is unjustly punished for acting in self-defense.

17-year-old Liang Qiang Qiang has an ineffectual father who uses his illness as an excuse to avoid his breadwinner responsibilities. Since young, Liang is made to undertake laborious household chores, and upon her mother's death, she is forced to quit school to provide for her family. Liang's preoccupation with familial duties leaves her with little time to socialize, and results in her naïve outlook on life. Liang fantasizes that she will be swept into a whirlwind romance that will rescue her from the banality of domestic life.

16-year-old Deng Bi Ni is the youngest of four children. She lives in the shadow of her three overachieving elder brothers and her family's male chauvinism. At home, Deng is subjected to her mother's vitriol due to her low academic status and her failures to conform to patriarchal standards of feminine passivity. Unable to find emotional security, Deng embarks on a search for affinity through ever more thrilling experiences.

Text Synopsis:

The Normal Academic students Ji Hong Quan, Liang Qiang Qiang and Deng Bi Ni live in dysfunctional homes where they are denied emotional safety and comfort. They seek solace and support in each other as their friendship blossoms. For Ji, life spiral downwards after he defends Liang from bullies and is harshly punished by the school. Ji finds himself ostracized by the disciplinary institutions of society: he is alienated by the patriarchal family and labelled an incorrigible delinquent by society (due to misperceptions of his teenage abrasiveness and his desperate attempts to make ends meet). Ji, hungry for intimacy and the desire to belong, soon descends into a vortex of drugs and a toxic love triangle.

Significance and Remarks:

The Spellbinding Vortex is You Jin's (pseudonym for Tham Yew Chin) first novella. The novella's title in Mandarin is 《瑰丽的漩涡》 (*Gui Li De Xuan Wo*).“瑰丽”(*gui li*) translates to the magnificence of a flower blossom and “旋涡”(*xuan wo*) refers to the spiral-like movements of a whirlpool or vortex. Central to the narrative is the metaphor of a traditional handloom weaving machine. The metaphor illustrates Singaporean teenage subjectivity as a becoming: teenage subjectivity is the dialectical process between the schizoid forces of teenage desires and the encroachment of authoritarian power structures and institutions that demand the individual's total submission and docility.

A master weaver, You Jin weaves together the interstices of Singaporean society. She captures the intense desires (for belonging and for escape from reality) of marginalized teenagers by writing about their alienation from their dysfunctional families and their stigmatization as Normal Academic students. You Jin's metaphor of the shuttle of a handloom is especially poignant: like the violence of the shuttle fired through the loom backwards and forwards, the unpredictable and schizoid teenage desire is constantly battered backwards and forwards within the structure of systemic and institutionalized patriarchy.

Potential areas of comparative analysis:

Singapore Literature, Post-Colonial Studies, Sinophone Studies, Ethnic Identity, Feminism, Cultural Studies, Social Commentary

瑰丽的旋涡

主要语言：中文
次要语言： -
翻译版本： -
页数： 225
作者： 尤今
出版年份： 1995
出版社： 教育出版私营有限公司

人物简介：

《瑰丽的旋涡》围绕三名普通学术源流（Normal Academic）的学生展开。因各种家庭因素，他们和家人的感情疏离。三人在彼此身上寻找到慰藉，满足了渴望被倾听、被重视、和被理解的情感需求。

纪宏泉是18岁的超龄生；他自小遭父亲家暴，母亲因胃癌逝世后，父亲的暴力倾向越来越严重，因不满父亲搞婚外情，纪宏泉不甘示弱反抗父亲，最后愤而离家。在学校，他下意识地模仿父亲，以暴制暴，伸张自以为的正义。校方一致认同他是问题学生，他干脆将错就错，主动退学。

17岁的梁蔷蔷的父亲是个不称职的一家之主——他总以病为由逃避养家糊口的重担。她自小被迫和母亲分担繁重的家务事；母亲意外逝世后，她被迫辍学、承担养家的重责大任。梁的世界围绕着家庭而转，社交圈子小、视野狭隘、思想单纯。她幻想遇见一场旋风式的爱情，将她从平淡无味的生活中解救出来。

16岁的邓碧妮是家中老幺，在典型的男权家庭中长大。她的母亲重男轻女，偏爱三名优秀的哥哥，对她恶言相向，蹂躏她的自尊以及践踏她的自信。她在家中备受冷落，活在哥哥的阴影中。极度缺乏安全感的她展开一场青春期的冒险旅程，试图填补内心的空虚。

文本概要：

纪宏泉、梁蔷蔷和邓碧妮三人在破碎家庭中长大，从未感受过家庭的温暖，内心极度缺乏安全感。在学校，他们三相互扶持，在彼此的友谊之间找到安慰。为保护梁蔷蔷，纪宏泉出手伤人，处以鞭刑，生活从此失控。纪宏泉发现，社会就像间惩戒所将他排挤在外：在家中，他是父权主义的受害者，不仅和父亲感情疏离，舅舅也认为他品性不良；在学校和社会，长辈认为他无可救药，给他贴上“不良少年”的标签；但他身上那些看似自暴自弃、难以被理解的行径，全是因为生活所逼。渴望一场亲密关系重新找回归属感的他，很快地便深陷毒品和三角恋万劫不复的深渊之中。

重点与备注：

《瑰丽的旋涡》是尤今的第一部长篇小说；“瑰丽”指的是灿烂绽放的花朵，而“旋涡”则是一个螺旋形往下降的形状。

作者用传统的织布机作为叙事的隐喻描写新加坡的青少年：纪宏泉、梁蔷蔷和邓碧妮就像是织布机上的“梭子”，而他们的家庭关系、校园生活和社会经历，分别就是织布机上的三条主线。这个隐喻刻画了新加坡青少年在追求主体性（subjectivity）的不确定性和变动性（as a becoming）：他们分裂的主体和权力制度展开一场辩证的过程，在这拉扯中，专横、具腐蚀性的结构对青少年的要求只有一个，那就是绝对的服从。

尤今是个编织大师，她把边缘人物的故事编进小说，从他们破裂的家庭关系，以及背负的普通学术源流班学生的污名，带出边缘青年内心的空洞和强烈的渴望——逃避现实，寻找归属感。作者使用的“梭子”隐喻尤为酸楚：他们分裂的主体在高度系统化和结构化的制度中不断地从四面八方遭受撞击，就像织布机上任人前后左右丢接、移动的梭子一样。

潜在的比较文学分析：

新加坡文学、后殖民研究、华语语系研究、民族认同、女性主义、文化研究、社会评论

GROWING UP PEREMPUAN

Primary Language: English
Secondary Language: Malay words, phrases, and sentences explained in the text and footnotes.
Translation Available: No
Number of Pages: 275
Editor(s): Filzah Sumartono, Margaret Thomas
Year of Publication: 2018
Publisher: Association of Women for Action and Research (AWARE)

Characterisation Notes:

The heartbreaking and brutally honest accounts are penned by female Muslim writers, who narrate the excessive and suffocating burdens, worries and struggles they encounter as they navigate restrictive societal and familial expectations.

Text Synopsis:

Growing Up Perempuan is an anthology of stories of female writers from the Muslim community. The collection begins and ends with "Essays", wherein Muslim women from all walks of life introspect on their lives and the cultures that bind or liberate them. The essays raise a multitude of topics that are addressed through a kaleidoscopic range of perspectives and experiences as recounted by the women. Sandwiched between "Essays" is a section entitled "Stories", a series by girls and young women aged 10 to 20 from welfare homes in Singapore. The stories document heartfelt incidents, thoughts, and feelings in the style of "Instagram stories", which are photographs that are accompanied by short and digestible passages.

Significance and Remarks:

Growing Up Perempuan immortalises the experiences of Singaporean Muslim women and megaphones them through text. It is the second of its kind, succeeding the anthology *Perempuan: Muslim Women Speak Out*.

Every story is tied to each other by the glimpses one gets into the cultures, customs, traditions, superstitions and laws that uniquely shape the experiences of a Muslim woman in Singapore. The motifs of a woman's filial responsibility crop up ever so often, as do the image of a modest Muslimah and the dangerous stereotypes of Malay/Muslims, among others.

The collection's strength lies in its embrace of diverse experiences. It constructs a space for any Singaporean Muslim woman to navigate the nuances of her identity and still belong. The woman of this anthology is not just a hijab-wearing Malay Muslim; she is an Indian woman navigating racial discrimination in the workplace and a Malay woman who passed as Chinese to avoid the same traps; she is an ex-Muslim who attended madrasah growing up and a Shia Muslim hoping to belong with her Sunni friends; she is a mother of two who is determined to break out of the vicious cycle of domestic abuse and a mother who broke out of that cycle; she is single by choice due to her advanced endometriosis and she is single by circumstance because marrying the same sex is still illegal in Singapore; she is also woman sustaining her family through sex work and a girl aspiring to be a police officer.

Refusing to be bound by their shared experience, the kaleidoscopic range of stories testify to the power of each woman to pave her own path. In a time where an empowered woman is a tireless career Superwoman who breaks out of her gender roles, *Growing Up Perempuan* provides a space in society's thought bubble for the ones who fall through the cracks of such monolithic representations of what it means to be empowered or, even more simply, to matter.

Potential Areas of Comparative Analysis:

Islam, Gender, Women in Singapore, Feminism, Traditional vs Modern Values, Malay Tradition, Races in Singapore, Family, Female Genital Mutilation, Stereotypes, Discrimination, Sexuality, Domestic Abuse, Sex Work

GROWING UP PEREMPUAN

主要语言：英文

次要语言：马来文(编辑在文中或注脚附上马来文词语、句子的解释)

翻译版本：-

页数：275

编辑： Filzah Sumartono, Margaret Thomas

出版年份：2018

出版社：新加坡妇女行动及研究协会 Association of Women for Action and Research (AWARE)

人物简介：

社会对穆斯林女性的期待给她们造成过度、令人窒息的负担、忧虑和挣扎；她们在这本汇集阐述，在克服社会期待的束缚的过程中，令人心碎、残酷且真实的故事。

文本概要：

Growing Up Perempuan 是一本由穆斯林女性作家执笔的创作汇集。该文集分为三个部分，以“散文”（Essays）开头和收尾，中间夹杂随性的“故事”（Stories）。“散文”触及众多议题，来自各行各业的穆斯林女性在文中呈现万花筒般多元、精彩的视角和经历，她们借此反思生命，以及当中或束缚或解放她们的文化传统。“故事”则是年龄介于10至20岁之间的福利院的少女的一系列随笔，她们透过社交媒体的限时动态（Instagram Stories），搭配照片以及简短、易消化的文字，呈现难忘的经历和心情。

重点与备注：

Growing Up Perempuan 是新加坡穆斯利女性的传声筒，它是继 *Perempuan: Muslim Women Speak Out* 之后，第二本聚焦穆斯林女性经历的作品汇集。

每一则故事各自独立的同时也相互关联——读者可在文中一窥穆斯林的文化、习俗、传统以及律法，以及他们如何一同形塑新加坡穆斯林女性独有的生命经验。穆斯林女性应该承担的孝道责任、必须保持的端庄形象，以及社会对她们危险的刻板印象等议题频频浮现在该文集中。

这一系列故事拥抱各种形形色色的经历，它为每一位穆斯林女孩提供了一个空间，帮助她们在异中求同，是该文集的优势之处。选集中的女性不仅是穿戴头巾的穆斯林：她是一名在职场上面对种族歧视、信奉回教的印度女性，也是一个为了避免同样遭遇的华巫混血儿；她是一个曾接触宗教学校教育的叛教着；她是希望能和逊尼派穆斯林做朋友、并找到归属感的什叶派穆斯林；她是渴望、并成功逃离家暴的两名孩子的母亲；她是因子宫内膜异位症（Endometriosis）而选择单身的女子；她也是个被迫单身的女子（因为同性婚姻在新加坡未合法化）；她也是为养家糊口而从事性工作的妈妈；她也是个立志成为警察的小女孩。

文集中的穆斯林女性拒绝让过去的共同经历所束缚，这些犹如万花筒般的人生故事恰恰证明了她们拥有开拓自己的道路的能力。在这个女性能摆脱固有性别角色（gender roles），实现自主权，成为职场女超人的年代，还有一群被遗忘的穆斯林女性，创作集正好在社会的思想泡泡（thought bubble）中腾出一个空间，让她们看到各种象征自我赋权（empowerment），或更简单的，自我被受到重视的表现。

潜在的比较文学分析：

伊斯兰教、性别、新加坡女性、女性主义、传统与现代价值观、马来文化传统、新加坡种族、家庭、女性割礼、刻板印象、歧视、性欲、家庭暴力、性工作

EDUCATION AND LANGUAGE POLICY

变调 (A CHANGE OF TUNE)

Primary Language: Mandarin
Secondary Language: No
Translation Available: No
Number of Pages: 137
Author: Zhang Xi Na (Teoh Hee La)
Year of Publication: 1989
Publisher: Grassroots Book Room

Characterisation Notes:

Bian Diao (*A Change of Tune*) is composed of a preface and four short stories. The protagonists are Chinese-educated students who are marginalized as Mandarin becomes second to English during the rapid modernization of the Singaporean education system. After leaving school, the protagonists struggle to adapt to the new Singapore, to the change of tunes of their lives.

Text Synopsis:

The journalist Chen Zi Juan is tired of the state of her life and career and decides to take a three-week break from work. On the first day of Chen's holiday, Miss Singapore Yin Bi Le commits suicide by leaping off a building. Two weeks after Yin's death, which invited widespread public speculation, Yin Bi Le's sister Yin Bi Yi contacts Chen and passes her a suicide note, requesting that she write a truthful and meaningful article on Yin Bi Le's death. Chen investigates and discovers the connections between Yin's death and Chen's elder brother Chen Zi Wen. At the same time, Chen finds the courage to face life anew.

Liang Shu Si breaks up with Pan Zhan Heng after her mother requests that she "stay away from politics." Liang gets engaged to He Le Da, the eldest son of the owner of the He corporation who was educated in Japan along with his other siblings. The couple has a daughter Ying Ying. Liang is appalled that Ying Ying's first words are Japanese and she leaves the He home with Ying

Ying against the wishes of her husband and his family so that her daughter can learn her mother tongue.

Hu Xin Rui is a Mandarin teacher. She is disheartened by the state of Mandarin education in Singapore—her students show no regard for the language and many perform badly in it. Meanwhile, Hu's boyfriend Qin Yi Min is disappointed in his career and decides to start his own business. Hu is alienated by Qin's superficiality and utilitarian worldview and breaks up with him.

Liu Wan Lin starts a fashion business with her classmate Ai Yun right after their graduation. After the latter's marriage, Liu heads to Taiwan to further their business and meets Jiang Mei. Liu invites and hosts Jiang as she visits Kuala Lumpur and Singapore to better understand the Southeast Asian market, hoping to begin a partnership with Jiang. Unfortunately, her other classmate Wang Ye had already taken the opportunity from her. Liu lingers at the neon-lit junctions of Orchard Road, melancholic and disappointed that she had let her father down.

Significance and Remarks:

Bian Diao (*A Change of Tune*) highlights the marginalization of Mandarin and Chinese education in Singapore through depictions of the predicaments of Chinese-educated students.

Chen Zi Juan has an intense hatred of the status quo. She feels as if she cannot belong in society and wonders why she persists in working and living. She contemplates resignation but continues to work because she sees little chance of securing a new job due to the incongruencies between her Chinese-educated background and the English-dominated Singaporean society. Chen had been a Mandarin teacher in a Normal Academic stream class and had resigned because she could not handle the stress and disappointment. At present, as Chen contemplates resigning from one of the few jobs available to the Chinese-educated student (she is a journalist), we can see that Chen's life follows the common fate of all Chinese-educated students: their career opportunities are always opaque and unknown.

The Chinese-educated always suffer the short end of the stick in comparison with the English-educated in Singapore. Qin Yi Min for example is subjected to the scorn of his superiors and is paid a lower salary than his English-educated counterparts; he is also derided and treated with prejudice in his job as a relief teacher in the "second language" Mandarin. These factors contribute to Qin's marginalization and his desire to enter the realms of business to prove himself. Similarly, Qin's girlfriend Hu Xin Rui also faces a similar predicament. Her students resist the study of Mandarin and express that "Mandarin is only useful in markets and hawker centres." Gradually, Hu loses confidence and her passion for Mandarin.

The dominance of the utilitarian paradigm in Singapore seems to accelerate the marginalization of Mandarin. He Le Da's younger brother, Le Si, believes that one must only study the language that "is most useful." If one does not study English, "even quotidian life would be difficult for her in Singapore." As Chinese schools disappear, Mandarin is demoted to an "optional" status. Liang is intensely shocked and fearful for the future upon hearing He's words. She attempts to defend the central role of Mandarin in her daughter's life by only speaking with her in Mandarin—she believes that her daughter cannot be a rootless, levitating "non-Chinese speaking Chinese monster."

The text suggests that Singapore's decision to sideline Mandarin caused great pain to an identifiable segment of the population. It argues that the lingua-cultural riches of its (majoritarian) population should not be so easily abandoned.

Potential areas of comparative analysis:

Post-colonial Language Environment, Chinese-educated vs English-educated students, Marginalization, Utilitarianism, Ethnic Culture, Identity, Singaporean Language Policy

变调

主要语言：中文
次要语言：-
翻译版本：-
页数：137
作者：张曦娜
出版年份：1989
出版社：草根书室

人物简介：

《变调》由一个代序和四个短篇故事组合而成。故事的主人翁们均受过中文教育，但在国家的现代化进程里，教育制度出现重大改革，中文被排挤到社会边缘，沦为“第二语言”。他们毕业后英雄无用武之地，开始另谋生路，生活开始变调。

文本概要：

陈子娟是名记者，她对目前的生活和工作现状感到无比疲倦，因此向报社告假，暂时休息三周。在休假前一天，模特儿鄞碧乐在摘下鱼尾狮小姐后冠不久跳楼自杀，引起众人非议。两周后，鄞碧乐的姐姐鄞碧仪主动联系子娟，将碧乐的日记和一封遗书交给她，希望她根据事实，写一篇有意义的报道。子娟步步追踪，竟发现碧乐的死和哥哥陈子文有关。当她逐渐揭开鄞碧乐自杀悲剧内幕时，也找回面对生活的勇气。

因母亲要求她“远离政治”，梁叔思与潘展恒分手，后嫁给和何氏集团长子何乐达，育有一女莹莹。何乐达和几个兄弟姐妹都曾赴日本留学，当叔思发现莹莹学会的第一句话是日语时，她不顾丈夫和婆家的反对，带女儿离开何家，让女儿能学好母语。

面对每况愈下的中文程度，华文老师胡馨蕊渐渐对中文教育失去信心。馨蕊的男友秦毅民在职场上郁郁不得志，他不甘心矮人一截，决定踏入商界，奉行功利主义的处世哲学，馨蕊对此感到不满，决定和他分手。

刘琬璘毕业后和同窗爱云靠批发时装起家。爱云结婚后，她到台湾寻找新商机，认识了江梅。为开拓东南亚的市场，江梅到吉隆坡和新加坡考察市场，琬璘殷勤招待，希望能争取和江梅合作，昔日同窗王业却在此时从她手中抢走了这个机会。徘徊在霓虹灯闪烁的街头，琬璘认为自己辜负了父亲的期望，陷入无限的惆怅和感慨。

重点与备注：

《变调》透过华校生面对的窘境，带出华文和华文教育在新加坡的边缘化。

陈子娟极度厌倦现状，不论是生活还是工作，她都感觉自己和社会格格不入，不知道为何而坚持。她曾萌生过辞职的念头，但作为中文系毕业生，在以英文为行政语文，华文逐渐丧失谋生功能的社会里，她在求职路上面对诸多局限。她曾是中文老师，由于承受不起普通班学生带来的挫折与震撼而离职，如今如果再次断绝一份中文系毕业生所能担任的工作（记者），她的未来将犹如其他华校生的命运，充满未知。

与其他英校生比起来，华校生总是吃亏，仿佛矮人一截。以秦毅民为例，他不仅受到上司冷言冷语的嘲讽，还发现待遇薪酬比英校生低。在当临时教师时，他因为被委派教第二语言中文而受到冷落与歧视，各种边缘化的际遇把他推向了商界。她的女朋友胡馨蕊也面对相同的困境。虽然热爱中文，但她的学生却不领情，认为华文只不过在巴刹和小贩中心用得上，面对抗拒学习的学生，她对教育渐渐失去信心。

奉行功利主义的新加坡无疑也是加速华文被推向边缘的帮凶。梁叔思的小叔（何乐达的弟弟）何乐斯认为，新加坡人只需要学习“最有用”的语言——英语。如果不谙英语，在新加坡的日常生活都将成问题，更何况随着华校消失，华文也变得无足轻重。这番言论让叔思感到胆战心惊、不寒而栗。因此，她不断和女儿说中文，避免她长大后变成没有根基、浮在半空中，不谙中文的“怪物”，凸显她对中文理想式的捍卫。

新加坡人丢弃中文和中华文化的决定让外国人感到疑惑和费解。我们为了生存而学习英文，但不论我们的英语说得多灵光，我们还是新加坡华人。如果学习英文就等同于丢弃母语，那我们终将沦为缺乏文化认同、民族认同，不中不西的四不像。

潜在的比较文学分析：

后殖民语境、华校生和英校生、边缘化、功利主义、民族文化、身份认同

THE RIVER'S SONG

Primary Language: English
Secondary Language: Several Chinese dialects, Mandarin, Malay and Singlish
Translation Available: No
Number of Pages: 306
Author: Suchen Christine Lim
Year of Publication: 2013
Publisher: Aurora Metro Books

Characterisation Notes:

Wong Ping Ping (Ping) is the daughter of Yoke Lan, the Pipa Queen of Chinatown. Ping spends most of her childhood with her childhood sweetheart Weng (Wong Fook Weng), along the Singapore River. In the meantime, Ping also learns how to play the Pipa under the mentorship of Weng's father. The novel also involves Ping's ex-husband, Rajeev and other inhabitants of the Singapore riverbank communities.

Text Synopsis:

Yoke Lan seeks a better life and wishes to rid herself of her daughter—she forces Ping to pretend that Yoke Lan is not her mother and only call her Ah-ku or Auntie. Yoke Lan then remarries a wealthy Mr Chang in Hong Kong, a property tycoon who owns land along the Singapore river. After a series of unfortunate events, Yoke Lan moves Ping out of the slums along the river and houses her in the Chang's mansion. Ping gradually develops a distaste for Weng and they are finally driven apart when Ping is forcibly uprooted to the United States, where she furthers her studies in music and embarks her career as a musicologist. In the meantime, Weng is incarcerated for being the voice of the illiterate inhabitants evicted from the Singapore River. More than 30 years later, Ping returns to a massively transformed Singapore that she finds unfamiliar.

Significance and Remarks:

Set against the backdrop of Singapore's modernization experience with especial focus on how it impacted the Singapore riverbank inhabitants, *The River's Song* grapples with the notion of identity on both personal and national levels.

Ping, who spends decades living in a foreign land, has always been ambivalent about her floating identity. As a child, she is derided for being a "mongrel" or a "chap jing" (offensive label for a person of mixed descent) on top of not being to acknowledge her mother. It is not until an involuntary relocation to the United States, and her return journey to Singapore after 30 years, that she eventually comes to discover the mystery behind her birth. Sensing her disorientation, Weng assures Ping that not only does she have her roots in Chinatown, she also has the prerogative, on her own act of will, determine who she really is (Chinese or mixed) and can be.

On the national level, the motif of "change" is central to the narrative. As Lim portrays, changes are first necessary and inevitable—in the name of progress and development, the inhabitants are shown the eviction order and made to move to public housing. Secondly, changes are met with resistance—the squatters, who grew emotionally attached to the river over the years, are reluctant to move into housing estates. Their dissatisfactions intensify as they are made culprits for unsanitary conditions and their licenses are revoked as a result, rendering them unemployed and obsolete. As such, the author invites readers to ponder if the rapidly changing landscape serves to heighten or damage the sense of belonging felt by denizens of the city.

The River's Song should be read in tandem with Lim's earlier novel, *A Fistful of Colours* (1993). Both novels raise questions about "home" and "identity"—in a country whose ideals are evanescent and dynamic, forging a shared sense of identity as well as belonging remains an uphill, onerous task.

Potential areas of comparative analysis:

Interracial Communication, Traditional vs. Modern values, Elderly Perspectives, Social Commentary, Languages in Singapore, Asian vs Western values, Hyphenated identities, Modernization in Singapore, Self-exile

THE RIVER'S SONG

主要语言： 英文

次要语言： 当地方言、中文、马来文、新加坡式英语

翻译版本： -

页数： 306

作者： Suchen Christine Lim（林素琴）

出版年份： 2013

出版社： Aurora Metro Books

人物简介：

女主人黄萍萍（Wong Ping Ping）是有牛车水琵琶皇后（Pipa Queen of Chinatown）之称的玉兰（Yoke Lan）的女儿。她大部分的童年时光和他的青梅竹马黄福荣（Wong Fook Weng）一起度过。与此同时，平也在荣的父亲的指导之下学习弹奏琵琶。小说也包含平的前夫拉吉夫（Rajeev）以及生活在新加坡河边的小人物。

文本概要：

玉兰向往更幸福、美好的生活，为了和女儿撇清关系，她逼萍萍以"阿姑"或"阿姨"称呼她。玉兰在香港和张姓富豪（新加坡河畔的地产大亨）结婚，并在一连串不幸事件后，将萍萍接到张家豪宅同住。萍萍搬到张家后渐渐对荣产生厌恶之情，萍萍被迫赴美留学后和福荣渐行渐远。萍萍美国专攻音乐，并成为音乐学家（musicologist）。与此同时，目不识丁的居民接获拆迁通知，荣也因为他们打抱不平而遭逮捕、囚禁。30多年后，萍萍再次重返新加坡，这个脱胎换骨、让她极为陌生的国度。

重点与备注：

The River's Song 以新加坡河为中心聚焦新加坡的现代化发展，在个人和国家两个层面上就身份概念进行探究。

在个人层面上，被迫离开新加坡、在异乡生活30余年的萍萍始终对自己漂移的身份（floating identity）感到困惑。除了被逼和母亲撇清关

系，她自小也被嘲笑是个“杂种”（mongrel）或是“什锦”（chap jing，冒犯混血儿的用词）。萍萍对身世一无所知，一直到她重返新加坡，才解开谜团；此时福荣察觉到萍萍的迷茫，并向她保证，她不仅能在牛车水寻回自己的“根”，也有权利根据自己的自由意志（own act of will）决定自己的身份（华族或混血儿），以及想成为的样子。

在更广大的国家层面上，“改变”是小说最核心的命题。就如作者所刻画，改变首先是必要且无可避免的：以经济发展和社会进步为名，生活在河边的荣以及其他村民接获拆迁通知，被迫搬进政府组屋。其二，改变的过程面对强大的阻力：小说人物多年来在河边生活、工作，积累了浓厚的情分，因此抗拒迁往组屋区。不仅如此，政府也将河畔不卫生的环境条件归咎在他们身上，并吊销他们的营业执照，导致他们顿时间失去经济来源，对政府的不满也越来越强烈。在此，作者向读者提出一个疑问——当快速、不断改变的城市景观使变化成为常态，是否会硬生生地切割国人对国家的归属感，使身份认同（sense of identity）开始变得飘忽不定。

The River's Song 应该和作者1993年出版的另一部长篇小说*A Fistful of Colours*并列阅读。这两部作品都否定了一个可能性——即一个固定的、对于家、对于身份认同的概念，毕竟在一个理想和价值观不断变化的国度，建构共同的身份认同感和归属感仍是艰巨且高难的任务。

潜在的比较文学分析：

跨种族沟通、传统与现代价值观、年长者视角、社会评论、新加坡语言、亚洲与西方价值观、多重连结身份（或带连字符的身份）、新加坡现代化进程、自我放逐

BATAS LANGIT (CONFRONTATION)

Primary Language: Malay
Secondary Language: No
Translation Available: Confrontation
Number of Pages: 187
Author: Mohamed Latiff Mohamed
Year of Publication: 1997; 2013
Publisher: Pustaka Nasional; Epigram Books

Characterisation Notes:

The protagonist, Adi, is a young Malay boy who grows up in Kampung Pak Buyung during the years of turmoil right before Singapore's independence from Malaysia. In the course of his life, we understand that Adi will experience massive political upheavals, race riots, gang wars and the *Konfrontasi* (confrontation) with Indonesia. Adi's life illustrates the personal and familial issues (especially racial and financial ones) faced by Singaporeans of the time.

Text Synopsis:

Set in the years before Singapore's independence, *Confrontation* brilliantly and emotionally stages the period of uncertainty and change that Singaporeans endured. The novel's protagonist, Adi, enjoys what little he has—he run errands for his neighbours to earn the odd ten or twenty cents to enjoy movies and snacks. However, his life is far from easy. Adi's father is a gambling addict and Adi is faced with financial and familial challenges early in his life. His domestic situation worsens when Adi's older sister, Ani, falls pregnant and decides to marry an Indian, non-Muslim man. Adi is forced to work multiple jobs on weekends—washing cars, cutting down coconut trees, selling stolen aluminium and copper scraps—to help his mother pay the monthly rent after his father's passing.

Adi is exposed to politics when politicians visit his village to encourage residents to vote to overthrow the white colonial masters. The politicians shout "Merdeka!" to rally the locals and engage them with the social issues of the time (especially regarding the equal access to secondary education for Malays). Adi also witnesses the violence of the Chinese school riots of 1956 (when students demanded that the British make Chinese the official language of Singapore) and gang fights occurring right at his doorstep.

In the second part of the novel, Adi is enrolled into the very first Malay secondary school in Singapore, following plans for the merger of Singapore and Malaya to form a single nation state. Adi learns new subjects such as Geography, History and Religion, in addition to Malay Language and Malay Literature, which are taught daily. Unfortunately, Indonesia launches the *Konfrontasi* (confrontation) and stages organised bomb attacks in Singapore, causing great political upheaval and instability. The novel ends with Singapore's separation from Malaysia and its new life as an independent country.

Significance and Remarks:

Confrontation brilliantly showcases the turmoil that ordinary Singaporeans were forced to endure during the tumultuous period that led up to the merger between Singapore and Malaysia. It is as if the reader can emotionally experience and witness the real lived experiences of people of the time.

The text also addresses issues of religion and race through its subtle references to the Maria Hertogh riots that took place between 11-13 December 1950 (protesters were enraged then that a Muslim girl had been forced to embrace Christianity).

The author Mohamed Latiff Mohamed constructs an interesting alternative perspective on Singaporean history, one that is told from the Malay perspective. Under British colonization, the Malays were stereotyped as "laid-back" and "contented." Counterfactually, Adi would have received only primary education and would have had to work as, say, a gardener or labourer if the Malay community had not demanded that a secondary school be built to serve their needs.

When the proposed merger to build a "Malaysian" Malaysia was brought up during rallies, campaigns promoting bahasa melayu were held and thousands swarmed to learn the language. Adi, together with his Malay counterparts, envisions a financially secure future as they will be advantaged due to their command of the Malay language. However, their dreams were shattered when the news concerning Singapore's separation from Malaysia was announced."

Beyond its portrayal of politics, the text also forces readers to confront the foundations of Singapore's multicultural social fabric. When the village is torn apart after the 1964 riots, Bibik, the old Peranakan Chinese woman, gives her disabled granddaughter to Adi's mother to look after. She laments: "For hundreds of years we've been living together, like brothers, without any fights, and now they all want to fight each other!" (153)

In sum, the text suggests that present-day Singaporeans are in a privileged position and that the racial harmony built up over generations is crucial to the country's prosperity.

Potential areas of comparative analysis:

Historical Fiction, Interracial Communication, Gender, Sexuality, Traditional vs. Modern values, Social Commentary, Politics, Religion, Culture, Colonialism, Family, Malay Education, Post-war Singapore,

BATAS LANGIT (CONFRONTATION)

主要语言： 马来文
次要语言： -
翻译版本： Confrontation
页数： 187
作者： Mohamed Latiff Mohamed（莫哈末 · 拉迪夫 · 莫哈末）
出版年份： 1997; 2013
出版社： Pustaka Nasional; Epigram Books

人物简介：

马来男孩阿迪（Adi）自小在甘榜布勇（Kampung Pak Buyung）长大。独立之前，新加坡的社会动乱不安——动荡的政治局势、种族骚动、街头帮派斗争以及马印对抗（Konfrontasi）伴随阿迪长大。此外，阿迪的童年生活也描绘了当时国人所面对，与自身以及家庭（特别是种族和经济问题）相关的课题。

文本概要：

作者把小说年代背景设在新加坡独立前的动荡岁月，精彩激昂地刻画了那段充满变数和未知的时代。阿迪平日为邻居跑腿，用赚到的额外一两毛钱购买零食小吃和观赏露天电影，点缀贫乏的物质生活。然，他的童年生活远没有那么轻松简单。由于父亲是个赌徒，他早早便面临着家庭经济状况陷入瘫痪的窘境；而随着姐姐阿妮（Ani）未婚先育、决定和印度（非穆斯林）男子结婚，以及父亲过世，阿迪的家境更是雪上加霜，他身兼多职，在周末洗车、砍椰子树，变卖偷来的废铝和铜，以帮助母亲支付房租等生活开销。

高亢的反殖民情绪和动荡的社会局势使阿迪和村民开始接触到了政治。政客拜访居民，高喊：猛地卡！（Merdeka，独立！）的口号，号召村民联合起来推翻殖民政府，也同时鼓励他们参与社会议题（尤其是马来族群接受中学教育）的讨论。此外，阿迪也目睹了由新加坡华校生联合会所发起的示威活动——他们向英殖民争抗议，希望当局能重视华文教育，并将中文列为官方语言，以及在家门口上演的街头帮派斗争。

在第二个部分，阿迪成为新加坡第一所马来文中学的学生；与此同时，新加坡正计划和马来亚合并成，成立马来西亚联邦。在学校，除了每天学习马来文以及马来文学外，阿迪也接触如地理、历史和宗教等新科目。不幸的是，印尼反对新马合并，开始对马来西亚展开对抗（Konfrontasi）政策，在新加坡策划多起炸弹袭击事件，以致社会局势不稳定、动乱不安。小说结尾，新加坡脱离马来西亚，以独立国家之姿迎接新的发展和生活。

重点与备注：

小说精彩地呈现新马合并之前最为动乱不安的岁月，以及当时人民被迫承受的混乱和骚动，使读者仿佛身临其境，目睹、体验当中人物的真实经历。

文本也触及宗教和种族议题。虽未明确指出事件，但文中所描述，强迫马来族女子信奉基督教的叙事应就是对1950年12月11日至13日所发生的“玛莉亚暴动”事件（Maria Hertogh Riots）。

有趣的是，作者从马来族的角度出发呈现另一个替代视角（alternate perspective）。一直以来，英殖民政府对马来族社群的刻板印象就是：他们“怠惰”且“容易知足”。事实是，如果他们没有站出来，向政府提出开办一所马来文中学的建议，阿迪在小学毕业后将无法继续升学，他下半辈子就只能和父亲或祖辈一样，成为园丁或蓝领工人。

当政治人物在群众集会上提出建构一个属于“马来西亚人的马来西亚”（Malaysian Malaysia）时，阿迪和他的同胞认为他们的语言优势能保障他们的经济地位，开始憧憬未来；与此同时，上千人蜂拥参与推广马来文的运动，积极学习马来语。然而，在听到新加坡宣布和马来西亚分家的消息后，他们的理想瞬间破灭了。

在描写政治之外，作者还迫使读者直视构建新加坡多元种族社会网的基石。1964年的种族暴动将社会四分五裂，人心惶惶、此时，一名娘惹老妇（她此前将残疾孙女交给阿迪的母亲领养）义正言辞地表示。“我们几百年来就像兄弟一般一直生活在一起，没有斗争，现在他们要我们自相残杀”。简言之，小说提醒我们今天所拥有的优势地位、以及由几代人辛苦建立起来的种族团结精神，对我国持续的繁荣和发展仍起着至关重要的作用。

潜在的比较文学分析：

历史小说、跨种族沟通、性别、性和情欲、传统和现代价值观、社会评论、政治、宗教、文化、殖民主义、家庭、马来文教育、战后新加坡

一个像我这样的男人 A MAN LIKE ME

Primary Language: Mandarin
Secondary Language: Some English
Translation Available: A Man Like Me
Number of Pages: 159
Author: Yeng Pway Ngon
Year of Publication: 1987
Publisher: Grassroots Book Room

Characterisation Notes:

The male protagonist Zhou Jian Sheng is a Chinese-educated executive in a Clan Association and an aspiring writer. For his part-time job, Zhou writes short essays and poems for a newspaper using the pseudonym Juan Sheng. Zhou's girlfriend Lin Zi Jun is a human resource manager and is paid more than three times Zhou's salary.

Text Synopsis:

The protagonist Zhou Jian Sheng had attained moderate fame in his youth as a writer. He believes that all good writers, including himself, need no certification for their talent. As a result, Zhou refuses to attend college and does not care to secure a better job. Zhou's girlfriend Lin breaks up with him as she feels that Zhou's lack of motivation will compromise the stability of their lives. After Lin's departure, Zhou hastily opens a bookstore with the help and support of his neighbour Mei Fen. Zhou develops a close relationship with Mei Fen, but remains enamoured with Lin. Zhou reaches out to Lin without Mei Fen's knowledge and the couple decide to get back together. Upon learning of their relationship, Mei Fen decides to leave Zhou, as she was upset that Zhou has remained tied to his past. Zhou's business falters without Mei Fen's help, and Lin leaves him yet again.

Significance and Remarks:

A Man Like Me is Yeng Pway Ngon's first full-length novel and was awarded the National Book Development's Book Award in 1988. The novel foreshadows the theme of the difficult conditions faced by Chinese-educated students that would appear in later works by the author such as *Art Studio*, *Lonely Face*, and *Trivialities about Me and Myself*.

The novel's protagonist Zhou faces many challenges that plague the Chinese-educated in Singapore: he is unable to make career advances, sustain his own business or his romantic relationships; he is marginalized in society. The young Zhou is idealistic and literary— he believes that he does not need to prove his talent and knowledge by attaining a "paper qualification" and that the pursuit of knowledge should be an end in itself—but such a personality is anathema to the utilitarian and capitalistic society of Singapore. Nevertheless, Zhou's (romantic and career) failings seemed to have arisen from his unambitiousness and complete disregard for his future rather than his idealism. It seems that Zhou had not been marginalized by society so much as he had been marginalized by himself. This theme of self-marginalization foreshadows the tragic end of the novel.

A Man Like Me is revolutionary in the 1980s Singapore sinophone literature scene for its bold and novel take on modernist literature. The novel's prose is saturated with lengthy passages of the protagonist's inner monologues to evince the protagonist's "anxious arousal" that had resulted from his setbacks in life. Yeng Pway Ngon explains that he drew inspiration from Canadian American author Saul Bellow's "psychological realism"[24] to narrate the tormented inner world of the intellectual Zhou. In all, *A Man Like Me* is a ground-breaking exercise of creativity that offers readers a fresh reading experience.

Potential areas of comparative analysis:

English vs Chinese-educated student, Post-Colonial Language Environment, Psychological Realism, Marginalization, Modernism, Erotic Anxiety

24 Liw Pei Kien, "Xinhua Dangdai Wenxue zhong de Xiandai Zhuyi" [Modernism in Singapore Chinese Literature] (Singapore: Global Publishing, SUSS Centre for Chinese Studies, 2017), p. 424.

一个像我这样的男人 A MAN LIKE ME

主要语言： 中文
次要语言： 零星英文
翻译版本： A Man Like Me
页数： 159
作者： 英培安
出版年份： 1987
出版社： 草根书室

人物简介：

男主人翁周建生（笔名：涓生）是一名华校生。他在一家公会担任行政助理，闲暇时热衷于在报刊上发表散文和诗作，希望能成为一名作家。他的女朋友林子君是名人事经理，薪资比他高出三倍有余。

文本概要：

建生自认为是小有名气的青年作家，深信当作家不需要一纸文凭；子君则希望建生继续升学、完成大学教育，但建生不打算转换跑道、找一份薪水更优渥、前景更光明的工作。子君不满他不思进取，最终以缺乏安全感为由提出分手。子君离开后，建生仓促地开设书店，开始和邻居美芬来往，后者主动入股，协助建生管理书店。然而，建生仍然念念不忘子君，瞒着美芬联系对方，后者得知他创业后，决定与其复合。美芬不满建生和子君藕断丝连，主动退出这三角关系，不告而别；少了美芬的帮助，书店的生意每况愈下，子君也再次选择离开，留下建生一个人孤苦伶仃。

重点与备注：

《一个像我这样的男人》是英培安的第一部长篇著作，于1988年荣获新加坡国家书籍理事会书籍奖 (National Book Development's Book Award)。英培安一向关注华校生社群所面对的挑战。在他的小说中 (如：《画室》(Art Studio)、《孤寂的脸》(Lonely Face) 和《我与我自己的二三事》(Trivialities about Me and Myself))，其核心命题离不开对华校生困境的审视，《一个像我这样的男人》也不例外。

和其他的华校生一般，建生的命途多舛：工作遇阻、情感受挫，创业失败，是重英轻华的社会底下，典型的边缘人物。建生痴迷文艺，理想是成为一名作家，但这在崇拜功利主义的资本主义社会极为格格不入，只能成为泡影。对建生而言，一纸文凭不足以判断一个人的学识或才智，求学也不应该以此为目标。然而，他胸无大志、苟且度日，从不为未来谋划（如：继续升学），引起子君和其母亲不悦。因此，与其说他被环境边缘化，不如说他主动地选择自我边缘化，提前预告其悲剧性的结局。

《一个像我这样的男人》是一部现代主义小说。大量且冗长的内心独白贯穿全文，再现身处边缘位置的建生，因面对生活中的各种挫败，而产生的“情欲焦虑”。英培安曾表示，他在创作时参照了美国当代文学作家索尔·贝娄（Saul Bellow, 1915-2005）的“心理写实”（Psychological Realism）叙事手法。[25] 此策略运用内省和自剖的手段揭示知识分子凌乱的内心世界。他参照此法以着重展现建生的情欲困厄，这突破框架、大胆新颖的表现手法，在当时的新华文坛实属罕见。因此，小说不仅为80年代的新华文坛开创新的格局，也为读者带来新鲜的阅读体验，是极具指标意义的颠覆性创新尝试。

潜在的比较文学分析：

华校生和英校生、后殖民语境、心理写实主义、边缘化、现代主义、情欲焦虑

25 刘碧娟：《新华当代文学中的现代主义》（新加坡：八方文化创作室、新跃社科大学新跃中华学术中心，2017年），页242。

末代华校生的网中岁月
ENSNARED: THE LAST GENERATION OF CHINESE EDUCATED STUDENTS

Primary Language: Mandarin

Secondary Language: A little English

Translation Available: No

Number of Pages: 279

Author: Zhang Hui (pseudonym of Cheong Weng Yat)

Year of Publication: 2013

Publisher: Society of Literature Writing

Characterisation Notes:

The characters in the book *Ensnared: The Last Generation of Chinese Educated Students* can be separated into two groups: the "converted teachers"—teachers who are forced to hold geography, history, and mathematics lessons in English instead of Mandarin; and the Chinese-educated students caught amid an era of transformation who are made to learn English.

Text Synopsis:

The book is a collection of micro stories and short stories. It has four sections: the first three include 58 pieces written by the author from the early 1970s to the late 1980s, and the last section comprises various responses to the collection penned by other authors.

In the late 1970s, in view of the declining population of Chinese-educated students, the Singaporean government abolished all Chinese schools and mandated that education can only be conducted in English. Mandarin, along with Malay and Tamil, is relegated to a secondary importance as a "mother tongue" language. Set in this context, the first story of this collection, "Wang Zhong Ren (loosely translated as *The Entangled Chinese Educated*)," invites the reader to empathize with the various stakeholders of the time. In the story the author narrates the challenges and setbacks undergone by a Chinese teacher surnamed Xu and his student Hong Ya Di after the educational transition. Xu enrols in an English-remedial class due to the new demands of his job, whereas Hong gives up on his education after he fails to overcome the English language barrier.

In addition, the author also discusses the loss of traditional virtues and values among students and parents after the transition. Students hurl profanities at their teachers, and parents criticize and file complaints against their children's teachers (in hopes of securing their children's grades from the negative influence of the "converted teachers" who are weak in English). The teaching profession is denigrated and undignified and morale is low.

In simple terms, the author intends to depict the indignance and anxiety faced by "converted teachers" and their Chinese-educated students during and after the educational transition to English. The transition side-lines the study of Mandarin, marginalising and sacrificing many teachers and students who cannot cope with the change.

Significance and Remarks:

The author Zhang Hui was a teacher in the early 1960s and directly experienced the Singaporean educational transition and its deleterious effect on Chinese-educated teachers and students. Like many other "converted teachers," Zhang continued to teach Mandarin and struggled with art lessons conducted in English. We can see traces of Zhang's painful experience in the unfair treatment and the grievances of Chinese-educated students in the collection; stylistically, the author expresses his strong identification with the Chinese-educated community through his highly emotionally charged expressions.

The first 13 stories of the collection are accompanied by reading guides penned by retired Mandarin teacher Xie Yue Xin. The guides aid the reader's understanding of the difficult challenges faced by Mandarin teachers in the wake of the educational reform. For instance, Xie explains that the Ministry of Education had organized a specialized crash course in English to help the "converted teachers" cope with the new teaching environment.

However, Xie argues that language cannot be grasped in such a short period of time; she shares that many teachers were unable to speak fluently after the course. These teachers had to face the scorn of their students and their parent's complaints, and many contracted a "fear of teaching" and chose to retire early.

Apart from their teaching duties, Singaporean teachers were also required to perform routine administrative duties such as drafting academic reports and recommendation letters for students. The "converted teachers" were doubly alienated by this requirement because all such administrative tasks were to be done in English.

Moving on, the Singaporean educational reform also sacrificed many Chinese-educated students. Students who were used to studying in Mandarin struggled to make the transition to English. As a result, their grades and morale suffered, and many of these students would choose to drop out of school.

The author also reveals that many "converted teachers" had been tragically scapegoated for the poor academic performances of their students. In the short story "*45.45 Hui Yi Ji Mi* (loosely translated to *Conference Confidential 45.45*)," the principal blames the school's declining passing rate in English on the "converted teachers" and not the English teachers. She believes that the "converted teachers," who comprise 45.45 percent of the teaching population, had adversely affected the overall English literacy in the school. The principal attempts to raise the student's performance in English by increasing the workload of the "converted teachers" in hopes that they would resign.

The Chinese title "*Mo Dai Hua Xiao Sheng De Wang Zhong Sui Yue*," the term "Wang" conjures an image that is particularly telling. The term, which means "net" or "web" is a metaphor for the pent-up frustration and perplexity of the Chinese-educated teachers and students in the face of drastic change. For instance, in the story "*Qing Qing De, Ta Qi Le* (loosely translated to *Gently, she cries!*)," the female protagonist Qiao Lian works as an escort to make ends meet. Qiao did not simply abandon herself to vice; instead, the Chinese-educated Qiao Lian was marginalized and forced to work as an escort to survive in the English-oriented Singaporean society of the 1970s and 1980s. In all, this collection is an elegy for all Chinese-educated teachers and students: they are trapped in a web and are kept from the realization of their hopes and dreams.

Potential areas of comparative analysis:

Chinese vs English-educated students, Post-Colonial Language Environment, Marginalization, Utilitarianism, Identity, Singaporean History, Singapore Chinese Education, Chinese Culture

末代华校生的网中岁月

主要语言: 中文

次要语言: 零星英文

翻译版本: -

页数: 279

作者: 张挥 (本名: 张荣日)

出版年份: 2013

出版社: 新加坡书写文学协会

人物简介:

《末代华校生的网中岁月》的人物可分为两组: 首先, 学校的"变流教员"——原本在华校使用华文教地理、历史和数理, 但在体制改革后, 被迫改用英文教学的师资; 其二, 在华校消失后、被迫学习英语的华校子弟。

文本概要:

短篇与微型小说集《末代华校生的网中岁月》共分为四部分: 前3辑收录58篇作者于70年代初至80年代末的创作; 最后一辑则包含个别作者对小说集的评论。

70年代末, 鉴于报名华校的人数逐渐减少, 教育部决定停办华校, 全国中小学统一以英语为主要教学媒介语; 而学生只能以第二语言修读母语(华文、马来文和淡米尔文)。小说集的开篇之作《网中人》正是时代的缩影, 使读者身临其境, 意义重大。在短文中, 作者描述许姓华文老师和学生洪亚弟在体制转型后所遭遇的挑战和挫折: 前者为应付工作需求, 硬着头皮报名英语进修班。后者始终无法克服学习英语的障碍, 主动放弃升学的机会。此外, 学生和家长也逐渐失去昔日尊师重道的优良传统价值观——学生向老师爆粗口, 家长也因为担心孩子的成绩一落千丈, 而向校长批评"变流教员"薄弱的英语基础。教职员的尊严瞬间荡然无存, 士气低落。

简言之，作者主要从“变流教员”和华校子弟这两个角度刻画华校师生在教育体制改革后所面对的无奈和彷徨。随着体制的转型，大环境不再重视华文学习。而无法适应体制的师生也承受巨大的精神压力，处在崩溃边缘，最终成为制度的牺牲品。

重点与备注：

张挥于60年代初开始从事教育工作，体制转型后，他难逃“变流教员”的命运——他一边用别扭的英语上美术课，另一边继续教中文。与此同时，他眼睁睁地看着周遭的华校师生在天翻地覆的改革中任人宰割。他将这切身之痛化为笔下一张张承受委屈以及不平等的待遇的华校生面孔，作品流露的唏嘘与愤慨显示他强烈的华校生情意结。

小说集的首13篇短篇后，附上退休华文老师谢月馨执笔的导读，以助读者体会华校师生面对的严峻考验。以其中一篇为例，谢老师解释，为帮助“变流教员”适应面目全非的教学环境，教育部为他们特别开设短期英语速成班，但语言的学习和运用，岂能立竿见影？他们上课时磕磕巴巴，不仅遭学生蔑视，还得面对家长的投诉，以致于他们患上“教学恐惧症”，一些老师也因此提早退休。

在教学之外，老师们也得负责行政工作，例如：填写成绩册、为学生写推荐信等，要用一个陌生的语言处理这繁琐的行政任务，可谓雪上加霜。至于惯用华文学习的学生，他们无法克服英语学习的障碍，跟不上学习进度、屡屡受挫，选择辍学，无疑是新加坡教育制度改革下的牺牲品。

“变流教员”也惨遭千夫所指，成为学生成绩不尽理想的代罪羔羊。在《45.45会议机密》这篇短文中，校长向老师指出，学生的英文及格率逐年下降，她非但没把矛头指向英文老师，反倒把原因归结到占总师资百分之45.45的“变流教员”身上，认为他们影响了学生的英文水平。为提高及格率，校长打算增加“变流教员”的工作量，以设法让他们自动申请转校。

《末代华校生的网中岁月》的“网”字是重要的意象，它暗喻着华校师生在骤变面前的迷惘和郁结。以《轻轻地，她泣了！》为例，为自力更生，女主角巧莲当起陪游女郎。或许有些读者会认为她自甘堕落，但在70至80年代的新加坡，职场相对重视英校生。身为华校生，她自然被排挤到边缘，为了生存，她选择当陪游女郎。《末代华校生的网中岁月》是华校师生的一部悲歌，他们即使有雄心壮志，却像是被困在网中，有志难伸。

潜在的比较文学分析:

华校生VS英校生、后殖民语境、边缘化、功利主义、身份认同、新加坡历史、 新加坡华文教育、华族文化

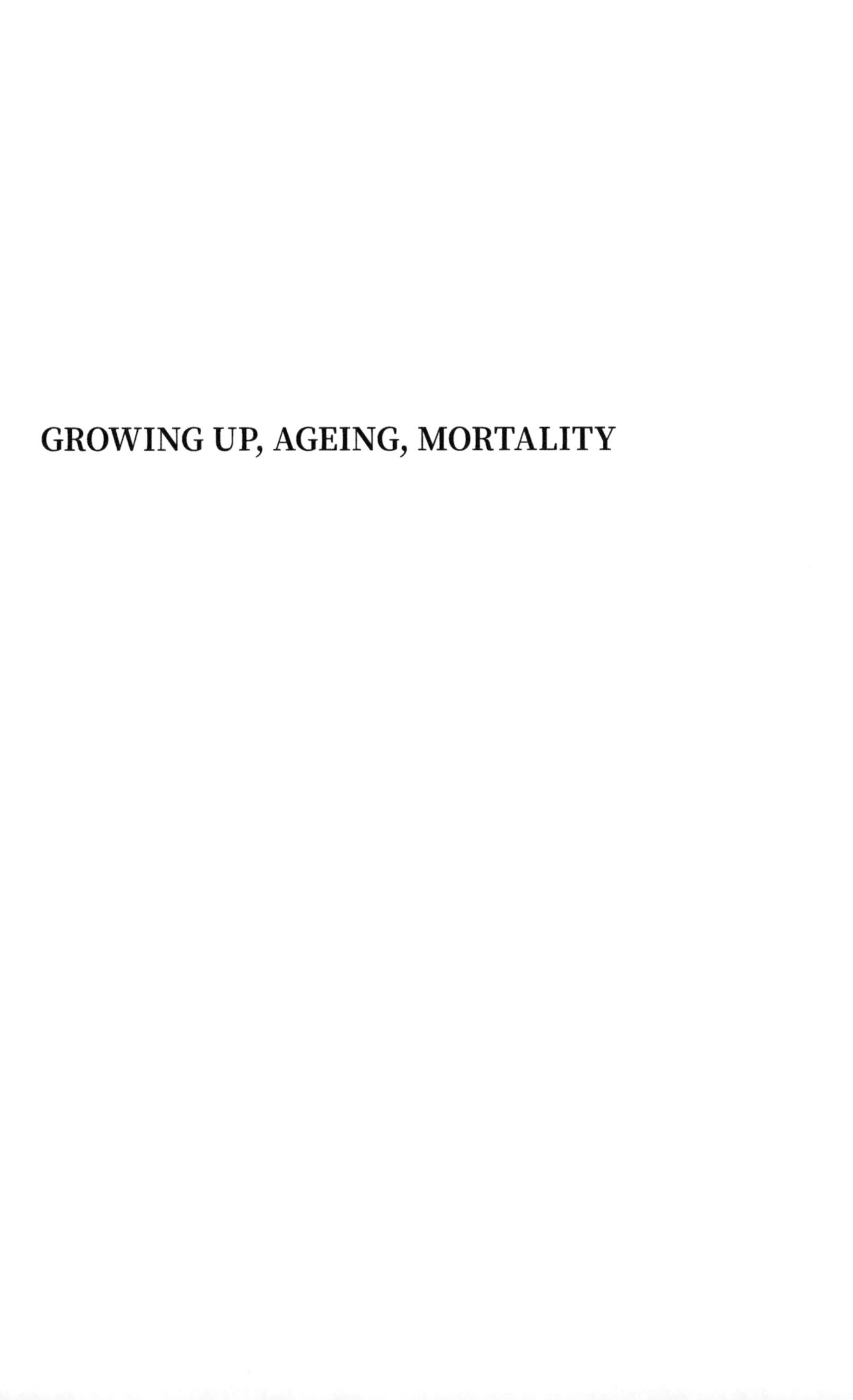

GROWING UP, AGEING, MORTALITY

放逐与追逐 EXILE OR PURSUIT

Primary Language: Mandarin

Secondary Language: English

Translation Available: Exile or Pursuit

Number of Pages: 238

Author: Chia Joo Ming

Year of Publication: 2015

Publisher: Full House Communications

Characterisation Notes:

The protagonist Hok Leong is a Chinese-educated student who does not perform well in school and fails all his subjects except for Mandarin and Physical Education. Hok Leong faces an uncertain future, but he is adamant that he does not want to be an "office boy" who serves coffee to his colleagues. Chiu-yun is an Indonesian transfer student. Hok Leong is delegated the role of tutoring Chiu-yun in Mandarin by their form teacher. In return, Chiu-yun also tutors Hok Leong in English. The couple grow close, but their romance comes to an end as Chiu-yun leaves for England to study after their graduation from secondary school.

Text Synopsis:

The story begins in the 1970s. Chiu-yun has just moved to Singapore from Indonesia, and her form teacher requests that her class support Chiu-yun in her adjustment. In particular, the teacher names Hok Leong to tutor Chiu-yun in Mandarin everyday half an hour before the start of classes. The arrangement turns out to be mutually beneficial: Chiu-yun achieves good grades in Mandarin, and Hok Leong passes his English and Mathematics exam for the first time in secondary school. One day, Chiu-yun introduces the song "Yesterday Once More" by the Carpenters to Hok Leong. Having learnt his first English song, Hok Leong overcomes his psychological fear of English. Due to the study sessions, the couple grow close—they watch movies, dine at cafes and skate together. Their relationship comes to an end as Chiu-yun leaves for England to further her studies.

For his efforts, Hok Leong is accepted into university but soon drops out due to his weak command of English. He starts work as a technician at a Japanese electronics company, and he soon meets and marries Hsiao-yuan. Twenty years later, Hok Leong chances upon Chiu-yun at a banquet in Shanghai. He notices that Chiu-yun is still wearing the bangle that he gave her in secondary school. Hok Leong himself still wears the watch that Chiu-yun bought for him. Both Hok Leong and Chiu-yun understood the gestures as symbols for their persisting love, but neither party chose to approach the other. On his return journey, Hok Leong hears the song "Yesterday Once More" playing through the headphones of his neighbouring passenger. As the music plays, Hok Leong relives the moment when he first met Chiu-yun.

Significance and Remarks:

The author Chia Joo Ming paints a delicate and detailed picture of his indignance towards the marginalization of Chinese language in Singapore. In Hok Leong's and Hsiao-yuan's navigation of the tension between the poles of "exile" and "pursuit," the novel presents the self-actualization of the Chinese-educated as a dialectical process.

Hok Leong is used to his "exile" to the margins of society. For instance, while helping his father at his stall in a hawker center, Hok Leong notices two girls. As he does not speak English, he was unable to communicate with them. As Hok Leong grows up, he realizes that society, too, labels people by "colour." In National Service, he discovers that the military has a colour-code for the recruit's language capabilities: dark green for English, orange for Mandarin, red for Hokkien (hence the term Hokkien-soldiers). Hok Leong finds himself among the minority who is labelled "pure orange" and derisively referred to as "Chinese Helicopters." In the face of stigma and scorn, Hok Leong self-deprecatingly adopts the derisive label of "1960s Helicopter" (87).

If Hok Leong had not met Chiu-yun in his youth, it is likely that he would have been "exiled" by society or willingly walked out on society by himself. As such, we can treat the meeting of the two as the turning point in Hok Leong's life. To Hok Leong, a hawker's son, Chiu-yun belongs to an utterly different world that is made up of "beautiful things". Nevertheless, the pair maintain a close friendship despite their class differences. During many of their idyllic afternoon study sessions, Chiu-yun patiently coaches Hok Leong to sing in English. Over time, Hok Leong overcomes his psychological barrier towards the language and starts to appreciate its beauty. Originally, "without speaking or listening to English, (Hok Leong) never knew that English songs were that moving" (21). Under Chiu-yun's tutelage, Hok Leong grows to appreciate singers such as John Denver—he would use a dictionary to clarify new words that he encountered. It was as if Hok Leong had entered a whole new world. At a time when most Chinese-educated students would give up their study of English after secondary four, Hok Leong persisted with the help of Chiu-yun and eventually is accepted into college. Thus, Hok Leong attains self-actualization by overcoming the barriers of language.

With the dawn of globalisation, it seems that the Chinese-educated no longer suffer the short end of the stick. In the novel, Hok Leong and his wife Hsiao-yuan visit Shanghai and Taipei in hopes of furthering their career. However, they basically encountered more pressure and stress. Hok Leong's superior had suggested that Hok Leong's career in China would be as easy as "fish in the water." Hok Leong is less optimistic, for he recognizes the inadequacies of his Chinese education. Hok Leong does not understand the nuances of Chinese history, politics, geography, and culture. In hopes of saving their children from future marginalization, Hok Leong and Hsiao-yuan decide to send their two daughters to Taiwan to study.

In all, the Chinese-educated Singaporeans face a double marginalization: for their weak command of the English language, they are "exiled" from Singaporean society; in an age of globalization, their command of Mandarin and Chinese culture is weak as compared to those of their Mainland and Taiwanese counterparts. In this regard, this novel serves as a timely reminder and indictment of Singaporean society. In the late 1970s, the Singaporean government had changed the primary language of all forms of education to English and banished the study of Mandarin to the realms of "mother-tongue," which accelerated the demise of Chinese language and culture in Singapore. In an age where progress reigns supreme, most people vacillate between the poles of "exile" and "pursuit." This novel, titled "exile and pursuit," crafts a space for reflection and adjustment for the modern reader: after all, only through the negation of "exile" can we return a modicum of agency to those who seek to "pursue" something.

Potential areas of comparative analysis:

Language Policy in Singapore, Chinese vs English Educated Students, Singapore History, Marginalization, Core and Periphery, Self and Identification, Globalisation

放逐与追逐 EXILE OR PURSUIT

主要语言： 中文
次要语言： 英文
翻译版本： Exile or Pursuit
页数： 238
作者： 谢裕民
出版年份： 2015
出版社： 富豪仕大众传播机构

人物简介：

华校生福良的学业成绩差强人意，除华文和体育，科科不及格。尽管对未来感到茫然，但他始终确信一件事：他不想给坐在办公室的人当跑腿、买咖啡。秋云是一名来自印度尼西亚的插班生，级任老师点名福良帮助她复习中文课文，尔后几年，秋云也成为福良的英文老师；两人的关系愈加亲密，但中学毕业后，秋云的父亲安排她远赴英国留学，两人渐行渐远，感情无疾而终。

文本概要：

上世纪70年代中，福良的级任老师希望大家多帮助来自印度尼西亚的插班生秋云，尤其点名福良帮秋云温习华文。两人相互帮助，成绩显著进步：秋云在华文考试取得佳绩，福良的英文和数学在升上中学后首次及格。在那些温馨的午后，秋云介绍福良听 The Carpenters 的“Yesterday Once More”。这是福良接触的第一首英文歌曲，也是卸下他学习英语的心房的关键。两人愈加亲密，一起看电影、到咖啡厅用餐和溜冰，但两人因秋云远赴英国留学被迫相隔两地，恋情无疾而终。福良虽然考上大学，但因为英文程度跟不上大学课业，中途辍学投入职场，在一家日本电子工厂担任技师，认识了妻子小愿。20多年后，福良在上海与秋云重逢。他发现秋云身上还佩戴当年他送她的玉佩，而他也还保留秋云赠给他的手表，暗示彼此相互的情感，但两人却装作不认识对方。在返回新加坡的班机上，福良听到从隔座乘客耳机流泻出的音乐，正是那首充满回忆的“Yesterday Once More”。随着音乐，福良仿佛回到第一次见到秋云的那天。

重点与备注：

谢裕民细腻地刻画中文在新加坡被边缘化的无奈，从中带出福良、小愿和那一代华校生在“放逐”和“追逐”的拉扯之间尝试自我实现的过程。

福良自小就是个被边缘化的人物，早已习惯被放逐的滋味。举例而言，他在小贩中心帮父亲经营面档时注意到两个女孩，但因不谙英语而无法和念英校的他们沟通。长大后，福良发现社会用“颜色”，给华校生贴上了标签。他在服兵役时发现兵营里以颜色名牌标签新兵身份：深绿色代表讲英语，橙色代表讲华语，红色代表讲福建话的福建兵，大部分新兵更把属于少数、纯橙色的华校生福良戏谑为“华文直升机”（Chinese Helicopter）。面对嘲讽，福良自嘲是“1960年的直升机”。

如果福良少年时没有认识秋云，他应该会因为被社会放逐而选择自我放逐。因此，秋云可说是福良人生的重要转折点。秋云于他而言是属于另一个世界的人：她是富家女，而他不过是小贩的儿子。即使存在明显的阶级差距，他们依然建立亲密的友谊。在那些慵懒惬意的午后，秋云一遍遍教福良唱英文歌，助他克服学习英文的心理障碍，颠覆了福良对英文的审美观。福良的英文程度薄弱，没有听英语歌曲的环境，也从来不知道英语歌那么好听（21），但因为秋云，他开始接触如约翰 · 丹佛（John Denver）的英文歌曲，并用字典查找歌词的意思，如同进入另个世界。当大部分的华校生认定只需要完成中学教育，福良在秋云的鞭策下逐渐掌握英文，不仅升上高中还考上大学。跨越语言的藩篱，福良尝到自我实现的硕果。

随着全球化时代的到来，华校生已不再吃亏。福良和妻子分别来到了上海和台北，原以为能在事业上取得更大的突破，但随之而来的却是另一波边缘化带来的危机感和紧迫感。福良的上司赞他在中国是如鱼得水，但他却有自知之明，自嘲那中文水平不过是皮毛，不足以让他理解中国的历史、政治、地理和文化。为避免下一代再次语言障碍被放逐，福良和小愿决定让两个女儿到台湾学中文。

福良年少时因英语程度不佳被社会放逐，成年后，全球化让他惊觉他的中文水平不过是冰山一角。福良的故事带出的各种被“放逐”的心情揭示华校生与社会的“距离”，延伸至今时今日，小说具有更强烈的警示意味。70年代末，政府大幅改革教育政策，把教学媒介由原本的母语改成英语，而学生只能以第二语言修读自己的母语，无疑加速华文华语在新加坡的没落。在计划赶不上变化的时代，不断在放逐和追逐间拉扯将成为大部分人的主旋律，而《放逐与追逐》正好给读者及时提供一个省思和匡正的机会。毕竟，不被放逐才有更多主动追逐的可能性。

潜在的比较文学分析：

新加坡语言政策、华校生VS英校生、新加坡历史、边缘化、边陲与中心、身份认同、全球化

双口鼎一村 (SHUANG KOU DING FIRST VILLAGE)

Primary Language: Mandarin

Secondary Language: Local dialects (Cantonese and Hokkien) and a few Malay words

Translation Available: No

Number of Pages: 358

Author: Zhang Hui (pseudonym of Cheong Weng Yat)

Year of Publication: 2015

Publisher: Lingzi Media Pte Ltd

Characterisation Notes:

The young protagonist, A-Ri, is born amidst the boom of distant artillery gunfire during World War II. He moves to Singapore and settles down with his mother in Shuang Kou Ding First Village, where he spends his childhood and obtains his education. In addition, there is also an imaginary talking horse which brays incessantly in the depths of Cheong's heart; its words and counsel weigh far more than his mother's — he only heeds the advice of the horse.

Text Synopsis:

The novel can be roughly divided into 2 parts: the first two-thirds of the novel focus on how Cheong moves to Singapore and settles down with his mother at Shuang Kou Ding First Village where he experiences the camaraderie between the villagers as a young boy. The later part of the novel portrays the tumultuous 1950s in Singapore: historical events such as the "1954, May 13 Riots" which would eventually lead to the protests against the colonial government fronted by the Singapore Chinese Middle School Student Union are portrayed. Understood within its historical context, the novel accentuates the sacrifices made by the Singaporean Chinese population in order to stay true to their ideals whilst laying a strong foundation for the nation.

Significance and Remarks:

Shuang Kou Ding First Village: The Yesteryears is an autobiographical full-length bildungsroman, wherein the aged protagonist Cheong Hui recalls his childhood years living in the Shuang Kou Ding First Village during the 1950s. Cheong was born in 1942 in Selangor, Malaysia and moved to Singapore with his mother when he was 3 years' old, eventually settling down at Shuang Kou Ding First Village located near the junction of Alexandra Road, Queenstown and Jalan Bukit Merah. Gambier plantations were then a common sight and apparently two ("*shuang*") bronze cauldrons ("*ding*") were located near Queenstown, and this gave rise to the name of the village.

Cheong employs intertextuality in the novel—he intersperses his short stories (for instance, "Xiu Ji's Lor Mee", "Youtu's sandals" and "Black Dog") into the main narrative, creating a multi-layered and multi-faceted structure consisting of multiple texts. Some characters in Shuang Kou Ding Village—Xiuzhi, Black Dog and Youtu—first appear in the above-mentioned fictions. While not in itself a text, the protagonist's imaginary talking horse injects an alternative perspective on events. Perhaps the most interesting "character" in the novel, the imaginary talking horse claims greater emotional verisimilitude in representing the protagonist's inner thoughts when guiding him onto the right track with its wisdom in moments of disorientation or turmoil.

The author identifies strongly with the Chinese-educated students (and the Chinese language), and this group is transformed into a recurring motif in his work. In an earlier work, *Ensnared: The Last Generation of Chinese Educated Students*, the author portrayed the insecurity and distress faced by the Chinese-educated during an era of great change. In *Shuang Kou Ding First Village: The Yesteryears*, Cheong highlights the growing anti-colonial sentiment and will to statehood developing againt the tumultuous backdrop of the 1950s inclusive of the May 13, 1954 riots. On that day Chinese educated students who were against the National Service ordinance promulgated by the British colonial government gathered to present a petition against it. However, the police intervened to break up the demonstration and arrested some of the petitioning students. The fallout from the incident fueled the disgruntled students to form the Singapore Chinese Middle School Student Union—the students organized campaigns and protests, shouting "Merdeka! ("Independence" or "Freedom" in Malay)", in hopes of overthrowing the colonial government. Notably, Cheong does not describe the heated demonstrations in detail, but instead foregrounds the solidarity of the Chinese Educated students and the unforgettable friendships they forged in their pursuit of revolution and national independence.

Potential areas of comparative analysis:

Singapore Story, History of Singapore, Traditional vs. Modern values, Elderly Perspectives, Kampong, Supernatural Elements, Family/ Domestic Life, Second World War, Feminism, Alternate Narratives, Mandarin, Childhood

双口鼎一村: 那些年那些事

主要语言: 中文
次要语言: 粤语、福建话和零星马来文
翻译版本: -
页数: 358
作者: 张挥(本名: 张荣日)
出版年份: 2015
出版社: 玲子传媒

人物简介:

少年阿日在炮火声中出生, 和母亲辗转从怡保来到新加坡落脚, 在双口鼎一村度过缤纷难忘的童年和求学时光。阿日的心中有一匹会说话的马儿, 它说话的分量比他的母亲还要更重他只听这匹马的话。

文本概要:

小说可分为两部分: 首先, 约三分之二的篇幅描述作者如何与母亲从马来西亚来到新加坡、并在双口鼎一村落脚、度过童年时光的故事。第二各部分则拉出局势动荡不堪的五零年代, 包括: 新加坡513学运以及随后应运而生的, 新加坡华校中学生联合会(简称"中学联")的反殖反黄反剥削等争取独立的游行运动。

重点与备注:

《双口鼎一村, 那些年那些事: 少年阿日记忆中的真实和幻境》(简称《双口鼎一村》) 是一部自传性质的长篇小说。阿日的故事便是作者张挥的个人经历——张挥于1942年出生于马来西亚雪兰莪州, 3岁时母亲带着他往南避难, 落户双口鼎一村。这座村子的位置大略位于现在的亚历山大路、女皇道以及惹兰红山交界处的附近, 据说当年亚历山大路附近种植、盛产来自廖内群岛的野生植物树甘蜜而女皇镇一带有两口熬煮甘蜜叶的大铜鼎, 这便是"双口鼎"村名的来由。

张挥在小说采用互文性的技巧: 他将一些微型或短篇作品(如:《有土的木屐》、《黑狗仔》和《秀记卤面》) 穿插进内, 使作品由多个文本构成;

《双口鼎一村》当中的人物 (例如: 秀芝、有土以及黑狗仔木得) 便源自上述创作。

虽然阿日和心中的那匹马之间的对话并没有出现在文本当中, 但这匹马儿依然为文本注入另一种视角。这匹马儿或是小说最有趣的“人物”。情绪上, 它更能代表主人翁的内心世界。每当心烦意乱、迷失方向时, 这匹有智慧、有分量的马儿总是会跳出来对他耳提面命一番, 提醒他走上正轨。

华校生（或华文）情意结是张挥作品中挥之不去的主题，在另一本微型小说创作集《末代华校生的网中岁月》中，他的作品就描述了华校生在教育改革中面对的窘迫与不安。在《双口鼎一村》中，作者以动荡的五零年代为背景，呈现华校生高亢的反殖民情绪以及对建国独立的渴望。1954年5月13日，华校生因不满征兵制度，向殖民政府提出免除国民服役的请愿书，镇暴警察却介入集会，逮捕多名学生。华校生对殖民政府的不满情绪持续高涨，促使他们成立新加坡华文中学校学生联合会（中学联）。他们万众一心，高喊：“Merdeka!”（马来语“独立”或“自由”的意思），期盼打倒殖民政府。张挥未过于描写游行示威的场面，反而聚焦华校生众志成城，一同争取建国独立的革命情谊。

潜在的比较文学分析:

新加坡故事、新加坡历史、传统与现代价值观的对立、年长者视角、甘榜、超自然元素、家庭生活、第二次世界大战、女性主义、另类叙述、华语、童年

SPIDER BOYS

Primary Language: English

Secondary Language: Singaporean colloquial English, Malay, and Chinese dialects

Translation Available: No

Number of Pages: 220

Author: Ming Cher

Year of Publication: 1995

Publisher: Penguin Books (New Zealand)

Characterisation Notes:

Kwang (also known as Shark Head and Monkey Boy) is the leader of a street gang in Singapore in the 1950s known as "spider boys." Kwang, together with Ah Seow, catch fighting spiders to sell or use in battles against neighbourhood rivals. Kwang makes a name for himself and attracts the attention of "smiling faced Yeow," the leader of another "spider boys" gang that is based in Chinatown. A man of vision, Yeow plots to extend his supremacy and island-wide domination by roping Kwang and his followers into his gang.

Text Synopsis:

In the 1950s, an opportunistic coffee shop owner known as Shoot Bird initiated the first official spider battle which would later become the prestigious Spider Olympic Games. The sport's popularity compelled street gangs to hunt for fighting spiders—the games promised not only generous prize money, but also respect from other "spider boys." Kwang, a school drop-out, is the leader of the "spider boys" at Bukit Ho Swee. He is dedicated to the catching and training of spiders for the games. He wins almost every spider battle in the run-up to the games; his followers and income multiply as a result. Kwang's popularity spread and gained the attention of Yeow, who plots to rebuild Hon Moon (Red Gate), an old Chinese secret society with the help of Kwang. Yeow finds himself smitten by Kim, Kwang's childhood sweetheart. Engrossed in wrestling spiders, Kwang risks losing Kim to the charismatic and dangerous Yeow.

Significance and Remarks:

Spider Boys is Ming Cher's first novel, in which he attempts to recount his growing up years in Singapore to his son, Marco. Set in colonial Singapore in the 1950s, Spider Boys is a true testimony of the innocent (flying kites, catching fighting spiders, and breeding fighting fish) but treacherous (open gang clashes between districts) street life in Singapore.

The spider fights, which the author elaborates in detail throughout the novel, is also a representation of the teenage protagonists' struggle for survival. The tumultuous years in the 1950s are marked by poverty—while the parents are away at work (some as live-in servants), children run the household and earn extra pocket money by gambling on fighting spiders. Kwang showcases his ingenuity by inventing a new method of spider feeding: when the spiders pounce for food, Kwang deliberately teases them by tugging their preys away, forcing them to jump higher and harder, and thus training them to be more aggressive in the process.

In contrast to Kwang's cunning, Yeow is the epitome of the brave and daring "street roamers." Yeow had been on the streets scraping for food since he was seven years old. His experience and vision allowed him to transform a group of leaderless street boys into a highly organized spying network in Chinatown.

Dialogues in the novel are peppered with local dialects and Singlish, a Singaporean pidgin English. In one scenario, the author uses the colloquial Cantonese 'water' to mean 'money' (134); in another, one character yelled, "don't look small at me" (100), which would literally mean "do not belittle or underestimate me" in Mandarin. In all, Ming Cher attempts an authentic literary representation of the language variants spoken on the streets of Singapore.

It is critical to note that *Spider Boys* was re-edited and published by Epigram Books in 2012. The language of the original novel may hamper readers who are unfamiliar with Singlish and dialects. The revision renders the narrative into grammatically correct standard English, with clear intent of improving the accessibility of the novel for readers both regional and international. However, one must be cognizant of the possibility that a homogenised English may result in the loss of authenticity and nuance with regards to the spoken language of the streets of Singapore. As such, it is unclear if the revision can retain the novel's essence.

Potential areas of comparative analysis:

History, postwar Singapore, growing up in Singapore, sexual awakening, superstitions, local traditions, traditional values, historiographies, colonialism, coming-of-age, gangster fiction, adolescence, Communism

SPIDER BOYS

主要语言：英文

次要语言：新加坡式英语、马来文以及地方方言

翻译版本：-

页数：220

作者：Ming Cher

出版年份：1995

出版社：Penguin Books（新西兰）

人物简介：

光（Kwang，绰号鲨鱼头、猴仔）是1950年代，街头帮派“蜘蛛男孩”（Spider Boys）的头目。顾名思义，“蜘蛛男孩”以斗蜘蛛为乐趣，光和好友萧（Seow）联手捕捉战斗蜘蛛（fighting spiders），一方面卖给同好，另一方面训练它们参与斗蜘蛛竞赛。光在斗蜘蛛的出色表现引起了居住在牛车水、另一名“蜘蛛男孩”笑脸姚（Smiling Boy Yeow）的注意。笑脸姚是个有远见的帮派头目，他计划拉拢光以及其追随者，以延伸、扩大他在岛上的影响力和霸权地位。

文本概要：

1950年代的新加坡，外号射鸟（Shoot Bird）的咖啡店店主看准商机，发起首个正式的斗蜘蛛大赛，这项活动后来也演变成享负盛名的“斗蜘蛛奥林匹克运动会”（Spider Olympic Games）。比赛广受“蜘蛛男孩”欢迎——赢得比赛的“蜘蛛男孩”不仅有丰厚的奖金，还能获得其他“蜘蛛男孩”的尊敬，因此燃起了“蜘蛛男孩”寻找、捕捉战斗蜘蛛的斗志。光是河水山“蜘蛛男孩”的领头羊，辍学后把所有时间和精力放在捕捉和训练蜘蛛上。他的战绩显赫，几乎赢得所有“斗蜘蛛奥林匹克运动会”前的比赛，名声大噪，收入和追随者也随之增加。此时，人气高涨的光引起了“笑脸姚”的注意，他打算拉拢光，一起重建古老的中国地下社团——洪门（Hon Moon，或者 Red Gate）。在这时候，“笑脸姚”被光青梅竹马的女友琴（Kim）所迷住，而成天沉浸在训练战斗蜘蛛的光，浑然不知自己即将把女友拱手让给既危险又富有魅力的“笑脸姚”。

重点与备注：

Spider Boys 是作者的首部作品，他希望透过小说，向儿子描述早年在新加坡的成长岁月。小说以1950年代英殖民时期的新加坡为背景，充分地呈现即纯真（放风筝、捉斗蜘蛛、养殖斗鱼）却同时又险象环生（街头帮派冲突）的街头生活。

在动荡不安的1950年代，家中经济拮据，父母外出打工（有的成为住家佣人，live-in servants），孩子一边操持家务，一边通过斗蜘蛛赚取额外的生活费；因此，作者详细刻画的斗蜘蛛比赛场面可说是光和萧等少年为生存而奋斗的一种象征。光在训练蜘蛛时展现了他的独创力：当蜘蛛扑向食物时，光故意将食物拽走，逗弄蜘蛛，迫使它们更卖力地跳，跳得更高、跳得更远，使它们更加饥渴、更具攻击性。

光的投机取巧和笑脸姚的勇敢和胆识形成强烈对比。笑脸姚是典型、无所畏惧的“街头游民”（Street Roamers）——他从7岁开始救灾街头拾荒，利用所累积的经验和本能的远见，他将原本散落在牛车水街头的男孩重组成一个高度严谨的的网络组织（spying network）。

小说的对话糅杂了当地方言和新加坡式英语。在其中一个场景中，作者用粤语口语“水”表示“钱”；而在另一个桥段，一人大喊“别看我小”（“don’t look small at me”），在方言或中文中都有“别看不起我”的意思；这些词汇出现在人物的对话之中，由此可见，作者尝试展现新加坡独立前众声喧哗的多元的语言生态。

至关重要的是，Spider Boys 于2012年由出版社Epigram Books重新编辑后出版。若不熟悉新加坡式英语和当地方言，原版小说的叙事语言无疑地将对读者造成阅读上的障碍。反之，修订版确保小说使用正确、标准的英语，目的很明确，那就是提高阅读性。吸引更多区域和国际读者阅读这本小说。然而，我们也必须意识到，单调统一的英语或许会导致小说失去原有的地方色彩，使读者无法体会新加坡真正的街头用语、并感受当中细小、微妙的差别。因此，修订版是否能保留小说的精髓还有待商榷。

潜在的比较文学分析：

历史、战后英殖民新加坡、成长小说、性启蒙、迷信、地方传统、传统价值观、史学、殖民主义、黑帮小说、共产主义

THE LIFE OF A BANANA

Primary Language: English

Secondary Language: A little Mandarin

Translation Available: No

Number of Pages: 269

Author: PP Wong

Year of Publication: 2014

Publisher: London Legend Press Ltd

Characterisation Notes:

The twelve-year-old British-born Chinese protagonist Xing Li is a banana—yellow like an Asian on the surface and white like a European on the inside. Xing Li's life is upended when her mother passes away in an accident; she then moves together with her sixteen-year-old brother Lai Ker to live with her maternal grandmother, eccentric Uncle Ho, and actress Auntie Mei. Unlike Xing Li and her elder brother who were both born and raised in London, their grandmother had grown up in Singapore before moving to the UK.

Text Synopsis:

On Xing Li's twelfth birthday, her mother is caught in a fatal accident at a restaurant when a faulty kitchen oven explodes unexpectedly. Her mother had dropped by the restaurant momentarily to collect a birthday treat for Xing Li. Following this incident, Xing Li and her brother are adopted by their very wealthy grandmother, who proves to be the stereotypical iron-fisted Chinese matriarch. Upon their arrival at their new home, their grandmother treats the two of them coldly and without any sympathy. She even threatens to cane them with a feather duster should they choose to misbehave or perform poorly in school.

Xing Li is also transferred to a private school called West Hill Independent Secondary School. It is at this school that Xing Li is confronted with the harsh realities of being an ethnic minority in a predominantly white European country. Xing Li is constantly bullied and ridiculed by her classmates, most notably by the tall and model-like Shils who has blonde hair. Regardless, Xing Li becomes close friends with Jay, a half-Chinese and half-Jamaican boy who enjoys classical music. With the help of her family as well as Jay, Xing Li is able to heal from the wounds of the past and eventually finds her own voice as a British Chinese.

Significance and Remarks:

The Life of a Banana presents the struggles of a British-born Chinese with her diasporic identity. In the eyes of the British, Xing Li is an outsider or a "Chink"—an ethnic slur commonly used to refer to a person of Chinese descent—while back in Singapore she would be shunned for her inability to speak Mandarin. As such, Xing Li's personal dilemma with her ethnic identity expresses how the notion of race and nationality proves to be an unstable and complex concept for many British Chinese.

The novel also depicts commonplace acts of discrimination and racism. As an ethnic minority person, Xing Li is subjected to many instances of school bullying. Her British classmates, who are unable to pronounce the sound of "X" in "Xing" make fun of her Chinese name and frequently harass her even during her lunch breaks. In order to find some peace and quiet, she hides in the toilet cubicle or the library, where she quickly gobbles down her meal. Jay, who is mixed-race, is also no stranger to crude remarks and racial prejudices. His parents' interracial marriage has led to the estrangement of Jay's grandparents, and provides gossip fodder for their neighbours. When Jay was just born, locals look at him like he was an animal in a zoo exhibit.

The story of Jay's parents proves to be instrumental in Xing Li's personal journey of finding her own voice and channeling what her brother refers to as "*CHM*" or "*Chinks have Mouths*". According to Lai Ker, "*CHM*" is a belief that the Chinese minority must continue to speak up for themselves in order to be heard. As the novel comes to a close, Xing Li finally musters enough courage to speak up for what is right and reports Shils for cheating during an exam. Auntie Mei also shows Xing Li some of her grandmother's old letters and Xing Li learns that her grandmother always has the family's best interest at heart despite her cold exterior. Xing Li finally realizes that "*CHM*" runs in the family and she becomes more determined than ever to speak her mind and stand up for the causes that are worth fighting for.

Potential areas of comparative analysis:

Diasporic Identity, Diaspora, Feminism, Singapore literature, Interracial Marriage, Liberalism, Hybridity, Nationalism, Campus Bullying,

THE LIFE OF A BANANA

主要语言： 英文

次要语言： 少许中文

翻译版本： -

页数： 269

作者： P P Wong

出版年份： 2014

出版社： London Legend Press Ltd

人物简介：

12岁的星丽（Xing Li，人名音译）是个英国华裔(British Born Chinese)，即大家俗称的外黄内白的"香蕉人"（Banana）。一场意外夺走了她母亲的生命，也彻底地颠覆了她的人生；她和16岁的哥哥来科（Lai Ker）一起搬进外婆家，和行径怪异的舅舅（Uncle Ho）以及阿姨（Auntie Mei）生活。和在伦敦出生、长大的星丽和来科不同的是，他们的外婆自小在新加坡生活，长大后才移居英国。

文本概要：

在星丽12岁生日当天，她的母亲到附近餐厅为她准备生日大餐，却不幸因餐厅烤箱意外爆炸而不幸丧命。她和哥哥后交由富有的外婆抚养。他们的外婆是典型的铁腕女族长——外表冷酷，对刚丧母的外孙没有丝毫的怜悯之心。她甚至威胁他们，如果不遵守学校纪律或表现不佳，绝对会拿出鸡毛掸子伺候。

星丽在外婆的安排下转校到一间私立学府。身为少数族裔（ethnic minority），星丽在这所以白人为主的学校惨遭巴霸凌，她经常遭到同学，尤其是"模特儿般高个子金发女郎"西尔斯（Shils）的欺凌和嘲笑。星丽在学校认识了热爱古典音乐的牙买加华裔男子杰伊(Jay)，星丽在他以及他家人的帮助下，治愈过去的伤口，最终找到属于自己、身为英国华裔的声音。

重点与备注：

The Life of a Banana 呈现英国华侨在面对自己的离散身份（diasporic identity）时的挣扎。在英国人眼中，她是个“Chink”（中国佬，一种针对亚裔的种族性侮辱用语）；回到新加坡，她是当地人眼中的华人（Chinese），但有限的中文程度使她遭到排挤。星丽所面临的种族认同（ethnic identity）的纠结和困扰，也同时表达了其他许多英国华裔对种族和国籍等概念的困惑和不确定性。

另，小说也刻画了普遍的种族主义与歧视现象。身为学校的少数族裔，星丽很快成了校园霸凌的对象。她的白人同学因无法发“星”汉语拼音的“X”这个音，常常嘲笑她的中文名字，到了中午休息时间也不放过耻笑她的机会。为了片刻的平静和安宁，星丽每到休息时间就躲在女厕或图书馆狼吞虎咽。同为少数族裔的杰伊对粗言秽语以及种族偏见并不感到陌生。杰伊父母的异族婚姻不仅导致杰伊的祖父母和他们的关系开始疏远，也成为大家茶余饭后闲言碎语的话题。杰伊刚出生时，更是引来大家异样的眼光，大家看他的眼神，就像看着动物园园区的动物一般。

杰伊的故事对星丽起着至关重要的作用。她在当中找到实践“中国人有话说”（“Chinks have Mouths”，“CHM”）的勇气，并找到属于自己的声音。根据来科的说法，“CHM”是一个信念，它鼓励身为少数华裔站出，让大家听见他们的声音。小说尾声，星丽终于鼓起勇气，向学校管理层举报西尔斯在考试中作弊的不当行为。回到家中，她的阿姨把她外婆的旧信件给她看，她才逐渐意识到虽然外婆外表冷酷，但始终以家人的利益为重。她也终于明白“CHM”早已流淌在家族的血液中，因此她比以往任何时刻都更坚定相信，她必须勇于表达己见，并在必要时、为值得坚守的信念挺身而出。

潜在的比较文学分析：

离散身份、离散、女性主义、新加坡文学、异族通婚、自由主义、糅杂/混杂性、民族/国族主义、校园霸凌

SON OF SINGAPORE

Primary Language: English

Secondary Language: A little Malay, Teochew and other Chinese words here and there

Translation Available: 新加坡仔：一个苦力的故事

Number of Pages: 132

Author: Tan Kok Seng

Year of Publication: 1972

Publisher: Heinemann Asia (Singapore)

Characterisation Notes:

Son of Singapore is the autobiography of Tan Kok Seng. The subtitle of the book is *The Autobiography of a Coolie*. The novel illustrates the author's impoverished childhood growing up in a village.

Text Synopsis:

Son of Singapore narrates the life of Tan Kok Seng in chronological order from 1944 to 1960. The book begins during the Japanese occupation of Singapore, as Tan recounts his childhood years growing up on a farm with his parents and six siblings. Tan describes how his oldest sister had to hide in the nearby mangrove forest whenever Japanese soldiers came to inspect the house and how his father had to work long hours at a small hemp factory to make ends meet. After the war, Tan started primary school, first at Dawn Private School then transferring to Holy Innocents Primary School, where he excelled in mathematics, but struggled with English. In order to support his family, a 15-year-old Tan worked as a coolie at the Orchard Road market during his adolescent years, where he was tasked with moving fruits and vegetables in and out of storage as well as delivering groceries to different households across Singapore. The book concludes with Tan moving to Kuala Lumpur to work as a driver for a British diplomat.

Significance and Remarks:

Tan Kok Seng may be considered a representative "working-class author" from Singapore. *Son of Singapore* is the first of his three-part autobiography cum documentary fiction work.

Son of Singapore offers a portrait of the rudimentary conditions in which poor farmers, such as Tan and his family, lived in during the early days of Singapore. Tan writes in an anecdotal manner without any pretensions of constructing a collective national history or a grand historical narrative. Instead, the book presents the early development of a young nation from a more personal perspective through the first-person account of the author. Tan, who only managed a Primary School qualification, shares his experiences as a labourer and writes extensively about his confusion and fascination with the diversity of spoken languages in Singapore—Teochew, Mandarin. English, Cantonese and Malay. As he is only able to comprehend Teochew and Mandarin, he often makes big blunders and receives complaints when he is working as a coolie.

It is worth noting that Singapore's *New Nation* newspaper voted Tan Kok Seng as one of the country's 'Top Ten Men of the Year' in 1972.

Potential areas of comparative analysis:

Interracial communication, Intergenerational communication, Traditional vs. Modern values, Elderly Perspectives, Languages in Singapore, Family/ Domestic Life, Autobiography Studies, Working Class Literature, History

SON OF SINGAPORE

主要语言： 英文
次要语言： 零星马来文、少许中文以及潮州方言
翻译版： 新加坡仔：一个苦力的自传
页数： 144
作者： 陈国盛 （Tan Kok Seng)
出版年份： 1972
出版社： Heinemann Asia (Singapore)

人物简介：

《新加坡仔: 一个苦力的自传》(Son of Singapore: The Autobiography of a Coolie) 是一部自传体小说，讲述作者陈国盛本身早年在农村长大的艰苦生活。

文本概要：

《新加坡仔：一个苦力的自传》线性叙述作者陈国盛从1944年至1960年的少年生活。小说从1940年代，日军占领新加坡期间开始，作者在小说开篇回忆起他和父母，以及其他6名兄弟姐妹在乡村农场长大的童年生活。陈国盛叙述，每逢日军进行突击检查时，他的大姐就必须逃到附近的红树林里躲避日军的追捕。他的父亲为了维持家中生计，到附近的麻布工厂长时间的工作。

日军投降后，国盛开始上学；他先是在一所私立小学上学，后转入圣婴小学（Holy Innocents Primary School），国盛的在校成绩除了数学之外，英语等其他科目都差强人意。因家中经济困顿，他小六毕业后辍学在家帮助父亲打理自家经营的农场。15岁时，他进入社会大学打滚，在乌节路的市场当苦力，负责运送蔬菜、水果等到个户家庭，并向他们收集订单。小说结尾，陈国盛决定辞去市场的工作，到吉隆坡担任英国外交官高志先生的司机。

重点与备注：

陈国盛是新加坡无产阶级文学（Working Class / Proletariat Writing)

的代表作家之一，《新加坡仔：一个苦力的自传》（以下简称《新加坡仔》）是他自传体小说三部曲的第一部。《新加坡仔》描绘了新加坡早期，作者以及其他农民的贫困生活。作者以阐述生活轶事（Anecdotes）的方式叙述童年生活，无意在过程中建构任何集体的国家历史或者历史叙述的意图，毫不做作。反之，他以第一人称的叙事，从更个人的角度呈现新加坡在独立之前的样貌和发展，实实在在展现一部"人民的历史"。

小说的叙事语言糅杂了日常方言和马来文，呈现1950年代新加坡多语多元化的语系生态。但对无产阶级、仅有小学教育程度的陈国盛而言，除了潮州话和中文，一概不谙其他语言（英文、粤语、海南话、福建话和马来文），因此在市场当苦力时，往往因语言障碍闹了不少笑话，甚至接到不少客人的投诉。值得注意的是，新加坡的《新国家午报》（New Nation）于1972年评选陈国盛为年度《十大人物》（Top 10 Men of the Year）之一，该报在评述《新加坡仔》时表示，小说取材于作者的自身经验，故事真实不虚，毫不做作。

潜在的比较文学分析：

跨种族沟通、代际沟通/跨代沟通、传统与现代价值观、年长者视角、新加坡语言、家庭、家庭生活、自传体小说研究、无产阶级文学、新加坡历史

DANCE WITH WHITE CLOUDS

Primary Language: English
Secondary Language: No
Translation Available: No
Number of Pages: 225
Author: Goh Poh Seng
Year of Publication: 2001
Publisher: Asia 2000

Characterisation Notes:

The protagonist, who is only known as "old man," is a successful businessman who is about to celebrate his sixtieth birthday. Despite the many successes in his career and family, the old man yearns for a simpler life. He creates a new identity and runs away from his family to live in the countryside. Ironically, the old man ends up repeating his old way of life when he decides to settle down with another woman and her two sons.

Text Synopsis:

Just before his sixtieth birthday party, the old man reminisces about the many successes in his life, including his thriving business, his exceptional children and grandchildren, as well as his beautiful mistress. He realises, however, that he has lost touch with his youth when he notices a group of boys loitering at a street corner. That very night, he decides to run away and begin his life anew without any ties to his current life. For months, the old man formulates his plan and creates a new identity as well as a secret bank account before running away. On the day of his escape, the old man takes a train to a small countryside town, leaving nothing but a note behind for his family.

He stays at a hotel and samples the joys of the countryside, including the simple but delicious food and the slower pace of life. He meets Chan Yew Sick, a former Chinese literature teacher and poet, during breakfast one day and they become fast friends. The old man is then introduced to Widow Lee

(Yoke Chun) by Mr Chan's wife during dinner at the Chan's house and the old man decides to rent a room in Widow Lee's house. Widow Lee is a strong and capable woman who has been single-handedly raising and supporting her two young sons ever since her husband was killed in an accident. After a year of living with Widow Lee, the old man proposes to her and they get married.

To support his new wife and her two young sons, the old man opens a modern supermarket in the town which becomes an immediate success. He makes two more friends Goh Khoon Teck and Chen Soo Peng. Together with Mr. Chan, they form the Hill Gang. The four old men visit seedy bars together and have affairs with other women, which eventually becomes detrimental to their everyday lives.

The novel ends with the old man reflecting on his life just before his seventieth birthday party. He realises that he is still discontented with the second life that he had created and thinks there should be more to life than this. It is as though he is discontented with the notion of attaining contentment itself.

Significance and Remarks:

Dance with White Clouds is a fable which accentuates the highly paradoxical nature of life, as it forces readers to examine what they consider contentment and the true necessities of life.

In the novel, the old man endeavours to reinvent himself by running away from his past relationships and settling down in a small town. However, the old man is only able to enjoy this slower pace of life for a brief moment, as his fear of boredom unwittingly drives him to make the same decisions he did in his previous life. The old man makes new friends, gets married and even becomes a successful entrepreneur, just like he did before running away. Ironically, the second life he has reinvented is not so different from the first.

Ten years later, on the old man's seventieth birthday, he supposes that he may have only five more years to live and wonders if there is more to life than simply being contented with the status quo. This ending brings the reader back to the beginning of the novel where the old man renounces his material comforts in favour of spiritual enlightenment, and at the same time, hints at the possibility that the protagonist will continue to reinvent himself innumerable times in his quest for personal realisation.

Potential areas of comparative analysis:

Existentialism, Self-Realization, Self Awakening, Desire, Paradox, Identity, Sexuality, Fables, Freedom, Social Commentary

DANCE WITH WHITE CLOUDS

主要语言: 英文

次要语言: -

翻译版本: -

页数: 225

作者: 吴宝星 (Goh Poh Seng)

出版年份: 2001

出版社: Asia 2000

人物简介:

无名无姓的男主人翁——"老头子" (old man) 即将迎来自己的60岁生日。"老头子"是名成功商人, 尽管事业有成、家庭幸福, 但他对现状感到不满, 渴望更简单的生活。为此, 他伪造身份、抛下家庭, 前往郊外小镇定居。他在镇上认识一名女子, 并和她以及她的两个日子安顿下来, 建立新的生活。讽刺的是, 这和他先前的生活并无差异。

文本概要:

在即将庆祝60岁大寿之际, "老头子" 回想他一生的成就, 包括他的事业、他杰出的子孙, 和他漂亮的情妇。然, 当他在街头瞥见一群少年时, 不禁意识青春早已离他远去。当晚, 他决定逃跑, 到没人认识他的地方展开新生活。"老头子" 用了数月的时间制定逃跑计划, 逃跑当天, 他带着伪造的身份证件和秘密的银行账户, 搭上火车前往郊外的小镇。除了一张字条, 他什么也没给家人留下。

"老头子" 在镇上一间旅馆落脚。他放慢节奏, 品尝简单的美食, 享受郊外生活的乐趣。一天, 他在享用早餐时认识了退休中文文学老师兼诗人陈耀锡 (Chan Yew Sick) , 两人一见如故。一日, "老头子" 受邀到陈耀锡家中作客, 经由陈太太的介绍认识李姓寡妇。她本名玉春 (Yoke Chun) , 在丈夫意外过世后独自抚养两名儿子, 是名坚强能干的妇女。"老头子" 决定租下玉春房子的其中一间房间, 成为她的租客。一年后, "老头子" 向玉春求婚, 两人结为夫妻。

为养活妻儿, “老头子” 在镇上开设一间现代化的超市, 超市的生意蒸蒸日上, 他不久便开始拓展业务。除了陈耀锡外, 老翁也结识另两名男子——陈书平 (Chan Soo Peng) 以及吴坤德 (Goh Khoon Teck) 。他们四人组成“山帮” (Hill Gang) 的小团体, 一起去乌七八糟的酒廊喝酒, 也个别有了新欢, 对他们原有的生活造成严重的威胁。

小说尾声, “老头子” 在庆祝70岁大寿的宴会前反思人生。他意识到, 他仍不满意所创造的第二人生, 认为生命应该还有其他事物可以品尝, 就像不希望因获得“满足感” 而感到心满意足一般。

重点与备注:

《白云之舞》是一则写给成人的寓言故事: 它迫使读者审视生命的真正所需, 并思考“知足” 的定义, 从而凸显生命 (人生) 极度矛盾的本质。

“老头子” 放弃舒适的生活、和家人切断联系, 在郊外小镇定居下来, 渴望重塑自我, 展开第二人生。然而, 缓慢的生活节奏并不长久。因为害怕孤寂, 他很快的结交新朋友、再婚, 甚至创业, 再次成为一名成功商人, 不知不觉走上回头路。“老头子” 的选择是具讽刺性的, 毕竟他所渴望的新生活同先前高度相似。

“老头子” 他的70岁庆生宴会上, 预测自己或许还有5年的寿命, 他思忖着: 生命是否还有更多可能性, 未必要满足于现状。这个结局使读者联想起小说开头所描述的情形: “老头子” 果断放弃安逸的物质生活, 转而追求精神启迪 (spiritual enlightenment) , 同时也暗示一种永恒的循环往复。“老头子” 为追求满意的生活, 将无限次重新塑造新的人生。

潜在的比较文学分析:

存在主义、自我实现、自我觉醒、欲望、悖论、身份、性和情欲、寓言、自由、社会评论

MEMELUK GERHANA (A SONG OF THE WIND)

Primary Language: Malay

Secondary Language: No

Translation Available: A Song of the Wind

Number of Pages: 474

Author: Isa Kamari

Year of Publication: 2007

Publisher: Al-Ameen Serve Holdings Sdn Bhd

Characterisation Notes:

The protagonist, Ilham grows up with his two childhood friends, Zul and Sevan in Kampung Tawakal. The trio fantasises about the village's sexiest woman—Kak Leha—who first aroused and awakened their sexual desires. Ilham subsequently enters three unsuccessful relationships with Nazira, Riyana and Syakila, all of whom drastically influence his life.

Text Synopsis:

Memeluk Gerhana is a bildungsroman or a coming-of-age story about a Singaporean Malay boy named Ilham. The novel interweaves the themes of love, friendship as well as the loss of childhood innocence. Covering the period from the 1960s to the 1990s, Ilham's growth parallels Singapore's own development, its transformation from a struggling young nation to a modern metropolis.

The narrative comprises three sections that cover Ilham's childhood, his adolescent years and his young adult life. These sections are further divided into specific chapters. The first section is primarily set in Kampung Tawakal and depicts Ilham's idyllic childhood. Seven-year-old Ilham goes on various adventures with his two friends, Zul and Sevan—they play games in the nearby Chinese cemetery, catch spiders, and construct toy weapons from bamboo.

The second section depicts Ilham's adolescent years. From the outset, the novel portrays Ilham's father as an earnest and hardworking individual who is willing to invest time and money in his son's education despite the economic downturn. He makes a point to save up money in order to move his family out of the village and into a HDB flat in Ang Mo Kio. He even tutors Ilham daily and assigns practices on top of Ilham's schoolwork. As a result, Ilham excels in school and gains admission to the prestigious Raffles Institution (RI).

However, Ilham struggles to keep up with his peers at RI. Compounding his misfortune, Ilham experiences three successive failed romantic relationships. The distraught Ilham then encounters Saifuddin, who is one of his schoolmates at RI. Under the pretense of collaborative research into Islamic studies, Saifuddin initiates Ilham into a clandestine religious fellowship known as 'Ikhwan'.

The third section depicts the complete decline of Ilham's life as it turns into a tragedy. His romantic interest since primary school, Nazira, is tragically killed in a road accident. Ilham becomes tormented by guilt and falls his 'A' level examinations, much to his parents' disappointment. At the same time, 'Ikhwan' is exposed by the authorities and is shut down for being an extremist group. Ilham is arrested and interrogated. Even after his release, Ilham finds himself under constant surveillance as the police continue to monitor his whereabouts. The novel concludes with a tragic poem, in line with the author's stylistic preference for ambiguous endings.

Significance and Remarks:

1. Childhood memories

Memeluk Gerhana is laden with rich descriptions of rural life in the 1960s and 1970s. In the novel, Ilham, Zul and Sevan head out for many adventures at the nearby Chinese cemetery where they catch and battle with spiders, make toy weapons from bamboo and steal chickens from their neighbours. Such episodes in the text capture the zeitgeist of village life in the early years of Singapore's independence and may resonate with older readers who grew up during that period.

2. Sexual awakening

The novel also explores the theme of sexuality and describes the sexual awakening of the three teenage boys. In one instance, Kak Leha (who is considered the sexiest woman in Kampung Tawakal) appears at the communal shower clad in a lemon-yellow nightgown that reveals her patterned underwear underneath. Ilham recalls how every man and boy at the bathhouse gulped in unison at the provocative sight. This scene was Ilham's first experience of being sexually aroused.

3. Romantic tragedy

Over the course of the novel, the protagonist experiences three different romantic relationships. The failure of all three relationships is largely attributed to Ilham's indecisiveness. Ilham passes up the chance to pursue his first crush, Nazira, because he was overly self-conscious about his family's socio-economic background. Years later, the couple reunite and declare their feelings for each other. However, the relationship abruptly ends when Nazira tragically dies in an accident. Ilham's second romantic interest, Riyana, was deemed unsuitable because of her disregard for religious doctrines (she refuses to wear a hijab, wears revealing clothes and kisses boys in public). Ilham's third romantic interest, Syakila, is a good listener and source of moral support. Unfortunately, the relationship ends as Syakila leaves for the United States to further her studies.

4. History/Historical Events

The author introduces many significant historical events from the 1960s and 1970s. Ilham often overhears the discussions between his father and his friends about current affairs—these include among other things the merger and separation of Singapore from Malaysia; the oil crisis of 1973; the Vietnam War; the assassination of President Kennedy; the formation of ASEAN; the triumph of communism in Indochina, and the landing of Apollo 11 on the moon. As such, the novel functions as a kind of historical memoir that documents the socio-political climate of the 1960s and 1970s.

5. Religious organizations

Almost all of Isa Kamari's writings engage the theme of religion. In this novel, Kamari attempts to explore and peel apart the Singaporean Muslim community and its extremist fringes.

Ilham's development (and eventual downfall) is largely shaped by his encounters with Islam. His first serious encounter with the religion only occurred because he sought spiritual refuge from his emotional distress. In his attempt to deepen his knowledge about Islam, Ilham mistakenly joins an extremist group. Under 'Ikhwan', Ilham studies the works of fringe Muslim scholars who espouse extremist ideas such as Maududi, M. Natsir, Sayyid Qutb, and Maryam Jameela. The politically debilitating rhetoric espoused by 'Ikhwan' eventually drew the ire and suspicion of the government, which moved in to break up the group, thereby catalysing the downfall of the protagonist.

Potential areas of comparative analysis:

Rural lifestyle, Childhood memoirs, Historical recollections, Islam, Religion, Extremist Organisations, Love, Friendship, Bildungsroman, Terrorism

MEMELUK GERHANA

主要语言: 马来文

次要语言: -

翻译版本: A Song of the Wind

页数: 474

作者: 伊沙·卡马里 (Isa Kamari)

出版年份: 2007

出版社: Al-Ameen Serve Holdings Sdn Bhd

人物简介:

马来少年伊利哈姆 (Ilham) 和他的两个童年玩伴祖尔 (Zul) 以及塞凡 (Sevan) 一起在甘榜塔瓦卡 (Kampung Tawakal) 一起长大。莉哈 (Kak Leha) 是村子里公认最性感的女子, 她激起并唤醒伊利哈姆等三人的性欲望, 因此莉哈可说是他们性启蒙的对象。在成长过程中, 伊利哈姆分别和娜齐拉 (Nazira) , 丽亚娜 (Riyana) 和莎齐拉 (Syakila) 有过三段失败的恋情, 而三人也急剧地影响了伊利哈姆的人生。

文本概要:

小说讲述马来小孩伊利哈姆的成长故事 (coming-of-age story) , 故事围绕着爱情、友情以及逝去的童真等主题。作者将小说背景设在上世纪60年代到90年代, 因此伊利哈姆的成长过程也与新加坡的发展并行。

小说分为三个部分, 分别概括伊利哈姆的童年生活、中学生活以及中学毕业以后的青年生活, 每个部分又细分成许多小章节。作者将第一个部分的场景主要设定在甘榜塔瓦卡, 描写伊利哈姆惬意的童年生活。他、祖尔以及塞凡三人常到附近的华人坟场探险、抓蜘蛛, 也一起用竹子自制玩具武器。

小说的第二个部分刻画伊利哈姆的青少年时期。伊利哈姆的父亲认真勤奋, 他将辛苦攒下来的积蓄购买宏茂桥的政府组屋, 举家迁出甘榜。不仅如此, 他也望子成龙——尽管经济不景, 他依然愿意投资时间和金钱在儿子的教育上,每天晚上都为伊利哈姆布置额外的作业。伊利哈姆也没辜负父亲的栽培,成功考上莱佛士书院。上中学后,他在学业上跟不上书院其他同侪的进度和步伐。于此同时,他连续三段挫折重重的恋情更是雪上加霜。在伊利哈姆情绪陷入低谷时,他结识了同校的赛福鼎 (Saiffudin) ,后者打着研究伊斯兰教的旗号,将伊利哈姆引入一个名叫"Ikhwan"(兄弟会) 的地下宗教团体。

第三部分,伊利哈姆的人生开始失控,逐渐成为一个悲剧。他自小学心仪的女孩娜齐拉在一起交通事故中不幸身亡,伊利哈姆因此饱受愧疚折磨,无心应战的他在A水准考试表现得一塌糊涂,令他的父母失望不已。同时,"Ikhwan"引起有关当局注意,最终遭取缔。无辜的伊利哈姆被逮捕,虽然接受审讯后被释放,但持续遭警方跟踪、监视。作者用一首诗歌作结,留下模糊又悲伤的结局,延续一贯的写作风格。

重点与备注:

1. 童年回忆

作者大量描写六七十年代的乡村生活。伊利哈姆、祖尔以及塞凡常到华人的坟墓附近冒险:他们斗蜘蛛、用竹子制作武器,甚至偷邻居家的鸡——这些描述新加坡建国初期的乡村生活和童年经历或能够唤起年长读者的生活记忆。

2. 性觉醒

小说也探讨了性相关主题 (Sexuality) 以及描绘了伊利哈姆三人的性觉醒。莉哈是村子最性感的女性,几乎村里的男人都深深为她着迷。其中一幕描述,她穿着柠檬黄色的紧身睡衣出现在村子的公共澡堂,睡衣下的印花内裤清晰可见。在伊利哈姆的记忆中,他不能忘记在公共澡堂排队洗澡的男子看着莉哈不停吞口水的模样,这一幕也是伊利哈姆第一次感受到性欲被激起的经历。

3. 爱情悲剧

伊利哈姆一共有过三段恋情,但均以悲剧收场,这很大程度上与他优柔寡断的性格有关。娜齐拉是伊利哈姆的初恋,可伊利哈姆因为贫富悬殊而感自卑,不敢进一步追求。两人多年后再次重逢,终于确认彼此心意,但娜齐拉却在一场车祸事故丧命。丽亚娜是伊利哈姆的第二段恋情，但伊利哈姆认为她无视宗教教义（虽然是穆斯林女生，却不戴头巾、穿着暴露，且敢于在公开场所和男生接吻），因此认为不适合与她发展感情。他的第三位恋人是莎齐拉，她一直是伊利哈姆的忠实听众、精神支柱，但最终选择赴美留学，与伊利哈姆的爱情也无疾而终。

4. 历史事件

作者在小说中穿插了许多60和70年代的具代表性的历史事件。伊利哈姆从小就常常听父亲与朋友们谈论世界发生的大事：如新加坡脱离马来亚、1973年的石油危机、越南战争、美国总统约翰·肯尼迪遇刺案、东盟的建立、共产主义在印度支那取得胜利、以及阿波罗X1登月。因此，这部小说可视为60年代末和70年代后期国际政治风气的回忆录。

5. 宗教组织

作者的作品主题大多涉及伊斯兰教，此部也不例外。他试图探索，并将新加坡穆斯林族群以及其极端主义的边缘群体剥离开来。伊利哈姆的成长（以及最终的失败）很大程度上，源于他和伊斯兰教（确切来说，极端组织“Ikhwan”）。他在情绪最低落、人生迷茫无助时选择走向宗教，加入“Ikhwan”。他想拉近和伊斯兰教的距离，加深对伊斯兰教的认识和理解，殊不知他加入的是一个极端的宗教组织，他们要求会员阅读毛杜迪（Maududi）、纳西尔（M.Natsir）、赛义德·库特布（Sayyid Qutb）以及玛丽亚姆·贾米拉（Maryam Jameela）等极端主义分子的书籍和文章。极端组织试图削弱政治力量的言论引起当局的怀疑和愤怒，最终遭取缔、逮捕归案。毋庸置疑的是，组织的瓦解对伊利哈姆悲剧性的结局起着催化剂的作用。

潜在的比较文学分析：

乡村生活、童年回忆、历史记忆、伊斯兰教信仰、宗教、极端组织、爱情、友情、成长过程、恐怖主义

NEW MIGRANTS

IF IT WERE UP TO MRS DADA

Primary Language: English

Secondary Language: No

Translation Available: No

Number of Pages: 143

Author: Carissa Foo

Year of Publication: 2018

Publisher: Epigram Books

Characterisation Notes:

The 51-year-old female protagonist, Cheryl Dada, suffers from an unknown medical condition after the passing of her mother. She moves into a nursing home to seek medical advice and to cope with her declining mental and physical health. It is also strongly suggested that Cheryl is experiencing the early onset of dementia as she has trouble recalling the past and could not recognise her own husband, Adam, and daughter, Clare.

Text Synopsis:

The events of the novel take place on a single day in the life of Cheryl Dada. It is Cheryl's birthday, which also coincides with Singapore's National Day. During the day, Cheryl makes astute observations about the people around her, from the workers at the nursing home—like Juwel, Lulu and Vikash—who are busy preparing for the evening celebrations, to Cheryl's fellow residents who seem less enthusiastic about the upcoming party. As the day progresses, Cheryl begins to look back on her past and the decisions that led to her checking herself into the nursing home. In particular, Cheryl reflects on her troubled relationship with her domineering mother, who was eventually diagnosed with dementia and passed away in a nursing home, as well as her adolescent affections for one of her classmates, Sarah. Slowly, Cheryl comes to realise how her life converges with the individuals around her and finds solace in her present circumstances.

Significance and Remarks:

The opening of the novel alludes to Virginia Woolf's *Mrs Dalloway*, where Cheryl contemplates whether or not she should purchase flowers for the party in the evening. Much like its literary precursor, Carissa Foo employs free indirect discourse to depict the protagonist's stream of consciousness and seamlessly weave personal narratives with national ones. *If It Were Up to Mrs Dada* also explores modern day anxieties that are the result of the increasing digitalisation of everyday life, as well as the constructed nature of national identity that is ultimately premised upon the act of myth-making.

At the same time, the novel also comments on Singapore's social attitudes and policies with regard to healthcare. The novel frames the country's approach to healthcare as efficient but lacking in compassion, especially when it comes to providing medical assistance for the elderly. In the novel, Cheryl laments the fact that the purchase of a wheelchair requires an assessor to evaluate the physical condition of the resident before the management team of the nursing home can approve the request.

Furthermore, the novel problematises the treatment and marginalisation of migrant workers in Singapore, which is unbecoming of such a multi-cultural and globalised nation. Juwel, who comes from Bangladesh, has no choice but to work extra hours washing cars in order to supplement his meagre income of $560, while Vikash left India for Singapore – the "land of opportunities" according to his brothers – only to discover the hard truths of life in a foreign land.

Potential areas of comparative analysis:

Singapore Story, History of Singapore, Traditional vs. Modern values, Elderly Perspectives, Family/ Domestic Life, Alternate Narratives, New Migrants, Spatial Relations, Identity, Ageism, Mortality and Death, Multiculturalism, Intertextuality, Digitalisation

IF IT WERE UP TO MRS DADA

主要语言： 英文
次要语言： -
翻译版本： -
页数： 143
作者： Carissa Foo
出版年份： 2018
出版社： Epigram Books

人物简介：

母亲过世后，51岁的女主人翁谢丽尔·达达（Cheryl Dada）患上不明病症。 由于身心状况逐渐恶化，她决定搬进疗养院接受专业的治疗。谢丽尔出现的症状，包括记忆衰退——她认不出丈夫亚当（Adam）和女儿克莱尔（Clare），表现了失智症早期的征兆。

文本概要：

小说的情节发生在谢丽尔生命中的其中一天，而这一天正好是她的生日，也同时是国家的生日。那天早上，谢丽尔敏锐地观察身边的人，从忙着准备庆生活动的外籍职员——朱威尔（Juwel）、露露（Lulu）和维卡什（Vikash）到对活动兴致缺缺的其他住客。当天，谢丽尔回顾她的过去：她忆起一生中所做的决定以及决定搬进疗养院的理由。谢丽尔尤其想起了她和母亲复杂的关系。她的母亲性格霸道，晚年患上失智症，最终在疗养院过世。她也忆起了青春期对女同学莎拉（Sarah）所产生的情感。渐渐的，谢丽尔在在与他们交流的过程中，逐渐地意识到她的生活是如何与他们的融为一体，并在现状中找到慰藉。

重点与备注：

作者借用弗吉尼亚·伍尔夫 (Virginia Woolf) 著作《达洛维夫人》（Mrs Dalloway）的框架。小说开头，作者描述翁谢丽尔是否应该为当晚的庆生活动添购鲜花而犹豫不决。如同她的文学前辈，作者采用意识流

（stream of consciousness）的文学创作手法，捕捉谢丽尔源源不断的意识活动，将个人故事以及国家叙事编织在一起。在个人层面上，小说描绘了因数码科技化转型而感到的现代焦虑（modern anxiety）。在国家层面上，它刻画了一个在神话历史的基础上建构的国家身份（national identity）。

此文建构一个即高效却又不近人情（特别在为乐龄人士提供医疗援助上）的医疗政策，作者就新加坡的社会态度和医疗制度做出评述：谢丽尔在小说埋怨到，若住客提出购买轮椅的要求，疗养院的管理层必须先安排评估员审核住客的情况，才能决定批准住客的申请与否。

小说也对新加坡对外籍劳工的恶劣态度和厌恶情绪提出质疑，作者认为，作为全球化当中一个拥抱多元种族的社会，新加坡的行为是不可取的。举例而言，来自孟加拉的朱威尔为了补贴560新元的微薄收入，不得不另外兼差（洗车）。另外，维卡什的哥哥告诉他，新加坡是一个机遇处处的国家。但在抵达新加坡后，他才猛然发现在异国生活的残酷现实。

潜在的比较文学分析：

新加坡故事、新加坡历史、传统和现代价值观的比较、年长者视角、家庭生活、另类叙述、新移民、多元种族主义、空间关系、身份认同、老龄化、死亡和死亡率、数码科技化

THE INLET

Primary Language: English
Secondary Language: No
Translation Available: La Ragazza Del Karaoke
Number of Pages: 371
Author: Claire Tham
Year of Publication: 2013
Publisher: Ethos Books

Characterisation Notes:

Wang Ling hails from an impoverished rural village in China. She graduated from a third-tier university in the northeast part of the country and now works as a laboratory assistant. Ling is unable to secure better economic prospects as she does not have a master's degree or a doctorate. Bright, ambitious, and hungry for more in life, she follows Ms. Fung (the managing director of a nightclub) to work as a karaoke lounge hostess in Singapore.

Text Synopsis:

The Inlet opens with Ling's unnatural death. Her naked corpse is discovered floating face-down in a private swimming pool of a seafront bungalow in "The Inlet", an exclusive enclave on a resort island just off the coast of mainland Singapore. The bungalow belongs to Willy Gan, an eccentric billionaire property developer. His nephew, Jasper Gan, had spent the night with Ling just hours before her death and is the prime suspect of the murder. The post-mortem report confirms the presence of swimming pool water in Ling's lungs and indicates that she suffered a knock on the head that resulted in a minor concussion or hematoma in the brain. To discover the truth behind Ling's death, the investigating officer Assistant Superintendent Wong Cheung Fai must hunt down Ling's ex-suitor as well as an oil trader nicknamed "Merrill Lynch."

Significance and Remarks:

The Inlet is a crime novel inspired by a real-life incident that made headlines in 2010. Li Hong Yan, a 24-year-old Chinese National karaoke lounge hostess, was found dead in the swimming pool of a luxurious waterfront mansion, which belonged to the chief executive of a property investment firm. Following a coroner's inquiry, Li's death was deemed an accident.

Tham employs a polyphonous storytelling strategy: each chapter is named after a character or a place and is narrated from the perspective of many different characters, including Ling herself, Ms. Fung, Jasper, Ling's ex-suitor Min Liang, Cheung Fai, and Cheung Fai's wife Li Ching, who is a newspaper crime journalist. The diverse viewpoints of these characters provide a comprehensive overview of the ever-changing demographics of modern Singapore.

Tham pens a series of vignettes that foreground the xenophobic attitudes of Singaporeans towards migrant workers. During her regular commute, Sanjana—a 15-year-old Indian girl who lives next to Willy's bungalow—is told off by a Singaporean Chinese man to return to where she came from. In another instance, the man who witnessed Li Ching being assaulted during one of her morning jogs boldly asserts that the assailant was "Indian or Bangladeshi" even though Li Ching herself was hesitant to make such an assumption since she did not get a good look at the culprit. As such, the novel reveals the underlying racial prejudices that Singaporeans have against migrant workers, thereby subverting the utopian notion that Singapore is a cosmopolitan haven.

Ultimately, this exclusive enclave known as "The Inlet" can be treated as a microcosm of modern Singapore: a 'melting pot' of different cultures that seek to lure the global elite into residing or investing in the country. As a result of Singapore's global interconnectedness, the life and well-being of an individual (such as Ling) is easily reduced to a single insignificant and transient moment. In the novel's final chapters, Cheung Fai fails to uncover the real identity of "Merrill Lynch" and consigns the cause Ling's death to that of an "accidental drowning."

Potential areas of comparative analysis:

Multiculturalism, Social class, Immigration Policy, Identity, Rich/Poor divide, Xenophobia, Migrant workers, Diaspora, Racism

THE INLET

主要语言： 英文
次要语言： -
翻译版本： La Ragazza Del Karaoke
页数： 371
作者： Claire Tham
出版年份： 2013
出版社： Ethos Books

人物简介：

王玲（Wang Ling）来自中国东北贫苦的乡村。从三本大学（即中国排名末端的学府）毕业后，从事实验室助理的工作。她若不继续深造、考取硕士或博士学位，不可能在事业上取得突破，改善生活条件。她聪明、雄心勃勃，因此决定到新加坡的夜总会当陪酒女郎，期待过上更好的日子。

文本概要：

故事以王玲的非自然死亡案开启：某天早晨，她全裸的尸身被发现面部朝下、漂浮在一座滨海豪宅"The Inlet"的私人泳池中。这栋豪宅位于新加坡外岛的一个度假胜地，豪宅的主人是性情古怪的新加坡亿万富翁、房地产开发商颜伟利（Willy Gan）。事发前几个小时，颜伟利的侄儿贾斯伯（Jasper Gan）和死者发生过两次性行为，是警方的首要嫌疑犯。尸检结果证实，在死者肺部验出泳池水，王玲死前头部也受到撞击，导致血肿。为厘清王玲的死的真相，助理警监黄祥辉（Wong Cheung Fai）必须找到王玲的前男友——绰号"Merrill Lynch"的石油交易员。

重点与备注：

The Inlet 的创作灵感源自一件不幸事故。2010年，24岁的中国女郎李红艳（Li Hong Yan）被发现全裸陈尸在一座滨海豪宅的泳池中，引起各界媒体强烈关注。豪宅的主人是一间投资顾问公司的创办人。经验尸庭研讯(Coroner's Inquiry)，确认李红艳的死因为意外溺毙(accidental drowning)。

作者采用复调（polyphony）的叙事策略：每一个章节以一个人物或者一个地方命名，呈现王玲、夜总会经理、王玲的追求者民良、黄祥辉以及丽清（黄祥辉的妻子，是一名意外线记者）等人的视角——他们的多元观点全面体现现代新加坡不断变化的人口结构。

作者在小说中穿插的一连串片段凸显新加坡社会的排外心态（xenophobia）。例如，新移民珊嘉娜 (Sanjana，颜伟利的邻居) 在一次例行的通勤中，被一名新加坡华裔男子无端数落，让她从哪里来 (印度) 便回哪里去。又如，丽清在晨运时遭不明男子袭击，目击者断言攻击者如果不是来自印度，那就是来自孟加拉，但丽清表示，她没有看清对方面貌，因此迟迟未下结论。小说揭示了国人在日常生活中对新移民的偏见，颠覆了新加坡是一个理想的国际大都会的乌托邦概念（utopian notion）。

高档的私人豪宅"The Inlet"是新加坡的缩影：她是个不断吸引全球精英移居此或进行投资的"大熔炉"。然而新加坡和全球各国的高度互联（interconnectedness）也使每个个体（例如：王玲）的生命化为一个微不足道的短暂片刻。在小说的最后几章，黄祥辉始终未能揭开王玲前男友"Merrill Lynch"的真实身份，她的死也以"意外溺毙"结案。

潜在的比较文学分析：

多元种族主义、社会阶级、移民政策、身份认同、贫富悬殊、排外情绪、外籍客工、排外/仇外心态、客工、离散、种族歧视

乌鸦 (CROWS)

Primary Language: Chinese

Secondary Language: No

Translation Available: No

Number of Pages: 373

Author: Jiu Dan

Year of Publication: 2001

Publisher: Lingzi Media Pte Ltd

Characterisation Notes:

Helen (Wang Yao) is a Chinese journalist. Upon her breakup with her fiancé, she leaves China for Singapore in search of greener pastures. She does so anonymously and without informing her family. Helen meets two other Chinese women, Fen, and Taxi in Singapore. The three women are united in their goals: to learn English, and more importantly, to obtain Singaporean residency through marriage. Risking deportation, the three women sell their sexual services in Singaporean nightclubs hoping to win the affections of wealthy Singaporean businessmen. They do not succeed in their goals: Helen and Taxi are eventually deported, whereas Fen languishes in a life of vice—constantly shifting from one man to another.

Text Synopsis:

The novel begins with Helen awaiting her flight to Singapore. She overhears a conversation between two Singaporean women discussing the murder of a Singaporean man by a Chinese woman. Helen shudders at the women's derisive attitude towards Chinese women. On the plane, Helen meets a wealthy Mrs Mai and tells her she intends to learn English and work as a Mandarin teacher in Singapore in the future.

Helen rents a room in Mrs Mai's mansion. She meets Fen and the psychology lecturer Li Siyan. Helen attempts to seduce Li to obtain residency in Singapore and improve her economic condition. However, Li's wife soon discovers this and forcibly separates the pair. Helen is ashamed that she had seduced a married man and decides to leave Li.

At a banquet, Mrs Mai introduces Helen to Liu Dao, a wealthy businessman in his 60s. Mrs Mai warns Helen that Liu Dao has endless female companions. Helen ignores Mrs Mai's warnings and engages in sexual contact with him. She pins her hopes on the man: she believes him when he says that he will allow her to stay in his apartment and love her like a daughter, and also when he offered to apply for her visa. At the same time, Fen breaks up with her boyfriend, and also attempts to seduce Liu Dao. Helen is disheartened by the promiscuous Liu Dao and leaves him.

Pressured by circumstance, Helen prostitutes herself. She is caught, and her student visa is revoked. Before leaving, a vengeful Helen tricks and drowns Liu Dao at the beach. At the end of the novel, Fen tells Helen that she had killed her only hope—Liu Dao had been faithful to her and was the only man who could solve her immigration problems. Overwhelmed by guilt, Helen turns herself in.

Significance and Remarks:

The author writes in the preface that *Crows* is a book about sin. Sin is an existential condition of humanity: in their natural struggles for self-benefit, humans inevitably harm society and other humans. Such is the sin committed by Helen, Fen and Taxi.

In the author's cruel world, human nature is twisted and nihilistic. Helen is principled and full of hope when she first arrives in Singapore. She tells Fen and Taxi that she does not wish to depend on men financially. She wishes to land a job as a Mandarin teacher and to "succeed" in life (to obtain Singaporean residency, a family, and a career). The three women share a dream of obtaining Singaporean residency. They want to be looked up to when they return to their homeland. Little do they know that their seemingly simple goal is at once unachievable and even pitiable.

Facing numerous pressures, and with no one to depend on, the women are driven to desperation; in their portrayal, humanity's ugly and twisted nature becomes apparent. Helen blackmails Li Siyan for $3000 by falsely claiming that she was pregnant. Helen then seduces Liu Dao because she loves his money and wants to copulate with him; she also tells Liu that she would not be able to survive without him. At the end of the novel, Helen tells Liu Dao that she does not mind sharing him with other women, that she can live at this beck and call.

The author describes sexuality down to the most explicit detail. The author explains in the preface that sexuality confronts us all in modern life and that it is impossible to avoid encounters with sex—particularly in a society where many women are forced to commodify themselves in order to survive. Pressured by circumstances, Helen initiates sex with Liu Dao, a man old enough to be her father. During sexual intercourse, Helen realizes that Liu is unable to climax—in fact, he had not been able to ejaculate for 20 years. Helen pretends that she does not mind and hugs him and consoles him. She services him repeatedly for the few thousand dollars he gives her every month, and for the stability and assurance he provides her in return.

The author appreciates that much of the reception to the novel was negative. She explains that she does not describe Chinese women as *Wu Ya* (crows) when she mentions the Singapore ordinance to shoot crows to reduce their population. Instead, the author intends for the metaphor "crow" to refer to human sin in general. To her, sin demands repentance. The three women Helen, Taxi, and Fen were unrepentant and never considered that they could live proper, dignified lives; they cast aside their dignity for money and the assurance that they can "conquer" men through their "sex." In their attachment complexes (to men), the women objectify themselves. To men, the women are no better than consumables to be thrown away after use. In sum, this tragedy highlights a significant problem for modern women: a woman must embark on a difficult journey, must move from a situation of subservience to that of agency and dignity.

Potential areas of comparative analysis:

Patriarchy, Chinese emigration, sexuality, sexual desire, diasporic literature, traditional femininity, modern feminism, women's representation, women's perspective, women's emancipation, sin, power

乌鸦：我的另类留学生活

主要语言： 中文
次要语言： -
翻译版本： -
页数： 373
作者： 九丹
出版年份： 2001
出版社： 玲子传媒

人物简介：

海伦（王瑶）原是报社记者，她与未婚夫分手后瞒着家人、隐姓埋名逃到新加坡。表面上，海伦、芬和湖南女孩Taxi三人在同一所语言学校学英文。但实际上，她们的目标只有一个，那就是获得新加坡的永久居民证。为达目的，她们依附在富商身上，不惜冒着被遣返的危险到夜总从事性工作。最终，除了一身伤痕，什么理想也没实现：海伦和Taxi被遣返回国，而芬依然是个周旋在不同男人身边、孤苦无依的女子。

文本概要：

海伦在候机室听见两名新加坡女子讨论起关于一名中国籍女子涉嫌谋杀一新加坡男子的新闻，言语间透露出对中国女子的歧视，不禁令她打了个寒颤。在飞机上，海伦认识了麦姓富太，并告诉她打算在新加坡学英文，然后当中文老师。

海伦成为麦太太豪宅的租客，同时认识了芬和心理学讲师李私炎。为了缓解窘迫的经济状况，海伦开始依附于私炎，幻想通过和私炎结婚，以配偶的身份申请居留权。两人的关系不久被私炎的太太捅破，海伦惊觉自己竟成了有妇之夫的小三，决定和他分开，她的生活再次陷入困境。

在一个宴会上，海伦透过麦太太认识了60余岁的富商柳道。麦太太警告她，柳道身边有无数名女子，千万不要和他发生男女关系。海伦对麦太太的劝告充耳不闻，把期盼寄望在柳道身上。柳道也承诺海伦，她可以住在他的公寓里，并会像疼女儿一样疼她，也答应帮她办签证。与此同时，芬的男朋友不告而别，理想破灭的她也主动攀上柳道。为此，海伦决定离开柳道。

海伦铤而走险，下海当妓女，但被逮个正着，学生证被移民局取消，被迫限时离境。在离开前，海伦把不会游泳的柳道引到海边，设计让他坠海身亡。芬告诉海伦，柳道对她有情有义，是唯一能帮她解决问题的人，但她却亲手毁了最后的希望，海伦万分懊悔，决定自首。

重点与备注：

作者在代序中坦言，《乌鸦》是本关于罪恶的书。人与罪恶共生共存，由于天性的弱点使然，人会为了争取自己的利益而努力挣扎，在过程中肯定对他人或社会构成伤害，这就是文中女子犯下的罪恶。

作者以其对残酷现实的描绘使扭曲的人性和道德的沦丧浮上台面。海伦刚抵达新加坡时，是有原则、且对未来充满希望的。她告诉芬和Taxi，她不愿意在经济上依赖男人，期望找到一份中文老师的工作，在新加坡过得有出息（得到居留权、结婚证或就业准证）。 她们都有共同的理想：在新加坡常住，偶尔回国，当是衣锦还乡。这个目标看似即简单，但同时又卑下且遥不可及。

在生存成为第一法则的严峻情况下，人的孤独无依、生存环境的严酷把她们逼上墙角。人性的扭曲、丑恶与异化也随之浮出台面。海伦开始堕落，不仅谎称自己怀孕，向李私炎勒索3000新元外，还委身于柳道，毫不讳言说就是爱他的钱，想和他融成一体——如果没有他，真的活不下去。她卑微地告诉柳道，她愿意和其他女人一样陪他吃饭、睡觉。

小说也有不少大胆、赤裸的性爱与情欲描绘。作者在代序强调，性是现实生活中无法回避的一部分。面对高昂的生活费，“性”是作为女人最有利的谋生武器。为了生存，海伦和足以能当她父亲的柳道发生性行为。第一次做爱后，她发现柳道患有性功能障碍，柳道坦言他是性无能，已经20年没有射精。然而，为了每个月几千元的生活费，她仍然装不介意，拥抱他、安慰着他，希望能在他身上获得依靠和稳定。

作者表示，大部分人对乌鸦的印象是负面的，但并不代表她把文中女性比作乌鸦。就如文中提到，新加坡政府曾命令射杀乌鸦，如果把乌鸦比喻成一种罪恶，并不完全恰当。所谓的罪恶必须也包含全人类所犯下的错。若有罪恶，就必须反省，但文中的女子没有一人愿意忏悔，或者通过其他途径让自己活得有尊严、有出息。她们自愿抛弃尊严依附于男性来获取金钱和内心的安稳，以为能用“性”来征服他们，但在她们委身于男人时，她们就已沦为男人可随时抛弃的附属品。小说中海伦、芬等一批中国女子的浓烈依附情结造就了这部悲歌，因此，要如何从被操纵到重新掌握主导权，为自己赢得尊重，才是所有女性必须思考的重要课题。

潜在的比较文学分析：

父权社会、海外华人、性、情欲、新移民、新移民文学、传统女性意识、现代女性主义、女性形象、女性视角、女性解放、罪恶、权利

陪读妈妈 (EDUCATION MAMA)

Primary Language: Mandarin
Secondary Language: No
Translation Available: No
Number of Pages: 203
Author: Min Zhou
Year of Publication: 2003
Publisher: Lingzi Media Pte Ltd

Characterisation Notes:

Pei Du Ma Ma is a work of documentary fiction. It narrates the story of Ye Ruo Dan, who quits her jobs and leaves her husband in China to care for her son Gao Xiang Ming during the course of his study in Singapore. Ye is faced with numerous uncertainties and hardships as she navigates a foreign educational system and the threat of Gao's "retainment" in school.

Text Synopsis:

Gao Xiang Ming has a weak grasp of English despite half a year of study in a language school. Upon moving to Singapore, he is retained for one year and must repeat primary three. Gao's mother, Ye Ruo Dan, heeds the advice of Gao's form teacher and hires a tutor for him. To sustain the cost of tuition, Ye decides to take up a job in Singapore. However, she soon realizes that no company would hire a worker who does not speak English.

In the face of economic pressures and constant rejection, Ye's confidence evaporates and she becomes easily stressed. Lowering her expectations even further, she finally finds two low-wage jobs: one as a laundrywoman for a hotel, and the second as a foot therapist. She lies to her husband and son that she works in insurance to save them from embarrassment.

Despite his mother's best efforts, Gao's academic situation does not improve. He fails his English, Mandarin, Mathematics, and Science subjects. Disappointed, Ye contemplates returning to China. At that time, she hears from a colleague that she can receive employment and medical benefits if she can attain permanent residency in Singapore through marriage to a Singaporean. Ye discusses this with her husband, and they agree to divorce in name. Unknown to Ye, her husband Zi Cheng had been sincere in the divorce because he had met another woman.

Ye meets Zhong Yong Qiang, a divorced man, through a marriage agency. Zhong helps Ye secure housing, a position as a relief teacher, and even Gao's transfer to another school. In her new job, Ye tutors primary school students in Mandarin phonetics. She then branches out to teach Mandarin to English educated adults, and her financial situation steadily improves.

Ye believes that marriage is necessary to her permanent residency and proposes to Zhong. Zhong refuses because he does not wish to be tied down by a marital contract. He argues that permanent residency has nothing to do with marriage, and relationships can thrive without marriage. This dispute leads to a severe schism between the couple, and Zhong eventually decides to leave Ye.

At the end of the novel, Ye starts to feel unwell and nauseous. She learns that she has a liver ailment and must be hospitalized. Ye remembers that she cannot afford to do so—her medical bills are not subsidized because she is not a Singaporean permanent resident (she links this to Zhong's adamant refusal to marry her) and she has no "CPF"—and faints on a sidewalk at midday.

Significance and Remarks:

The novel documents the emotional experiences of some women in Singapore. The author Min Zhou (the pseudonym of Chen Hua) is an experienced news reporter. In the course of writing the novel, she drew upon interviews with dozens of emigrant mothers in Singapore (Ye Ruo Dan's character is based on one such "classical" account). As a result, the author can portray life in Singapore to a high degree of specificity and emotional reality.

"Accompanying mothers" such as Ye Ruo Dan are a common sight in Singapore. The author explains that many agencies process up to 990 visas for emigrating mothers in a year—an average of two or three mothers a day. Like Ye, most of these mothers give up their families and career in hopes that their children can receive a bilingual education in Singapore.

The term "accompanying mothers" has a negative connotation in Singapore. The media vilifies such mothers as "gold diggers" or "little dragon girls" (a euphemism for prostitute) who ruin families. Thus, "accompanying mothers" face a double marginalization in Singapore: they are alienated by a language barrier and by the invisible prejudice of Singaporeans.

The novel establishes the symbolic significance of marriage to the "accompanying mothers." The strange scenes of a fake divorce and a fake marriage to obtain permanent residency in the novel can be understood from such a perspective—to the "accompanying mothers," marriage is a social symbol that is instrumental for their concrete plans. As such, the mothers pay little heed to the qualities of their husbands: to Ye Ruo Dan, it does not matter if her husband has a low social status, or if he earns lesser than her and is physically unattractive.

To the "accompanying mothers," permanent residency is a proof of social status and a ticket to a dignified life in Singapore. As Ye Ruo Dan explains, if she doesn't get married, her son will view her as another "accompanying mother" who makes a living by seducing married men and engaging in sex work. In addition, permanent residency also offers a sense of belonging to Ye. She explains that, if she doesn't attain permanent residency, her relationship with Singapore will always be ephemeral, like a lover whom one does not truly possess. To Ye, the "true possession" of a lover can be likened to concrete improvements to her livelihood (such as a high-salaried job and the ownership of a house in Singapore).

The author empathizes with and even attempts to rationalize the actions and motivations of the "accompanying mothers." To the author, the common stereotype of "accompanying mothers" unjustly demonizes their attempts to seek marriage and permanent residency. After all, these mothers are but ordinary women who are afraid of poverty and have to stay off the streets together with their children. The author hopes that she can dispel the stereotypes and misunderstandings associated with the label "accompanying mothers" by giving voice to them through her work. However, it is arguable that the text only portrays the indignation and loneliness of the "accompanying mothers"; little of their professed desire to integrate into Singapore society comes through. In so doing, the author may have highlighted the victim mentality of the women she writes about. For instance, Ye's borderline-psychotic insistence on following through with a fake marriage, along with her disregard for her choice of husbands, evinces an absolute instrumentalization of love and relationships. If we take Ye as a representation of all "accompanying mothers," the text may have deepened the very stereotypes that it intended to dispel.

Potential areas of comparative analysis:

Chinese Emigrants, New Migrants, New Migrants Literature, Cross-Culture Dialogues/Interaction, Diasporic Experiences, Symbolic Identity, Cultural Identity, Marriage, Sense of Displacement/Loss

陪读妈妈

主要语言： 中文
次要语言： -
翻译版本： -
页数： 203
作者： 悯舟
出版年份： 2003
出版社： 玲子传媒私人有限公司

人物简介：

《陪读妈妈》是一篇纪实小说。叶若丹为儿子高向明辞掉工作、抛下丈夫子城，带着他到新加坡求学，成为全职的“陪读妈妈”。面对和中国截然不同的教育体制，向明迎来海外生活的第一个危机——留级，充满未知与辛酸的留学生生活也随即展开。

文本概要：

尽管上了半年的语言学校，向明的英语基础仍然非常薄弱，必须留级一年，从三年级开始读起，若丹也听取老师的建议为儿子聘请补习老师。为了支付补习费用，她开始找工作，但没有一家公司愿意聘请不谙英语的人工作。面对高昂的生活费，她的自信逐渐瓦解，变得焦躁不安，失去耐性。她把标准降低，最后找到两份工作：一份在酒店熨床单，另一份则在按摩院当足底按摩师，赚取微薄的收入。为了不让丈夫和儿子感到自卑，她隐瞒实情，骗他们自己从事保险业。

向明的英文成绩没有进步，除了华文，其他科目都不及格。若丹动了回国的念头，同时，她从同事口中得知，如果和新加坡人结婚，就能以配偶的身份申请永久居民（Permanent Resident, PR）。有了PR，她可以享有政府的医疗津贴、购买房子以及找到薪水更好的工作。她和丈夫协议假离婚，子城毫不犹豫地签了一份离婚协议。若丹没想到的是，子城在中国有外遇。

若丹透过婚姻介绍所认识了离异男子钟永强，钟永强帮她找房子，帮向明转学，也帮她争取在小学当义务老师的机会。进入教书的圈子后，若丹有越来越多教中文的机会，除了给小学生上拼音课，也帮受英文教育的人补习华文，生活打开了另一扇窗。若丹认为结婚是成功申请永久居民的前提，主动提出结婚，但永强不愿意被一纸婚姻束缚，认为能否取得永久居民证和结婚无关，人与人也不一定要以结婚为前提而来往。两人就结婚和申请永久居民证这个问题僵持不下，永强也不再包容若丹，决定离开她。

小说尾声，若丹身体不适，呕吐不止，接受检查后发现肝功能不正常，必须住院治疗。当她想到永强不愿意结婚，自己不是新加坡永久居民，没有医疗津贴，没有公积金可以支付高额的医药费时，她在暑气最猛烈的正午昏倒在路上。

重点与备注：

《陪读妈妈》除了是一篇纪实小说，也可以是一篇情感实录。作者悯舟（原名陈华）曾为报社资深记者，她以报道新闻求真求实的手法，采访了数十名陪读妈妈，最后选择其中一个最经典的案例（若丹的原型），记录她在狮城生活的喜悦悲欢。因此，故事的人物、遭遇、细节和心情等刻画都真实有效。

陪读妈妈并不罕见，根据她们提供给作者的情报，负责办理出国的中介公司，一年可办990个陪读妈妈的签证，平均每一天就有两三名母亲决定陪孩子留学。和所有陪读妈妈们一样，若丹抛家别业投奔新加坡只为一个目标：让孩子接受双语教育。关于陪读妈妈的负面新闻层出不穷，在主流媒体的大肆渲染之下，她们成了“捞钱捞男人”，破坏家庭的“小龙女”（情妇和妓女的代名词）。面对有形的语言隔阂和无形的歧视，陪读妈妈们的海外生活可说是赔了夫人又折兵。

我们不得不提小说描绘的怪像：假离婚、假结婚以及申请永久居民，以及其所延伸关于婚姻和永久居民对陪读妈妈的标志性意义。婚姻的意义远超于配偶的名分，因此若丹对对方的身份地位毫无要求，就算收入少一点、长相差一点也没关系，把结婚和申请永久居民的急迫全写在脸上。永久居民是身份的提升——有了它，她们可以有自尊地在新加坡生活。用若丹的话说，没有婚姻，向明会以为她和部分陪读妈妈一样是新加坡男人的情妇，出卖肉体换取金钱。永久居民也代表了归属感。没有它，她对新加坡的感情像是和情人相处一般，若有似无。所谓的拥有，是指改善生活条件的筹码，例如：薪资更优渥的工作以及属于自己的房子。

作者不但怜悯陪读妈妈的遭遇，也尝试合理化她们的行为和想法。在陪读妈妈们背负的标签之外，若丹认为，她们想嫁人，想申请永久居民，无非因为她们不过也是平凡的女子，她们害怕身无分文、无瓦遮头。随着《陪读妈妈》的发表，作者希望更多陪读妈妈的声音能被听见，许多人对她们的误解也能稀释或消散，但读者在小说中仅能看见陪读妈妈自认为的无奈与孤独，缺乏她们尝试融入社会的过程，难免有受害者心态的嫌疑。例如，文中若丹以假结婚之名，行申请永久居民之实的执着几乎接近病态，再加上她毫不讳言她对配偶毫无要求，更加坐实了她把婚姻当工具的事实。如果若丹的际遇是所有陪读妈妈们命运的缩影，这难以让读者不产生负面的想法。

潜在的比较文学分析：

海外华人、新移民、新移民文学、跨文化交流、离散经验、身份象征、文化认同、婚姻、位移感（sense of displacement/loss）

永发街事 (ENG WATT STREET HAPPENINGS)

Primary Language: Mandarin
Secondary Language: some English
Translation Available: No
Number of Pages: 270
Author: Chen Ji Zhou
Year of Publication: 2019
Publisher: Linking Publishing

Characterisation Notes:

Yong Fa Jie Shi (loosely translated as The Happenings of Eng Watt Street) is a collection of 12 short stories. The characters hail from a variety of backgrounds: some are Singaporean, while others are tourists and emigrants from China, Europe and the United States. Their seemingly independent life trajectories interweave at Eng Watt Street, where they leave deep imprints on each other.

Text Synopsis:

Eng Watt Street is a site where the seemingly anarchic trends of human migration and globalization intersect—people of different nationalities, race, religion, sex, sexual orientations, and generations meet and form relationships there. The author depicts the experiences of the myriad inhabitants of the street. These include the transformative experience a young man from Sichuan, the romance between a construction worker named Zhang Qiang and a girl from Fujian, the forbidden love beating in the heart of a young professor, the elderly grandmother who lives alone but who puts great effort into looking after her non-Chinese grandson, and the emptiness encountered by a middle-aged man after divorce.

Significance and Remarks:

The author Chen Ji Zhou was born in Sichuan, China. His life experience spans three continents: he lived in Singapore for 10 years (he moved to Singapore to study from the age of 17), six of which was spent at Eng Watt Street. Chen then lived in Heidelburg, Germany during his college years, before moving to the United States for his PhD candidature in Harvard University in 2015.

The novel deals with the theme of the transformative powers of migration and movement. For instance, in the first story "Species and beginning," the author discusses the metamorphosis of the Sichuanese youth Li Xiao Yi after his emigration to Singapore. Li's childhood coincided with a natural calamity and his father had sent him to live with his relatives because the family could not afford to raise him. As he grew up, Li changed his surname to Zhang and moved to Singapore. During canoeing practice, Zhang becomes lost in the Singaporean rainforest and finds himself transformed into a large insect the next day. The author then brings the speculative short story to a shocking climax to emphasise his point about the transformation and evolution of a human being as he moves from place to place.

Aside from its significance in the author's lived experience, Eng Watt Street is also significant to the collection's themes of migration and movement for historical reasons.

Eng Watt Street takes its name from the shipping merchant See Eng Watt, and is in Tiong Bahru, a neighbourhood where multiple immigrant communities have gathered since the 19th century. Many of Tiong Bahru's streets are named after early Singaporean Chinese entrepreneurs such as Eng Hoon Street (after Koh Eng Hoon), Seng Poh Lane (after Tan Seng Poh), Lim Liak Street (after tin mine owner Lim Liak). Interestingly the name "Tiong Bahru" is an amalgamation of Hokkien and Malay: "Tiong" means "the end" in Hokkien whereas "Bahru" means "new" in Malay. Thus, the combination of the "end" and the "new", along with Tiong Bahru's history, evokes the interweb of emigration, beginnings and ends that accompany migration and movement. In this collection, the author discusses the lives and movements of his own generation in Eng Watt Street, foregrounded by the historical figures of Tiong Bahru.

The author reveals that he was inspired by the Taiwanese author Wu Ming-Yi to compose a "long story" through "short stories." *Yong Fa Jie Shi* reflects this dual focus: the individual short stories revolve around Eng Watt Street, but only as a site among many others. The characters meet at Eng Watt Street and will soon move elsewhere; they will then be replaced by new inhabitants who will begin anew the cycle of stories. In the unceasing process of immigration and emigration, the author explores the flow of life and the excitement, hopes, and loneliness of the unknown.

Potential areas of comparative analysis:

Overseas Chinese Communities, New Migrants, New Migrants Literature, Sinophone Literature, Cross-Cultural Discourse, Diasporic Experiences, Sense of displacement/ loss, Globalization and Migration, Interracial Love, Homosexuality, Singaporean Language Policy, Chinese-educated students, Identity

永发街事

主要语言： 繁体中文
次要语言： 零星英文
翻译版本： 无
页数： 270
作者： 陈济舟
出版年份： 2019
出版社： 联经出版事业股份有限公司

人物简介：

短篇小说集《永发街事》共收录12篇作品，故事人物背景多元：除了在地居民，也包含来自中国、欧洲和美国等的移民或过客。他们原本看似平行的生活在永发街交织在一起，在彼此的生命中留下或深或浅的雪泥鸿爪

文本概要：

四川少年一夕之间失踪变形、福建小妹和建筑工人张强喝粥谈情、巴黎男子为爱漂洋过海、从北京回新的失婚妇女邂逅印度裔保安人员、青年教授的禁忌恋情、独居老妇照顾不似华裔的孙子、中年男子离婚后的空虚，全球化的迁徙与流动将看似不可能有任何交集的男男女女聚集到新加坡。在永发街上演绎一出出跨越国籍、种族、宗教、性别、性向和世代等的生命碰撞。

重点与备注：

作者陈济舟生于中国四川，十七岁南来狮城升学，客居星洲10年间曾在永发街生活6年；他在大学期间曾旅居德国海德堡，2015年毕业后负笈美国哈佛深造，目前正攻读博士学位，生命经验横跨亚欧美三大洲。

小说处理和关注移动带来的变化，以开篇〈物种与起源〉为例，作者叙述四川少年李效益移居他乡后的蜕变。李效益幼时碰上天灾，家中困顿，父母将他过寄给亲戚，他长大后改名换姓成张孝义移民狮

城。离开熟悉的故乡，少年居然在一次皮划艇训练后神秘消失在雨林深处，一夜之间变成巨型爬虫类。作者超现实的处理方式将故事带推向骇人听闻的高潮，也折射出异乡人为适应迁居，通过变异而产生的进化。

对作者而言，永发街是他旅居新加坡期间的居住地，具备特殊意义。但除此之外，扣紧小说集关于"移动"和"移民"的主题，永发街也具有历史性的象征意义。

位于中峇鲁的永发街取自船运商人薛永发（See Eng Watt），自19世纪以来便是移民汇聚之地，也因此中峇鲁后来有不少街道取自新加坡华社的企业家，除永发街外，还有以华商许行云命名的行云街（Eng Hoon Street）、侨领陈成宝的成保巷（Seng Poh Lane）和锡矿主林烈的林烈道（Lim Liak Street）等。值得注意的是，中峇鲁的英文拼音"Tiong Bahru"是方言和马来文的结合："中"(Tiong) 原为"塚"或"终"的福建读音, 意味"结束", 反之, "峇鲁"(Bahru) 在马来语则意味着"新"。"终"和"新"的结合，加上中峇鲁的故事，唤醒了伴随迁移和流动，由移居（旅居）、开始和结束所串联成的移动网络。但这些都属于历史。陈济舟在小说要刻画的是属于他这一代人的流动故事。

陈济舟在书中揭露，台湾作家吴明益给了他用"短篇"建构"长篇"的启发，而《永发街事》正是一本见微知著的作品。虽然故事扣紧永发街，但严格来说，它只是座驿站——各路人马在此聚集，或逗留或羁旅，再从这里走向世界各处。他们搬走后，依然会有一批接一批的过客取而代之，在川流不息的迁进与迁出之间，探索流动的生命带来的未知和精彩、孤独与希冀，人来人往、周而复始。

潜在的比较文学分析：

海外华人、新移民、新移民文学、华语语系新加坡文学、跨文化交流、离散经验、全球化迁徙和流动、异族恋情、同性爱情、新加坡语言政策、华校生、身份认同

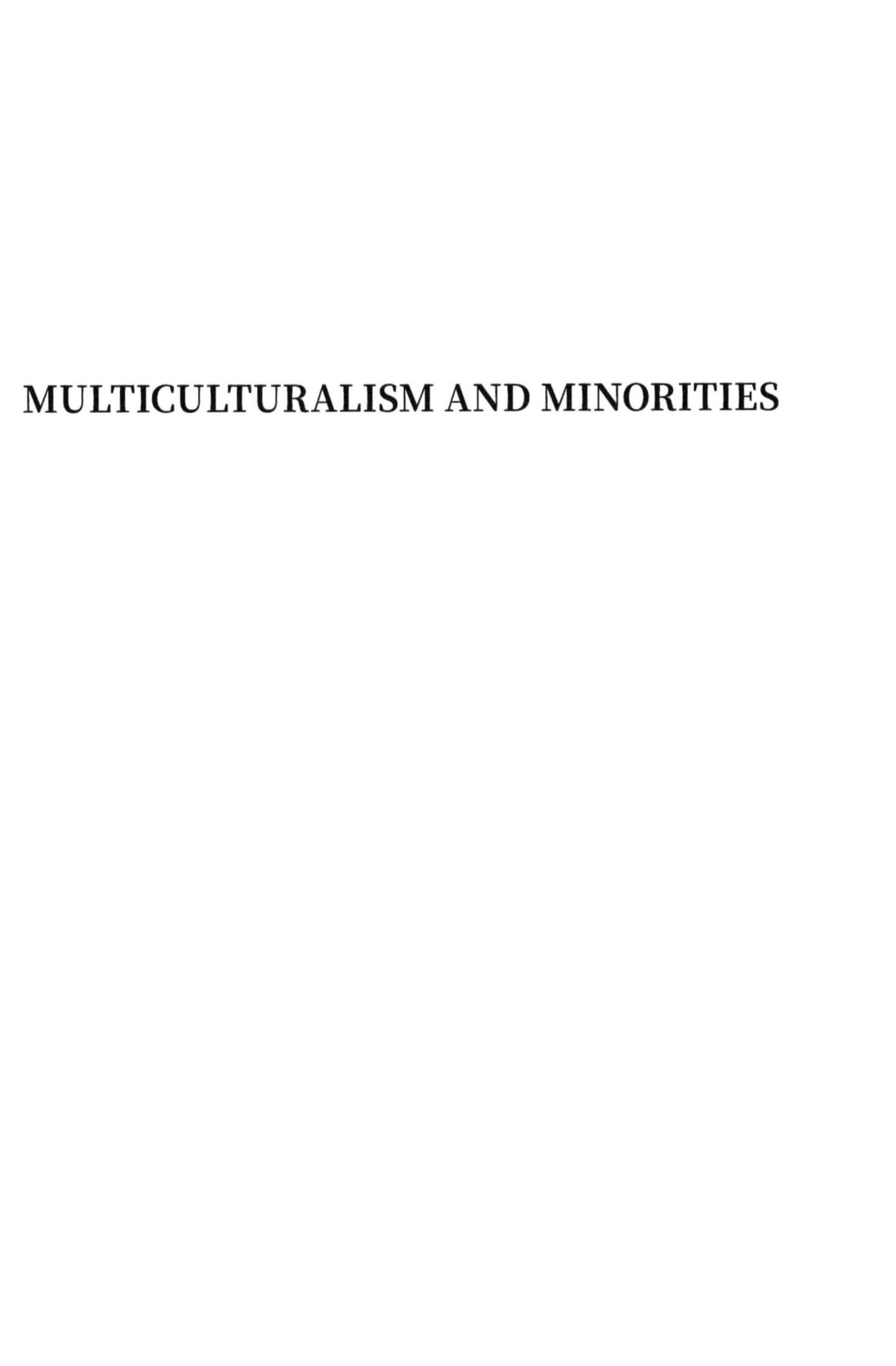

MULTICULTURALISM AND MINORITIES

FISTFUL OF COLOURS

Primary Language: English
Secondary Language: Some Singlish
Translation Available: No
Number of Pages: 362
Author: Suchen Christine Lim
Year of Publication: 1993
Publisher: EPB Publishers

Characterisation Notes:

The main protagonist Suwen is an aspiring artist and a full-time art teacher at a college. She has a close-knit circle of friends who are avid lovers of art and literature: Jan, Mark, Nica and Zul. Jan and Mark are Suwen's colleagues from the same college, whereas Nica is an accomplished sculptor who also acts as Suwen's mentor. Jan and Zul are a long-term couple and are engaged by the end of the novel, while Mark and Suwen express a romantic interest in each other. Nica's boyfriend Robert Lim also plays a minor role in the novel.

Text Synopsis:

Suwen grew up in the Ong Mansion with her mother, half-sister and stepfather—Ong Tay Luck—the proprietor of the largest Chinese-owned bus company in Singapore. Ever since she was a teenager, Suwen has resented her stepfather for attempting to sexually assault her in her sleep, as well as her mother for not fully acknowledging the incident. Suwen is only able to find solace in her life through the act of painting and hopes to organise her own art exhibition. She develops a close relationship with a small group of friends who seek to defy cultural stereotypes and racial prejudices in Singapore. In the course of the novel, Jan struggles with the disapproval of her Chinese-Christian parents over her relationship with a Malay-Muslim man. Nica, who is the daughter of an Indian-Hindu father and a Baba-Catholic mother, unabashedly opposes her father's expectations of a "Proper Indian Girl" by becoming an outspoken and openly promiscuous artist. Even Mark, who is an expatriate of Irish, Italian, and Scottish descent, seeks to complicate the conventional binary between the European colonisers and the colonised Asians, since Ireland, Scotland and Wales were previously colonised by the English.

Scattered throughout the novel are stories about the Ong family that are set against the backdrop of the major historical events in Singapore, from the patriarch Ong Ah Buck's humble beginnings as a coolie and rickshaw puller in the early 1900s, to his marriage to the daughter of a wealthy towkay (business owner). The novel also covers the various trials and tribulations that the Ong family endured during the Japanese Occupation, after which the family business was inherited by Ong Tay Luck, the son of Ong Ah Buck's second wife and concubine.

As the novel progresses, Mark eventually falls in love with Suwen and tries to kiss her while they were out on a morning walk at a Chinese cemetery. Reminded of her childhood trauma and unable to confront her own prejudices against European men, Suwen decides to cut off all contact with Mark. During this period of separation and in order to spite Suwen, Nica propositions Mark to pose nude for one of her artworks. This deeply upsets Suwen and prompts her to create an abstract painting that is charged with her own repressed sexuality and feelings of betrayal. Suwen's painting is subsequently exhibited at the Art Gallery of the National Museum, where it draws public criticism for its erotic and vulgar subject matter. The novel concludes with Suwen on a train to Kuala Jelai in Malaysia—the rural village where Suwen was raised by her maternal grandparents prior to moving into the Ong Mansion—and Mark admiring Suwen's painting at the gallery, both unable to arrive at any form of reconciliation.

Significance and Remarks:

As a work of historical fiction, *Fistful of Colours* sheds light on the lives of early immigrants in Singapore, particularly through the rags-to-riches story of Ong Ah Buck, the patriarch of the Ong family. The novel follows his journey from an impoverished rickshaw coolie to a wealthy rickshaw towkay, while also depicting the historical reality of life in Singapore during the early 1900s.

Additionally, the novel also explores the importance of language in shaping an individual's cultural identity. Unlike the majority of Chinese

Singaporeans who can read and write in Mandarin, Suwen grew up speaking Cantonese to her grandparents before learning English while she was in school. She subsequently enrolled in Durham University to read English and the History of Art in the Western World. As such, Suwen feels alienated from the Chinese community in Singapore since she is only fluent in English and is unable to understand Mandarin. She even laments how the Mandarin-speaking majority are quick to brand people like her as "half-Chinese" and Westernised "geh angmohs." Suwen's anxiety about her cultural identity is, in turn, contrasted with her half-sister Sulin, who is Chinese-educated but is unable to find a job after graduating from Nantah. Consequently, this comparison between the two sisters only seek to demonstrate how language is an important determinant of an individual's social position within the community. While Suwen is shunned by the Mandarin-speaking community for being English-educated, Sulin becomes marginalised by the switch to English as the primary language of administration in Singapore.

In the same instance, the novel examines the value of history and whether an individual's present circumstances are the result of his or her own actions or are merely the product of the past. Throughout the novel, members of the Ong household continue to repeat the Cantonese saying, "Umbrellas have different handles, people have different fates" (15), suggesting that an individual does not have agency in his own life. For instance, even though Ong Ah Buck was able to escape the harsh living conditions of a rickshaw coolie, his legacy was ultimately undermined by the fact that he was not afforded a grand funeral after passing away only a few days before the Japanese surrendered. Hence, the novel demonstrates how life is ultimately the subject of external forces, such as an individual's socio-economic background as well as the events that occur during his or her lifetime.

Yet, *Fistful of Colours* also posits that history is malleable and that an individual's past can ultimately be changed according to his or her own subjective perception. This is epitomised in Nica's proclamation that "Our lives are for us to mould into whatever shapes we want." (115) Indeed, art and history are shown to be interrelated in the novel, where art becomes a means by which the individual is able to assert his or her own autonomy. This is reflected in Suwen's own artistic journey in the course of the novel. Evidently, Suwen began her investigation into the history of the Ongs in the hopes of disclosing the family's secrets through her paintings. However, after she discovers that Nica had made a series of nude sketches of Mark, Suwen decides to paint an abstract piece that functions as both an assertion of her identity as an artist and an acknowledgement of her past trauma.

Potential areas of comparative analysis:

Interracial Communication, Interracial Love, Gender, Sexuality, Traditional vs. Modern values, Social Commentary, Languages in Singapore, Singaporean Religions, Asian vs Western values, Eurasian communities, Art in Singapore, Multiculturalism, New Migrants, Sense of Identity

FISTFUL OF COLOURS

主要语言： 英文

次要语言： 零星中文、马来文以及新加坡式英语

翻译版本： -

页数： 362

作者： Suchen Christine Lim（林素琴）

出版年份： 1993

出版社： EPB Publishers

人物简介：

素雯（Suwen）是一名老师，同时有是名雄心勃勃的艺术家。她的挚友马克（Mark）、妮卡（Nika）、珍妮（Jan）以及祖尔（Zul）和她一样热爱文学和艺术。珍妮、马克和素雯是同事，雕塑艺术家妮卡则是素雯的艺术指导。珍妮和祖尔则是一对跨族情侣，两人相恋已久，在小说最后互订终身。马克和素雯相互倾慕。妮卡的男友罗伯特（Robert）在小说中扮演次要的角色。

文本概要：

素雯和她的母亲、同母异父的妹妹素琳（Sulin）以及继父王第六（Ong Tay Luck）一同在王家大宅生活。王第六是新加坡最大的华资巴士公司的大当家。由于继父曾企图在她睡梦中性侵犯她，素雯自青少年时期就对继父、以及并不承认此事的母亲充满厌恶之情。她只能在绘画创作当中寻求慰藉，希望有一天能举办自己的画展。与此同时，她也和马克、妮卡等好友试图挑战新加坡社会的文化刻板印象（cultural stereotypes）以及种族偏见。随着情节的发展，珍妮因父母亲不认可她和穆斯林男子祖尔的跨种族恋情而和他们产生冲突。妮卡是一名华印混血儿(Chinese-Indian)——她的父亲是印度族，信奉兴都教。而她的母亲是信奉天主教的土生华人。妮卡的父亲希望她和其他印度女孩一样做一个“端庄的印度女子”(Proper Indian Girl，PIG)，然而她违逆父亲的意思，成为一名离经叛道、生活放荡的雕塑艺术家。由于爱尔兰、苏格兰和威尔士都曾是大英帝国的殖民地，拥有爱尔兰、意大利以及苏格兰血统的马克，试图将欧洲殖民者以及亚洲殖民

地之间传统的二元对立（conventional binary）关系复杂化。

从王第六的父亲王阿木（Ong Ah Buck）在上世纪初当苦力、拉人力车的卑微开始，到和头家的女儿结婚、成家立业，小说穿插以新加坡重大历史事件为背景王家家族历史，同时也描述王家在日占时期经理的苦难。日军投降后，王阿木将公司交给他的第二任妻子的儿子王第六掌管。

马克和素雯渐渐对彼此产生好感。一日早晨，他们在华人坟场散步时，马克试图与她有亲密接触，使素雯想起了童年的创伤。另外，素雯始终放不下对白人的偏见，而与马克保持距离。在两人分开的这段期间，为了刻意伤害素雯，妮卡向马克提出为她的作品当裸体模特儿的建议。素雯感到难过和沮丧，但同时也激发她的创作欲。她将内心压抑的情欲和被背叛的情绪完整地呈现在一幅抽象画中。素雯的画作在国家美术馆展出，然作品却因其情色、粗俗题材而舆论哗然。小说尾声，素雯准备从新加坡前往瓜拉日莱（Kuala Jelai）的老家，这是她搬进王家大宅前，外公外婆抚养她长大的偏僻乡村。同时，马克正在国家美术馆欣赏素雯的创作。两人各在一方，彼此未达成任何形式的和解。

重点与备注：

《斑斓色彩》（Fistful of Colours）是一本历史小说，它透过王家掌门人王阿木如何从贩卖劳力生活到咸鱼翻身的故事，揭示早期南来移民在新加坡的故事。同时，小说也描述上世纪初新加坡生活的历史面貌。

语言在塑造个人文化身份（cultural identity）扮演举足轻重的角色。和大部分能阅读以及书写中文的新加坡人不一样的是，素雯自小习惯使用粤语和外祖父母沟通，一直到上学后，开始学习英语。素雯后负笈英国攻读英语以及西方艺术史。由于她只精通英文，当她回到新加坡时，她无法融入华人社群。她甚至感叹，精通中文的新加坡人是如何迅速地给她这贴上如“半个华人” 或西方的“假洋鬼子”的标签。素雯的文化身份焦虑和同母异父的妹妹素琳形成强烈的对比。素琳是典型的华校生，从南洋大学毕业后迟迟找不到工作。两姐妹的对比彰显了语言是决定社会地位的重要因素——素雯不谙中文，遭新加坡的华人社群排挤。而由于社会改用英语为行政用语，素琳逐渐成为社会的边缘人物。

小说也检验历史价值，并探讨个体身处的境况是自身努力的结果抑或仅仅是历史的产物。贯穿小说的是王家成员不断挂在嘴上的广东谚语——“同人不同命，同伞不同柄”，暗示我们不可能通过自身努力主导命运。举例而言，虽然王阿木成功摆脱了人力车夫恶劣的生活环境，但一场战争大大削弱了王家的财力，以致于当他在日军投降前几天过世时，他的家人无法帮他风光大葬。小说向我们展示，人生总是受制于如社经背景以及人生中不可控的外在力量。

小说也探讨了历史的可塑性（malleable），即个体的过去可以因为自己的主观意识而改变。妮卡认为，“我们必须要像一个雕塑家一样塑造我们周围的事物”，“而不是反过来让它们来塑造我们”。事实上，艺术和历史相互关联、密不可分。这一点在素雯的艺术道路上得到了体现。很显然，素雯一开始挖掘家族的历史，是希望在作品中披露家族的秘密。然而，当她发现妮卡为马克画了一系列裸体素描后，她决定创作一幅抽象画，透过这幅作品，她既宣誓了她艺术家的身份，也接受、正视了童年的创伤。

潜在的比较文学分析：

跨种族沟通、跨种族恋情、性别、情欲、传统与现代价值观、社会评论、新加坡的语言、新加坡宗教、东方与西方文化、欧亚裔社群、新加坡艺坛、多元文化主义、新移民、身份认同

PENGHULU YANG HILANG SEGALA-GALANYA (PENGHULU)

Primary Language: Malay

Secondary Language: Transliterated Arabic verses from the Quran

Translation Available: Penghulu

Number of Pages: 215

Author: Suratman Markasan

Year of Publication: 1998

Publisher: Penerbit Fajar Bakti Sdn Bhd; Epigram Books

Characterisation Notes:

75-year-old Pak Suleh was once a well-respected *penghulu* (village headman) of Pulau Sebidang, a small island off the coast of Singapore. He is married to his 65-year-old wife Mak Timun and have six children between the ages of 18 and 45, four daughters, Piyah, Leha, Bedah, and Sohrah, and two sons, Lamit and Juasa. Pak Suleh's sons-in-law Maiden and Syed Farid wish to be voted into Parliament and the Islamic Religious Council of Singapore respectively.

Text Synopsis:

Along with all the other inhabitants of Pulau Sebidang, Pak Suleh had been forced to relocate to the mainland by the Singaporean government in order to make way for urban development. Pak Suleh is unable to adapt to living in a HDB flat and suffers from asthma due to the poor air quality on the mainland. He insists that he should return to the island (and he eventually does so) despite the disapproval of his wife and children. At the same time, Pak Suleh struggles to keep his family together, while also dealing with the delinquent behaviours of Sohrah and Juasa as well as the sinister political ambitions of Maiden and Syed Farid. Both Maiden and Syed Farid pursue their own personal agendas under the guise of acting for the greater good of the family. The novel closes with Maiden arriving on Pulau Sebidang to detain Pak Suleh, Mak Timun and Sohrah, only to discover that the island is completely deserted and that Pak Suleh and his family have mysteriously disappeared.

Significance and Remarks:

Penghulu Yang Hilang Segala-galanya is a meditation on loss, displacement and desire. The novel paints a distressing picture of the incommensurability between old and new through an elderly man's inability to keep up with the times after spending his entire life on an island untouched by the forces of modernisation.

Plagued by the difficulties of modern life, Pak Suleh obstinately chooses to remain true to his faith and traditions. On the one hand, Pak Suleh must cope with the delinquent behaviours of his children, believing that his children's misdemeanours are the result of the negative influences of living in a modern society. On the other hand, Pak Suleh must deal with the constant harassment of his ambitious sons-in-law Maiden and Syed Farid, who attempt to manipulate Islamic teachings in a bid to coerce Pak Suleh into leaving Pulau Sebidang permanently.

In questioning the selfishness of an individual's personal ambitions, the novel highlights the contrast between faith and religion. Many characters in the novel employ Islamic terms and directly cite the Quran to prove their argument. While some of these characters do have altruistic intentions, there are others who manipulate Islamic teachings only to further their own agendas. For instance, Syed Farid cites a verse from the Quran in order to persuade his in-laws not to allow Pak Suleh to return to the island. According to Syed Farid, Pak Suleh should try to adapt to his new life on the mainland, as Allah would never make changes to our lives should we choose not to embrace such changes. Ultimately, in this clash between tradition and modernity, the novel suggests that there can be no happy conclusion without a mutual accommodation of differences.

Potential areas of comparative analysis:

Transition from old to new, Sense of loss/displacement, Traditional vs. Modern mindsets and values, Islam, Faith vs. Religion, Family life, Island Narrative

PENGHULU YANG HILANG SEGALA-GALANYA (PENGHULU)

主要语言： 马来文

次要语言： -

翻译版本： Penghulu

页数： 215

作者： Suratman Markasan

出版年份： 1998

出版社： Penerbit Fajar Bakti Sdn Bhd; Epigram Books

人物简介：

75岁的苏莱（Pak Suleh）原是瑟比当岛（Pulau Sebidang）上的彭古鲁（Penghulu），即岛上德高望重的村长。他和65岁的妻子提曼（Mak Timun）育有6名介于18至45岁的子女——其中包括4名女儿琵雅（Piyah）、蕾哈（Leha）、比达（Bedah）和索拉（Sohrah）；以及2名儿子拉米特（Lamit）和朱萨（Juasa）。苏莱的女婿麦登（Maiden）和赛义德·法里德（Syed Farid）积极参选，分别希望能进入国会和新加坡回教宗教理事會（Islamic Religious Council of Singapore）。

文本概要：

为配合政府的都市发展计划，苏莱一家连同岛上其他居民被迫迁移至新加坡本岛上的政府组屋。苏莱无法适应住在组屋的生活，也因不良的空气素质饱受哮喘折磨。他不顾妻儿的反对，坚持返回岛上居住（他最后得偿所愿）。

苏莱艰难地维系家人的关系。他不但要应付女儿索拉和儿子朱萨的叛逆行为，还得面对两名女婿险恶的政治野心。不论是麦登还是和赛义德，都打着为家人谋福祉的幌子追求个人目的。小说最后，麦登来到瑟比当岛，准备逮捕苏莱、提曼以及索拉，却发现岛上荒芜一人，苏莱一家已神秘失踪。

重点与备注：

《彭古鲁》是一部关于失去、移居（displacement）和渴望的小说。苏莱在未经现代化发展所破坏的瑟比当岛生活了一辈子，作者透过他被迫举家迁往本岛而迟迟无法适应现代生活的艰辛过程，向读者描绘一幅传统与现代生活的不可比性（incommensurability）的沉重画面。

被现代生活种种困难所困扰的苏莱固执地忠于自己的信仰和传统。一方面，他认为现代生活充满不良影响，污染了索拉和朱萨，导致他们性差踏错。另一方面，他选择返回瑟比当岛居住，当他的女婿发现后，野心勃勃的他们不断骚扰他，企图以伊斯兰教义之名，迫使苏莱永远离开瑟比当岛。

《彭古鲁》就个人私欲大胆提出质疑的同事，也强调信仰和宗教这两个概念的差异。小说许多人物为证明自己的观点，都选择引用伊斯兰教用语或者《可兰经》，虽然部分人物的确出于好意，但也有另一部分只是为了满足个人私欲。例如：赛义德为说服家人不让苏莱返回瑟比当岛，引用真主的话以证明他的论证：苏莱必须适应新加坡本岛的新生活，这是因为若我们不拥抱改变，真主也不会改变我们的生活。因此，苏莱应该勇敢改变生活方式，并适应新加坡本岛上的新环境。作者在小说所刻画地传统与现代价值观的冲突也暗示读者，唯有相互包容、相互体谅，才能拥有一个令人满意的圆满结局。

潜在的比较文学分析：

新加坡发展史、位移感、传统和现代价值观、伊斯兰教、信仰和宗教、家庭生活、岛屿叙事

THE MINORITIES

Primary language: English
Secondary language: No
Translation available: No
Number of pages: 243
Author: Suffian Hakim
Year of Publication: 2018
Publisher: Epigram Books

Characterisation Notes:

The protagonist, a Malay-Chinese landlord, is also the narrator of the novel. Prima facie, the author is naïve and charitable: his desire to forge a community for marginalized minorities through his new inventions drives the plot.

However, many aspects of the narrator's personality remain opaque: the reader is never told the narrator's name and is never provided with an explanation for the narrator's constant preoccupation with a piece of almond. As such, the narrator is both familiar (the novel is told from his point of view) and defamiliarized (the narrator himself seems invisible).

The narrator strives to develop a technology called "SoundLoft" which is capable of translating brain waves into music. He enlists three of his friends (also his tenants), all of whom had been displaced from their job or familial duties, to help: the Singaporean Indian laboratory technician Shanti Rathasattama, the Bangladeshi artist Cantona Bin Fawwaz and the Mainland Chinese Chang "Tights" Ying Hao.

In all, the characters in *The Minorities* seem like an attempt to exhaustively include every single marginalized group in Singapore—the racial minorities, migrant workers and even the "paranormal" (in the novel, the narrator welcomes and affirms Diyanah's identity as a "pontianak" or Malay vampire). The juxtaposition of these diverse groups of people evinces a common human condition that underlies all their experiences.

Text Synopsis:

Four friends—the narrator, Shanti, Cantona and Tights—embark on a quest to confront the apparition of the narrator's recently deceased father. At one point, Tights defecates on a banana tree, and finds that the flat is haunted by the "pontianak" Diyanah.

Murdered by her former lover almost 70 years ago, Diyanah seeks their help to return to her hometown in Malacca for closure. They befriend Diyanah and agree to fulfil her wish via a road trip, agonising a mob of supernatural entities in the process. During the journey, the reader is shown the characters' liminal identity and their desire to belong to a community (even for Diyanah).

Significance and remarks:

The Minorities problematises the concept of "minority" and foregrounds the lived experiences of people deemed to be "minorities." In the novel, the narrator desires to attain closure by seeking acceptance from his deceased father. Similarly, the other characters Shanti, Cantona, Tights, and Diyanah too desire closure and acceptance by their respective communities. Despite the characters' drastically different backgrounds, they are united in their similar experiences of marginalization due to their identity as a "minority" within their communities. To sum, *The Minorities* invites its readers to ruminate on their own society's treatment of its minorities and to look past the reified concept of "minority", such that all can participate and share in the identity of the collective.

Potential areas for comparative analysis:

Social Commentary, Identity, Hybridity, Multiculturalism, Multiracialism, Modernisation and Development, New Migrants

THE MINORITIES

主要语言：英文

次要语言：-

翻译版本：-

页数：243

作者：Suffian Hakim

出版年份：2018

出版社：Epigram Books

人物简介：

男主人翁是名马来华裔房东，同时也是小说的叙述者。从表面上看，作者是天真且宽厚的：他希望透过他的发明将社会上的少数族群凝聚在一起。尽管他的渴望推动了情节的发展，然而关于叙述者的个性和其他特点依然显得隐晦——首先，我们并不知道这名房东的姓名；其二，男主人翁一直执着于一块杏仁，但作者并没有向读者解释缘由。因此，叙述者对读者而言即是熟悉（小说从他的角度叙述），但同时也是陌生（叙述者本身似乎是个隐形人）。

男主人翁找了三个朋友（也是他的房客）：印度实验室技术人员珊迪（Shanti Rathasattama）、孟加拉艺术家康托纳艺术家（Cantona Bin Fawwaz）以及来自中国的张英豪（Chang Ying Hao），一起研发一款能将脑波转换成音乐的科技——“SoundLoft”。三人当中，康托纳和张英豪两人是非法逗留在新加坡的无业游民，珊迪则为了躲避暴力的丈夫，暂时和他们一起住。

小说人物涵盖新加坡所有的边缘族群，包括少数族群、外来客工，还有科学无法解释的超自然事物（男主人翁等人在小说中欢迎并确认迪亚娜（Diyanah）马来女鬼（Pontianak）的身份）。作者将形形色色的人物并置在一起，正好揭示，虽然他们来自不同群体，但他们拥有类似的经历，而这源于他们共通的生活境况。

文本概要：

叙述者的父亲过世后，他和房客四人展开行动，迫使父亲的灵魂再次出现在他眼前。张英豪一次在香蕉树下排便，不久后他们四人居然发现家中来了个不速之客——马来女鬼迪亚娜。她告诉他们，她在70多年前遭情人谋杀，希望四人能帮助她的魂魄回到故乡马六甲，以做了结。四人决定帮助迪亚娜，开车前往她的故乡完成她的心愿，途中引起一群超自然存在物的不悦。在这段旅途中，读者可以感受到他们的边缘身份，以及他们（包括迪亚娜在内）想融入群体的渴望。

重点与备注：

作者在小说强调“少数民族”的生活和经历，并对“少数民族”这一概念提出质疑。在小说当中，男主人翁希望透过得到已故父亲的接纳以获得解脱。同样的，不论是珊迪、张英豪、康托纳或是迪亚娜，他们都渴望被所属的个别族群接纳，以获得一种了结和宽慰。尽管人物的背景大相径庭，但他们“少数民族”的身份造就了相似的边缘化经验。简言之，作者透过小说邀请读者反思社会对“少数民族”的待遇，并放下传统的固有概念，使所有人成为集体的一部分，一同参与、共享集体的身份认同（collective identity）。

潜在的比较文学分析：

社会评述、身份、混杂/杂糅、多元文化主义、多元种族主义、现代化与发展、新移民

潮州老汉 (OLD TEOCHEW GENT)

Primary Language: Chinese
Secondary Language: Some English words
Translation Available: No
Number of Pages: 191
Author: Hong You He
Year of Publication: 2012
Publisher: Xinhua Cultural Enterprises(S) Pte Ltd

Characterisation Notes:

The 68-years-old titular protagonist Luo Pan is an elderly widower who lives alone. He suffers from chronic diseases and must go for follow-up checks every 2-3 months; he too has just undergone cataract surgery and his vision gradually improves. He has two middle-aged sons (Yi Wen and Yi Lun) and two middle-aged daughters (Yi Qian and Yi Dan); his eldest son Yi Lun marries Sangeetha, an Indian nurse.

Text Synopsis:

The elderly widower is largely alienated from his middle-aged children and their families. Despite his efforts to connect and communicate with them, the members of his family continue to ignore his efforts and take his generosity and kindness for granted. Yi Wen and Yi Lun harbour evil intentions and conspire to mortgage Luo Pan's apartment, causing the latter to suffer from a stroke once again. Above all, there is still true love and genuine connection: the lonely Teochew speaking widower and the cast out daughter-in-law Sangeetha find solace in each other's company, and the unlikely duo begins to reshape the dysfunctional family dynamics.

Significance and Remarks:

This novel highlights the common issues of generational gaps and language barriers within many modern Singaporean households. The elderly widower, a paradigm of traditional views and values, finds an unlikely source of care and companionship in the newest addition to the family—an Indian daughter-in-law. This novel combines traditional values and modern sentiments to challenge racial prejudices and question the abuse and neglect of the elderly by the younger generations today. As a commentary on Singapore's domestic issues, the novel also highlights the linguistic barriers between generations and reveals them to be excuses to not communicate at all: in the novel, the Teochew-speaking widower and his English-speaking daughter-in-law learn to bridge and transcend their linguistic and cultural differences.

Potential areas of comparative analysis:

Interracial communication, Intergenerational communication, Traditional vs. Modern values, Elderly Perspectives, Social Commentary, Languages in Singapore, Family/ Domestic Life.

潮州老汉

主要语言： 中文
次要语言： 少数英文
翻译版本： -
页数： 191
作者： 洪有和
出版年份： 2012
出版社： 新华文化事业（新）有限公司

人物简介：

68岁的罗盘老先生是一名独居鳏夫，他长年饱受慢性病折磨，每隔两三个月就得回医院复诊。他不久前刚切除白内障，视力逐渐恢复正常。罗盘膝下有二男（一文、一伦）二女（一丹、一茜），其中一文的太太桑吉达（Sangeetha）是名印度籍护士。

文本概要：

罗盘老先生和家人的感情日渐疏离：虽然他用尽心力想与他们保持联系，但罗家成员居心叵测、各怀鬼胎，不仅对他的宽容与友善视若无睹，一文和一伦甚至串谋起来，将父亲的房子擅自抵押给银行，导致他再次中风。但人间自有真情，一口操潮州话的罗盘竟然在桑吉达身上找到慰藉，渐渐将原本失调的家庭关系重新找回平衡点。

重点与备注：

语言隔阂造成的代沟是普遍现代新加坡家庭所面临的课题与挑战。罗盘老先生是传统的潮州老汉，而新加入的家庭成员——印度籍媳妇桑吉她——原本看似最不可能给家翁带来关怀与陪伴的人，却出乎意料成为罗盘老先生心灵的慰藉。作者融合传统价值观与现代关系之间的情感，使它们产生碰撞，并对种族歧视与对年长者忽视（Neglect of the Elderly）等现象提出挑战和质问。小说可视为就新加坡家庭议题提出的社会评述：两代人之间因语言隔阂导致沟通障碍，以此为不沟通的理由，但这是借口——在《潮州老汉》中，口操潮州话的老先生与说英语的媳妇努力突破语言与文化之间的差异，找到沟通的桥梁，成为彼此的慰藉。

潜在的比较文学分析：

族群沟通、跨代沟通、传统与现代价值观的对立、年长者视角、社会评述、新加坡语言、家庭生活

恋念德港情 (PULAU TEKONG LOVE)

Primary Language: Mandarin
Secondary Language: No
Translation Available: No
Number of Pages: 244
Author: Chong Han
Year of Publication: 1992
Publisher: Long House Publisher

Characterisation Notes:

The protagonist Jiang Ya Shu lives with her husband Zhou Jia Yu, along with seven children: four boys and three girls. Jiang is forced by the family's poor economic situation to send her eldest daughter Su Ying to live in a monastery. To sustain the remaining eight members of his family, Zhou runs a small ferrying business with his neighbor Wan Shu to ferry commuters to and from Pulau Tekong and Changi pier. Unfortunately, Zhou succumbs to chronic asthma despite having visited many notable physicians to treat his condition. Jiang manages to provide for her family by tapping rubber and working many other odd jobs. In all, through his depictions of the lives of Jiang and her family, the author accentuates the natural beauty and simplicity of life on Pulau Tekong.

Text Synopsis:

The novel begins with the death of Jiang Ya Shu's husband Zhou Jia. Before Jiang could sell the assets of her husband's company, Yu Liu Gen, the son of a local provision shop owner, sabotages and burns the entire fleet of ships. Jiang's economic situation becomes difficult. To maintain family finances, Jiang's eldest and second son Song Hai and Song Jiang work in the ferrying and fishing business; her second daughter Shu Ying, third son Song He, and youngest son Song Xi leave for the Singaporean mainland to work as apprentices as they come of age.

Song Hai meets and falls in love with a Malay woman Fatimah. Both parents vehemently oppose the relationship: Jiang cannot accept that her descendants will be "mixed blooded," whereas Fatimah's mother Siti is prejudiced against Chinese (especially the widowed Jiang) and insists that Fatimah marry a fellow Malay. Siti tells Song Hai that he may only obtain the hand of Fatimah if he returns with a "sizeable dowry" within a year as part of the "conditions of marriage." Jiang adamantly objects to the marriage as she felt that her son had been blackmailed. She asserts that her "Malay in-law" and her "bastard grandchild" will never be allowed into her home.

Against his mother's wishes, Song Hai moves to Singapore to work to earn his "sizeable dowry." He engages in illegal cigarette trafficking and is soon caught and sentenced to prison. After his early release due to good behaviour, he returns to Pulau Tekong to meet with Fatimah but unfortunately drowns in a marine accident (his body is later found by the coast guard). Fatimah falls into a stupor and never completely regains her sanity: she mopes around all day, and occasionally goes to the beach to reminisce about Song Hai. Fatimah refuses to marry, and no man would marry her.

Moving on, Shu Ying meets the radical leftist teacher Shi Bi Hua in Singapore. She is infected by Shi's revolutionary enthusiasm and his beliefs that one must fight and not cower or prostate oneself in the face of injustice. They are persecuted for their anti-colonialist activities and they flee to the Thailand-Malaysia border, eventually settling in Beijing.

Song He takes up an apprenticeship in a traditional Chinese medicine shop. He is highly regarded by his master and soon opens a medicine shop by himself with the assistance of his father-in-law. Song He's comfortable but superficial and materialistic life induces him to forget his roots and alienates him from his mother Jiang. Lastly, Jiang's youngest son Song Xi participates in a kidnapping attempt and is incarcerated.

After many years, Jiang reunites with her eldest daughter Su Ying after the latter publishes an article seeking her mother. Su Ying tells Jiang that she lives separately from her husband with her boyfriend, with whom she runs a salon. She has two sons who are under the care of her husband's family. Lastly, in the mid-1980s, Jiang Ya Shu and Song Jiang, together with the latter's children, move to the Singapore mainland to stay in a HDB flat as Pulau Tekong is converted to a military base.

Significance and Remarks:

The author was born and raised in Pulau Tekong. His colourful depictions of the relationships and ups and downs of everyday life on the island in *Lian Nian De Gang Qing* (which translates as Nostalgia/Love for Pulau Tekong) serves as a personal recollection and memory of his hometown.

The narrative is centred around the life of Jiang Ya Shu. Jiang's life is a tragic one: she is widowed in mid-life, and she subsequently lost her daughter-in-law to drowning, and her second daughter goes missing.

However, like all traditional women, she does not wallow in self-pity but instead takes up multiple jobs to support her entire family. Jiang resilience stands in stark contrast to her weak physical appearance. Further, Jiang's experiences allow her to deeply empathize with the difficulties of those around her on Pulau Tekong. For instance, Jiang empathizes with the plight of a fellow widow and helps her by offering her own kitchen-helper job to her. In all, through the author's characterization of Jiang, he highlights the spirit of fortitude and independence among the traditional women of Singapore.

Next, *Lian Nian De Gang Qing* also incorporates the richness of Singapore's culture: the reader is treated to festivities such as the annual opera in appreciation of the gods, the Hakka mountain song soiree, open air theatres, circuses, Malay weddings and Christmas dinner parties. The author presents these festivities as the highlights of an age in which material comforts are scarce, and in so doing, invokes a shared memory of older Singaporeans.

Interracial love is the most prominent source of conflict in the novel. Jiang Ya Shu opposes Song Hai's marriage to Fatimah because she believes that all Chinese people must be "rooted" and that marriage with a non-Chinese will disqualify Song Hai from Chineseness and his "roots."

Chinese "rootedness" is also evident in the Chinese people's emphasis on education. Song Jiang's wife Du San Niang reminds him: no matter how poor or difficult their lives, they must support their child's education—even if they must haul human waste to afford doing so. In contrast, Fatimah's father Zahari is an avowed utilitarian who sends his daughter to a Chinese school so that she can learn Mandarin and eventually help at his stall. Given his motivations, we can understand why Zahari would never allow his daughter to marry the poor Song Hai.

The novel briefly touches upon the political history of Singapore as seen/ unseen from the perspective of the inhabitants of Pulau Tekong. The novel's portrayal of the life of the teacher Zheng Chun Ji reflects the tumultuous years of Singapore's independence—from the first parliamentary elections, through the violent racial riots, to eventual independence. Zheng is arrested for conspiring against the government, sentenced to two years of imprisonment and then conditionally released to Pulau Tekong.

In the 1980s, Pulau Tekong is designated for military use. Prior to their eviction, the inhabitants of the island sigh and express that they "will never get to see another opera after this year's." Nevertheless, the rubber plantations, farms, pigpens, ocean, and coconut trees of the island, all of which bore witness to the lives—the blood, tears, love, hate, hopes, and dreams—of its inhabitants, will remain as the collective memory of a generation.

Lian Nian De Gang Qing is a novel dedicated to the people of Pulau Tekong, and to the island itself. While the dreams that the people once had about a "prosperous gathering" on the island may never materialize, the author has carved a space for them to reexperience the place of their childhoods.

Potential areas of comparative analysis:

Nostalgia, Singapore History, Family Life, Religion and Faith, Interracial Marriage, Traditional Practices

恋念德港情

主要语言：中文
次要语言：-
翻译版本：-
页数：244
作者：崇汉（本名：邹昔璆）
出版年份：1992
出版社：长屋出版社

人物简介：

姜雅姝和丈夫周加一共有4男3女，但因经济拮据，把长女素樱交由寺院寄养。周加和邻居胡万叔合股经营渡船生意，载客来往于德光岛和樟宜码头，养活一家八口。他长期饱受咳嗽、气喘折磨，拜访许多名医都无法治好，不久病入膏肓、逝世。中年丧夫的雅姝靠着割胶和打其他散工勉强维持家计，抚养子女长大。透过描写雅姝和其子女的遭遇，作者将德光岛淳朴的风土人情和自然风光呈现在读者眼前。

文本概要：

丈夫病逝后，雅姝打算卖掉他的渡船套现，但却被杂货店的少东余六根恶意纵火，生活顿时困窘不堪。为贴补家计，雅姝的长子松海和次子松江分别在渡船和奎龙工作。次女书樱、三子松河、老幺松溪成年后先后离开德光岛到新加坡本岛当学徒。

松海和马来籍女子花蒂玛情投意合，但遭双方父母反对。雅姝反对异族通婚，无法容忍后代子孙都是混血儿，花蒂玛的母亲娜茜对华人有偏见，看不起雅姝是个寡妇，认为女儿必须嫁给同种族的男子。娜茜告诉松海，若他想迎娶花蒂玛，必须在一年内以“巨额聘金”作为“结婚条件”。雅姝不满儿子被变相勒索，坚决反对这门亲事，再三强调马来媳妇不准踏进她的家门，更不喜欢自己的孙子是“杂种”。

为了爱情，松海不顾母亲反对，毅然到新加坡工作。为赚取巨额报酬，他铤而走险走私烟酒，锒铛入狱，但因行为良好提早被释放。他出狱后回到德光岛和花蒂玛团聚，却不幸因舢舨翻覆坠落海里失踪，尸体后被水警发现。花蒂玛虽侥幸捡回一命，但却从此神志不清，状况时好时坏。岛上马来男子不愿意娶她，她也不愿意嫁人，天天静静消磨时间，偶尔到海边缅怀松海。

书樱在本岛认识了左倾分子史壁华老师，面对不公的待遇，她幡然顿悟：面对不合理事物必须拥有反抗的勇气和精神，不能一味忍气吞声，任人宰割。她和史壁华等人参加左翼反殖民运动，后被通缉，逃往泰马边境，后落脚北京。

松河在中药铺当学徒，受老板器重，婚后在岳父的资助下开了中药铺。虽然他的生活变得优渥，但却数典忘祖，在铜臭味的世界打滚，和母亲的关系愈发疏离；幺子松溪则误入歧途，参与绑架富商案，被判坐牢。多年后，雅姝的长女素樱透过登报寻亲终于和母亲相认、团聚；她告诉母亲，她和丈夫已经分居，两个儿子交由婆家照顾，目前和情夫同居并合股经营理发店。80年代中期，随着德光岛被列为军事基地，雅姝、松江以及两名孙子一同迁往本岛的组屋。

重点与备注：

作者生于、长于德光岛，他在《恋念德港情》中描绘岛上朴实但多彩的生活图景、纪念岛民的与悲欢离合，为故土留下一份念想。

故事围绕雅姝而展开。她是个带有悲剧性色彩的人物：中年丧夫、长子坠海身亡、次女音讯全无以及媳妇意外溺毙等。但如同所有传统女性，她不自怨自艾，身兼多职，以柔弱的身躯扛起家庭的重担。岛民各有各的生活，也各有各的艰难，虽然雅姝被生活所辜负，但也因此更能感同身受他人的难处与困境。为了帮另一名寡妇维持生计，她将心比心，主动把包办伙食的工作让出来。作者透过雅姝不幸的际遇，展现旧时代妇女坚毅与自立自强的典型精神面貌。

其次，作者也在《恋念德港情》融入了富的本土色彩。一年一度的酬神戏、客家山歌晚会、露天电影院、马戏团表演、马来传统婚礼舞会和圣诞节联欢晚会等不仅是岛民的集体记忆，更是在那物质缺乏的年代，点缀生活的奢侈。

小说最明显的冲突体现在松海和花蒂玛的异族恋情上。雅姝反对松海娶花蒂玛，认为华人必须有“根”，而异族通婚将使他丧失作为华人的身份特征，希望他“现实一点”。 关于华人对“根”的执着，从教育对华人的重要性可见一斑。松江的妻子杜三娘不时告诫他：家境再困难，人再苦，卖屎缸也要让孩子上学，可见她非常重视教育。花蒂玛的父亲查哈里则很明显是个功利主义者，他把女儿送进华校，目的是为了让她学习和华人交谈，协助他一起经营杂货店，因此他不愿意女儿嫁给一贫如洗的松海。

从新加坡自治后首届的立法会议选举，回教徒和华族发生的暴力冲突，到新加坡独立，岛民也若有似无地见证着新加坡的建国之路。在书中刻画不多、来自本岛的郑春纪老师是这段历史的缩影：他因涉嫌反政府活动而被逮捕，在监牢蹲了两年后有条件被释放，只能住在德光岛。

80年代，政府将德光岛划入军事管辖区。迁往本岛前，岛民无不感慨，感叹："看了今年的大戏，就没有得看了"。德光岛的胶林、菜园、猪舍、海洋和椰子树等交织着岛民的血泪、爱恨、希望与失落，谱写一代人的共同回。《恋念德港情》是一部献给岛民和故土的长篇小说，德光岛人迷恋的"繁华盛会"，或许不能在梦里上演，但能在书中回味哺育他们成长的故土。

潜在的比较文学分析：

怀旧、新加坡历史、家庭生活、信仰、宗教、跨种族婚姻、传统习俗

'OTHERS' IS NOT A RACE

Primary Language: English

Secondary Language: Kristang (Portuguese-Eurasian mother tongue) and Malay; Glossary of terms included in references

Translation Available: No

Number of Pages: 101

Author: Melissa De Silva

Year of Publication: 2017

Publisher: Math Paper Press

Characterization Notes:

This book is a collection of short pieces that revolve around Eurasian identity in a Singapore context. The stories span many different genres of writing and attempt to construct a multifaceted discourse on the subject. The synopsis on the back of the book is succinct: "*'Others' is Not a Race* is a tapestry that weaves together the multiple genres of narrative fiction, creative nonfiction, literary food writing and family memoir, to offer insight into the micro-minority Eurasian community through the lens of the writer's own experiences. Throughout the book, the author interweaves the themes of memory, loss, language identity and cultural reclamation."

Synopsis:

The book begins by introducing "some very quick facts" about Eurasians in Singapore. The rest of the book features a series of historical accounts interspersed with commercial-like interjections of recipes and the author's (not so) successful attempts at whipping up traditional Eurasian dishes.

In the first story, De Silva shares a dramatized version of the events that led her on her quest to connect with her identity—she begins by learning her native tongue, Kristang, in the hopes of consoling her ailing grandmother. Next, the author expresses her dismay at the quality of sugee cakes today. We then return to the historical narrative, in which she compares Malacca today to the places of her childhood. De Silva describes Malacca as a place frozen in time, its way and pace of life untouched by the corrupting influence of modernity. To supplement this account, the author includes a short story told by her mother about her childhood home. We are then abruptly whizzed to the present, where the author, ashamed of her lack of knowledge of tradition, tries (again) to cook Debal curry.

Moving on, we then have an odd piece of creative fiction in which a mosquito narrates the story of De Silva's great-grandfather, who died working on a Japanese-assigned farmland in Malaya during the world war. After this creative interlude, we are then treated to even more recipes of pineapple tart, belachan and chinchalok, as well as a modest treatise defending Eurasian tea from charges of plagiarism made by certain 'British' parties. The author then recalls her school days, during which she had to study Malay as her mother tongue instead of her native Kristang.

At this point, the author embarks on a tirade against an "anonymous policy maker" for banishing her racial identity to the container called "others." She states polemically that: "We are Singaporeans. And we are Eurasian too. We belong and we deserve rightfully to be named." (81) The book then concludes with another fictional story, one in which the last two remaining Eurasian men meet in a bar and bemoan the loss of their cultural identity.

Significance and Remarks:

This book will undoubtedly be informative for those seeking insight into Eurasian culture in Singapore. It presents valuable recollections of the author and her parents, all of which shed light on the ways of life of members of the Eurasian community. However, the excess of juxtaposition with the present arguably distorts the picture—the Eurasian heritage seems to be viewed through the rose-tinted lenses of nostalgia. This quote speaks for itself: "Yet this place too, is having its identity eroded by the relentless claw of development... What I do know is that this is the only patch in the world where I don't have to explain who I am, or why." (33) In terms of cataloguing Eurasian food heritage, the book is also not particularly successful for it is based on personal anecdotes and is neither systematic nor disciplined.

On the other hand, the book can be seen as an expressly political pushback against the marginalization and dilution of Eurasian identity. A quote from the last fictional story sums up this fear: "We aren't even 'Others' anymore, we're invisible." (95) Through these stories, the author invites us to contemplate the slippery slope of labels—when we identify certain races with "others," they lose their distinctive qualities forever. The author blames the bureaucracy: "This is the price of your administrative convenience. The fruit of your tidy solution: 'Others.'" (81) For all the rhetoric, however, the solution is still social and cultural. This book probably stems from the core belief that it is possible to preserve the unique Eurasian identity by means of storytelling, and by engaging the reader with the products of authentic Eurasian culture. In that, we can share De Silva's optimism.

However, we must recognize two assumptions in De Silva's argument. Superficially, we see that she has appropriated the term "Others" for Eurasians. As she has mentioned, rather ironically, in the introduction, the term is also used to contain Filipinos, Caucasians, Africans and Japanese. It seems that, in her righteous fit, the author has implicitly endorsed the marginalization of other, even smaller cultures. More insidiously, we must examine the implications of such a call for the strengthening of a particular racial identity. While this may lead to the preservation of a fading cultural heritage, it may also deepen the practice of racial stratification in Singapore. One must be cognizant of the possibility that a stronger racial identity may come at the expense of the Singaporean one. In this respect, De Silva's message must be taken with care.

Potential Areas of Comparative Analysis:

History, Oral History, Modernization, Traditional vs Modern Values, Familial Life, Preservation and Dilution of Heritage, Racial Diversity, Eurasian Culture, Marginalization, Social Commentary, Food Culture, Cultural Reclamation, National Identity

'OTHERS' IS NOT A RACE

主要语言：英文

次要语言：克里斯坦语（Kristang，葡萄牙裔欧亚社群所使用的混合式语言）以及马来文；作者在书末附上词汇供读者参考。

翻译版本：-

页数：101

作者：Melissa De Silva

出版年份：2017

出版社：Math Paper Press

人物简介：

'Others' is Not a Race （《"其他"不是种族》）是一本讨论新加坡欧亚裔社群（Eurasian）身份认同的短文故事汇集。作者创作的短篇风格迥异，试图从多个面向就此议题进行论述。小说背后的介绍简明扼要——《"其他"不是种族》将不同种类的叙事类型，包括虚构叙事（narrative fiction）、非虚构创意写作（creative nonfiction）、文学美食写作（literary food writing）以及家庭回忆录（family memoir）编织在一起，作者的经历为欧亚裔社群提供富有洞察力的独到见解。小说也贯穿记忆、失去、语言与认同（language identity）和文化收复（cultural reclamation）等主题。

文本概要：

作者先为读者介绍生活在新加坡的欧亚裔社群的基本概况，紧接着再呈现一系列的历史叙述(historical accounts)。此外，作者也在书中夹杂着像似广告的欧亚裔的食谱以及她烹煮欧亚裔传统美食的失败经验。

在第一个故事中，一连串戏剧化的事件也驱使她开始寻找她和欧亚裔社群的联系。为了安抚病危的祖母，作者开始学习她的母语——克里斯坦语。接下来，作者表达了对如今市面上苏吉蛋糕（Sugee Cake）质量的失望。紧接着，作者穿插一片历史叙述，作者在这里对如今的马六甲以及她童年的回忆做比较。她表示，马六甲就就像一个被时光冻结的城市，其生活方式和步调都没有因为现代化的发展而改变。为补充说明，作者在这里也加入一个由她母亲口述的、关于她童年家乡的小故事。我们后突然地回到当代，在这里，作者因对传统缺乏了解而感到愧疚。此时，她也再次尝试烹煮欧亚裔咖喱（Debal Curry）。

接下来，作者加入了一篇诡异、由一只蚊子负责叙述的虚构创作。故事讲述作者的曾祖父于世界第二大战期间，在马来亚的一座由日军掌管的农田工作而不幸丧命的故事。在这段饶富趣味的小插曲过后，作者和读者分享黄梨塔、峇拉煎辣椒酱（Belachan）以及配料虾酱（Chinchalok）的制作方式。另外，作者为欧亚族裔的传统茶饮进行辩护，否认英国人对其族裔的剽窃指控。接下来，作者回忆起了她的求学时光，当时，她必须以母语的形式在学校修读马来文，而不能选择克里斯坦语或者英文。

紧接着，一名匿名的政策制定者将新加坡的欧亚裔族群归类为"其他"，此举引起作者不悦，她抨击该名政策制定者："我们是新加坡人，我们同时也是欧亚族裔，我们属于这里，我们理应有切确的命名。"小说以另一个虚构的故事做结尾——两名欧亚裔男子在酒吧一同哀悼丧失的文化身份（cultural identity）。

重点与备注：

小说呈现作者和她父母的宝贵回忆，揭示了欧亚族裔过去的生活方式。因此对于想要更深入了解新加坡欧亚族裔文化遗产的读者来说，《"其他"不是种族》无疑是具有参考价值的。然而，作者将大量的过去和现在并置在一起，难免使过去的描述有些失真。作者透过玫瑰色眼镜看待欧亚族裔的文化遗产，然而现实是有目共睹的——作者写到："然而，这个地方的身份象征也被无情的发展爪子所侵蚀……我所知道的是，这里是世界上唯一一块我不需要解释我是谁、或者为什么的地方。"就编目欧亚族裔的饮食文化遗产而言，由于作者基于个人经验而非系统化的研究，小说在这方面还尚缺火候。

另外，小说可被视为对已被边缘化、已被淡化的欧亚族裔身份的明确的政治反击，最后一个虚构故事中的其中一句话概括了这份恐惧："我们甚至不再是'其他'，我们是隐形的。"作者恳请我们思考贴标签所导致的滑坡谬误（slippery slope）——即当我们把欧亚族裔归类为"其他"后，他们将永永远远失去他们的独特品质，毫无挽回的余地。对此，作者把矛头指向官僚制度："这就是你们为了方便行事所必须付出的代价，你们选择了整齐的解决方案，将我们归类为"其他"，而这就是你们现在所看到的结果。"撇开所有的政治空谈，解决方式还需从社会和文化这两个层面着手。这本书的创作契机大概源自于这样的一个核心：作者相信以故事的形式引起读者对欧亚族裔文化传统的兴趣，或许能守护独特的欧亚族裔身份。在这一点上，我们可以和作者一样感到乐观。

但是，我们必须意识到作者在文中提出的两个假设。首先，作者肤浅地将“其他”（others）的概念挪用（appropriate）到欧亚族裔以外的族群身上。在小说的绪论，她表示“他者”也涵盖了菲律宾人、洋人、非洲人以及日本人。这是具讽刺意味的，作者似乎为了伸张正义，默默地将其他更小的文化社群也边缘化了。

其次，我们必须更小心检验呼吁强化特定族群身份认同带来的影响。尽管这将帮助我们守护消失的文化遗产，但这或许也将加剧新加坡种族分化的现象。而我们也必须意识到，在强化种族身份认同的同时，或将牺牲对新加坡人的身份认同。在这方面，我们必须谨慎看待作者所传递的信息。

潜在的比较文学分析：

历史、口述历史、现代化、传统与现代价值观、家庭生活、遗产的守护与淡化、种族多样性、欧亚族裔文化、边缘化、社会评论、饮食文化、国家认同

SUGARBREAD

Primary Language: English
Secondary Language: No
Translation Available: No
Number of Pages: 278
Author: Balli Kaur Jaswal
Year of Publication: 2016
Publisher: Epigram Books

Characterisation Notes:

The protagonist Parveen (Pin) is a 10-year-old Punjabi-Sikh girl. Her family speaks Punjabi—a language not commonly heard in Singapore. She receives financial assistance to attend an all-girls' elite Christian school, where she is subjected to racial slurs and derisive remarks from her classmates and the school bus driver. Farizah, Pin's best friend and a devout Muslim, is adept at gracefully brushing off racist comments directed at them.

Pin's mother, Jini (Ma) oversees the household. Ma suffers from a skin condition that causes her to break out in rashes. The novel also features Pin's extended family: Pin's ailing maternal grandmother Kulwant (Nani-ji); Jini's siblings Sarjit (or Mama-ji) and Bilu, and Sarjit's wife and Jini's sister-in-law Birender (Fat Auntie). Pra-ji (meaning "elder brother" in Punjabi), the two-faced oracle at the Sikh temple, also makes an appearance.

Text Synopsis:

Pin grows up being told by Nani-ji and Ma that she must never become like her mother. She never gets an explanation until late in the novel when the debilitated Nani-ji moves in with Pin.

During her teenage years, Jini believed that her skin condition was a punishment for her "filthy thoughts." At one point she sneaks out to seek treatment from Pra-ji, a reputable oracle in the Sikh community, only to be sexually assaulted. Jini narrowly escapes. At the same time, Jini's disabled brother, Bilu, dies from ingesting bleach from a coke bottle. Tragically, Jini has no alibi as Pra-ji denies that he had even met her. Rumours start to spread that Jini was a loose woman who had been meeting other men at the time of Bilu's death, and the rumours lead to Jini's estrangement from the family.

In the present, Pin is confronted with insensitive racial taunts in school. The school bus driver mutters "Mungalee" (a derogatory label for Indians) to her face and her classmates poke fun at her skin colour.

Other students who are racial minorities are also tormented: Pin's Chinese classmate, Abigail Goh, ridicules her Indian classmate Gayathiri for reeking of coconut oil; Abigail also proclaims that Muslims do not consume pork as they are descendants of pigs themselves. As the novel unfolds, Pin understands the hard truth of life as a racial minority in Singapore and learns to approach conflict with tact and wisdom.

Significance and Remarks:

This novel is narrated by Pin, a fair-skinned girl who is a practising Sikh. She is a student at First Christian Girls' School. Taken as a whole, Balli Kaur Jaswal's novel is a welcome commentary on the lives of racial and religious minorities in Singapore because it empowers the Singaporean Sikh community by giving them their own voice.

The novel characterises the lived reality and racial discrimination faced by a Singaporean Sikh in a way that is deeply relatable to Sikh readers and educational for non-Sikh readers. For instance, Sikhs experience discrimination for their mere existence as a "rare" racial minority and for the kara that they must wear around their wrists. This is a worrying feature for a nation that prides itself on its racial and religious harmony.

Jaswal also highlights issues such as the hypocrisies and the toxic emphasis on family reputation within the Sikh community. The characters in the novel live in fear of being caught performing inappropriate or forbidden acts, even if such acts are unintentional or otherwise justified. For instance, Ma is embarrassed and compelled to hide her rashes because of the Sikh community's skewed perception that rashes are a physical manifestation of guilt or wrongdoing. For Pin, her desire to appear perfect in front of God leads to paranoia and a delusion that God will punish her for even the most trivial of actions.

It is implied in the novel that the Sikh community's obsession with social normativity ultimately conceals and furthers their arrogance and self-servitude, as evinced in Fat Auntie's sycophancy and Pra-ji's exploitative behaviour. Such behaviour endangers the more vulnerable members of the community such as Jini, where family members choose to preserve their reputation within the Sikh community over Jini's own well-being.

In *Sugarbread*, Jaswal's comments on a broad swathe of contemporary Singaporean social issues through a child's eyes. The analysis is deliberately superficial to engage and shock the uninformed reader. Pin's naivete as a 10-year-old allows the author to present the experience of discrimination in a raw and visceral manner, especially since Pin herself is not knowledgeable about the nuances of social interactions. In the scenes where Abigail asks a seemingly innocuous question, or when Pra-ji displays a change in behaviour, the author successfully creates a sense of unease and alarm that invites the reader to investigate these social issues for themselves.

Potential Areas of Comparative Analysis:

Sikh Religion, Faith, Sikh Culture, Racism, Classism, Elitism, Disability, Traditional vs Modern values, Rich-Poor Divide, Surveillance Culture, Sexual Assaul, Elite schools, Caste System, Multi-Culturalism, Religion

SUGARBREAD

主要语言：英文
次要语言：-
翻译版本：-
页数：278
作者：Balli Kaur Jaswal
出版年份：2016
出版社：Epigram Books

人物简介：

小说的主人翁是年仅10岁的旁遮普族（Punjabi）女孩帕维恩（Parveen，小名Pin），她和家人信奉锡克教（Sikh），在家中使用旁遮普语（一个大多数新加坡人闻所未闻的语言）沟通。她也是一名接受经济援助、在一所由基督教教会创办的精英女校的学生。身为少数民族，她在学校承受着来自同学以及校车司机，带有种族歧视意味的侮辱和嘲讽。帕维恩最要好的朋友法丽扎（Farizah）是一名虔诚的穆斯林，和帕维恩不同的是，她总能以最优雅的姿态面对、化解因种族主义言论引起的争端。

帕维恩的母亲吉妮（Jini，也称Ma）是家中的掌舵手，多年来饱受皮肤病折磨，一旦爆出红疹，就会全身发痒，难以忍耐。小说也包含帕维恩延伸家庭的成员，其中包括：她病重的外婆库尔婉特（Kulwant，也称Nani-ji））、吉尼的手足沙尔吉特（Sarjit，也称Mama-ji）和毕鲁（Bilu）、沙尔吉特的妻子碧琳德（Birender，绰号“胖阿姨”）。Pra-ji（旁遮普语中“大哥”的意思），两面三刀的神谕（Oracle）也出现在小说当中。

文本概要：

吉尼和库尔婉特自帕维恩小时候就不断告诫她：长大后千万别和她的母亲一样一副德行，使她倍感困惑，一直到她病危的外婆搬进家中，她才了解当中的含义。

年少时期的吉尼误以为，她的皮肤症状是上帝对她“污秽思想”（filthy thoughts）的惩罚。因此，她偷偷地向Pra-ji，一个德高望重的神谕求助，希望他能医治她的症状，却惨遭Pra-ji性侵。她虽然逃过一切，但她残疾的弟弟毕鲁却因为独自留在家中，不幸误食在可乐瓶的漂白剂而身亡。Pra-ji否认曾和吉尼见面，后者因无法提出不在场证明而遭千夫所指，有关于她抛下弟弟，和男人私会的谣言开始流传开来，渐渐导致她与家人疏远。

回到现在，帕维恩在学校面对各种形式的种族歧视——不仅学校的巴士司机在她面前嘟囔着“Mungalee”(诋毁、贬低印度族的标签)，她的同学也拿她的肤色大做文章。除此之外，其他少数族群同学也难逃被羞辱的命运：帕维恩的华族同学艾碧佳（Abigail）不但嘲笑印度同学盖亚特里（Gayathri）身上散发椰子味，甚至声称穆斯林本身是猪的后代，因此他们不食用猪肉。随着小说情节的发展，帕维恩渐渐体认身为少数民族的艰难处境，同时也学会以更巧妙、更明智的方式处理冲突。

重点与备注：

小说由帕维恩叙述：她皮肤白皙、信奉锡克教的女孩，同时也是第一基督女子学校（First Christian Girls' School）的学生。锡克族是新加坡的少数民族之一。作者透过小孩的视角赋予他们话语权，因此小说可视为就新加坡少数民族、宗教社群等议题所发表的社会评论。

小说刻画新加坡锡克族的生活以及所面对的种族歧视，不仅能和锡克族社群产生极大的共鸣，对非锡克族（或者非少数民族）而言，其教育意义不可忽视。锡克族不因其他，只因属于少数族群、甚至因为根据锡克族传统手上必须佩戴的手镯（Kara）而受歧视。以上社会现象对以种族和谐为荣的国家来说，是令人担忧的现象。

作者也点出了锡克族内部的问题：他们的伪善以及他们对家族声誉几近苛刻、偏执的要求。小说的人物活在恐惧之中，害怕行差踏错（即便是无心的或情有可原）。例如：锡克族认为皮肤出现红疹是愧疚感或行为错误所导致的身体现象，对吉尼投以异样的眼光，导致后者尴尬不已，在最热的天也穿着长袖以遮蔽身上的疹子。另外，帕维恩意识到上帝的存在，认为上帝在监控她的举止行为，开始变得诚惶诚恐，为了讨好上帝，她尽力地在祂面前呈现最好的一面。

小说也暗示，锡克族对社会规范性(social normativity)的执着不仅掩盖，同时也助长社群的傲慢和自私。我们可以从阿谀奉承的胖阿姨身上以及Pra-ji对锡克族社群的剥削行为看到这一点。这使原本就处于弱势的吉尼成为受害者：事发当天，她被Pra-ji性侵犯，Pra-ji滥用大家对他的信任，否认曾见过吉尼。他的信徒为维护自身利益相信Pra-ji，使吉尼成为整个事件的牺牲品。

小说就当代新加坡的社会议题进行评论，覆盖面广泛，但由于作者透过一个10岁小孩的眼睛进行观察，议题缺乏更深层次的讨论。但有趣的是，作者刻意流于表面的观察却是帕维恩发自内心、最赤裸裸的感受，足以震撼读者。在小说中的一些桥段，如华族同学艾碧佳提出一个看似无害的问题时、或者当作者带出Pra-ji的另一面时，作者成功地给读者造成不安和引起警觉，引导他们重新审视社会议题。

潜在的比较文学分析：

锡克教、信仰、锡克教文化、种族主义、阶级主义、精英主义、残疾、新加坡文学、传统与现代价值观、贫富差距、监视文化、性侵犯、精英学校、种姓制度、多元文化主义、宗教

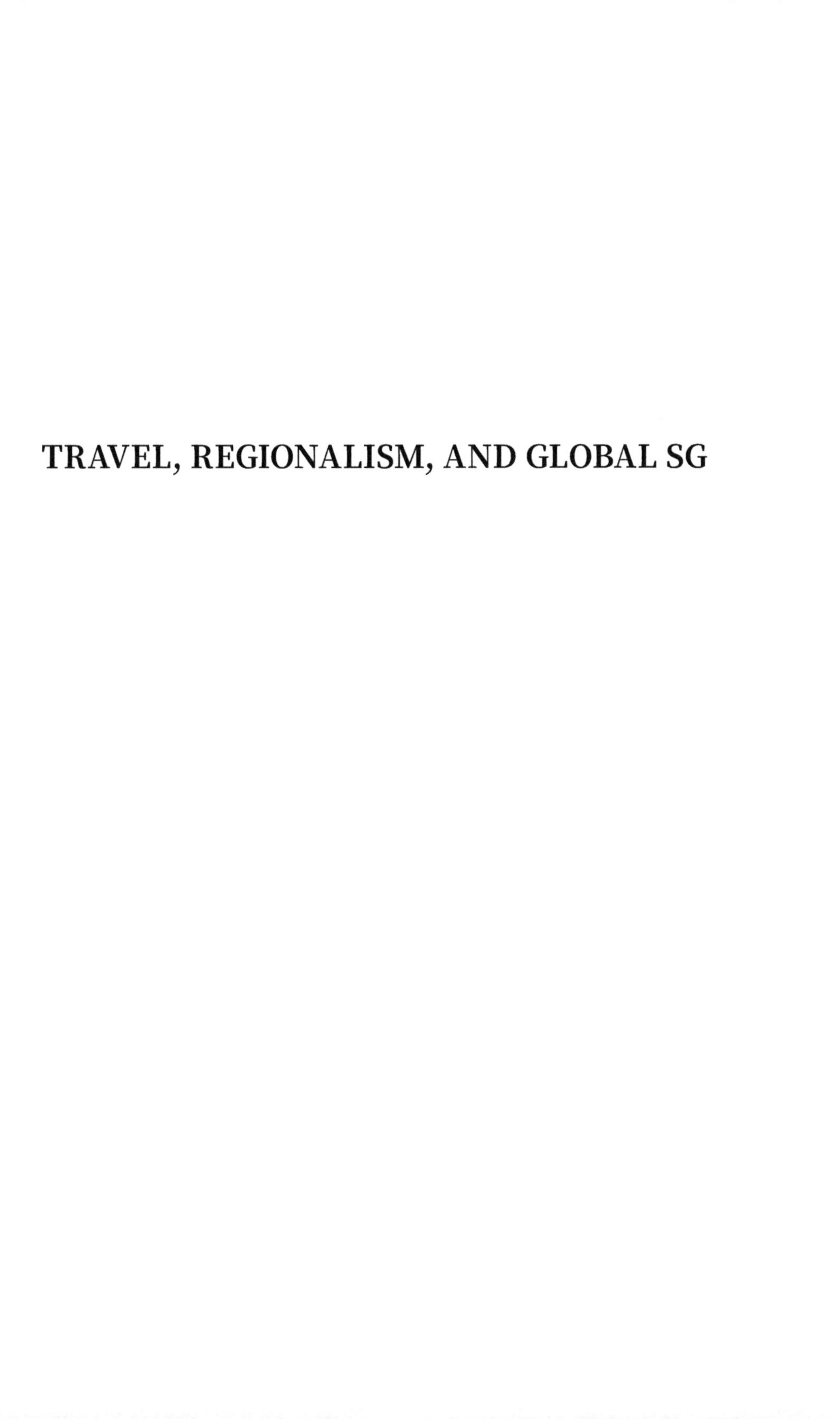

TRAVEL, REGIONALISM, AND GLOBAL SG

THE IMMOLATION

Primary Language: English

Secondary Language: No

Translation Available: No

Number of Pages: 189

Author: Goh Poh Seng

Year of Publication: 1977

Publisher: Heinemann Educational Books (Asia) Ltd

Characterisation Notes:

The protagonist, Thanh, is a 22-year-old man who yearns to be a revolutionary. He becomes obsessed with the smile on a Buddhist monk's face as the latter commits self-immolation in public. Thanh joins and becomes fiercely loyal to a group of freedom fighters who seek to topple the ruling government. However, over time, he becomes increasingly sceptical about the primary goal of the revolution as he partakes in missions that challenge his morals and his concept of freedom.

Text Synopsis:

The text begins with Thanh witnessing the immolation of a Buddhist monk named Tran Kim. The latter's serene smile at the moment of death continues to haunt Thanh throughout the course of the novel.

Thanh visits Superior Thi Tung at the Thing Hoai Pagoda in the hopes of understanding the meaning behind Tran Kim's smile. The monk corrects Thanh when he describes Tran Kim's self-immolation as a suicide. To the Superior, Tran Kim's death was not for "Abhaya", which is the desire for non-existence through an act of self-destruction, but was instead a constructive self-sacrifice for the good of others.

Thanh dismisses his father's worries that his group of friends was being monitored by the secret police and continues to meet with them. Unlike his comrades who come from working-class backgrounds, Thanh comes from a wealthy family and had gone overseas to study. He is particularly smitten by

My, an 18-year-old teacher who is also one of the revolutionists.

In fear of capture, Thanh's group goes underground and moves to a communist training camp in the countryside. Thanh begins his military training and eventually participates in a mission to ambush an enemy supply convoy. However, Thanh's faith in the revolution begins to waver and he starts to question the necessity of violence after he kills an enemy soldier for the first time during the operation. Thanh's comrade Quang Tuyen, who is a former newspaper reporter, advises him about the dangers of being too serious and fanatical. Quang tells him that confusion and being uncertain is part of being human, and that having "godlike certainty" is destructive because it inadvertently leads to a blind faith in overzealous leaders.

Nearing the end of the novel, the camp is destroyed by an airstrike. The survivors are forced to return to the capital and are split up to carry out different missions. Thanh finds himself lost and trapped after he is assigned a high-risk mission to attack the Presidential Palace on New Year's Day. He visits My and begs her to escape with him before his deployment. My, however, ruthlessly rejects him and Thanh leaves her.

The novel ends with Thanh narrowly escaping from the battle at the Presidential Palace and stumbling upon a homeless man named Old Lam. Thanh learns that the city is on curfew and shares a meal with the elderly man. They both fall asleep and Thanh dreams about Tran Kim's smile. Thanh wakes up the next morning to find that Old Lam has died in his sleep.

Significance and Remarks:

The Immolation exposes readers to the moral and ethical dilemmas faced by revolutionists.

During an argument between Thanh and his father, they debate about whether it is better for an individual to act nobly and speak out against a corrupt government or to act less scrupulously and work within the system to ensure one's own survival. This discussion demonstrates how the question of right and wrong is not as clear-cut as it appears and that the actions of each individual cannot be measured according to the same moral yardstick. Thanh himself does not single-mindedly follow the orders of his military superiors and occasionally questions his involvement in the revolution. In the course of the novel, Thanh's loyalty to the cause steadily declines as he continues to witness firsthand all the violence and bloodshed that the conflict has brought about. As such, the novel challenges the notion that an individual has a fixed identity and demonstrates how personal experiences and trauma can transform a person's thoughts and opinions that initially seemed unquestionable.

Ultimately, *The Immolation* prompts the reader to question the delicate binary between loyalty to a cause and crazed fanaticism. Just like Tran Kim's act of self-immolation, the action that an individual takes for the betterment of society can either be regarded as altruistic and courageous or overly extreme and self-destructive.

Potential areas of comparative analysis:

Violence, War, Trauma, Identity, Communism, Social Commentary, Religion, Culture, Asian vs Western values, Family

THE IMMOLATION

主要语言： 英文

次要语言： -

翻译版本： -

页数： 189

作者： 吴宝星（Goh Poh Seng）

出版年份： 1977

出版社： Heinemann Educational Books (Asia) Ltd

人物简介：

22岁的阿单（Thanh）立志成为一名革命者。较早前，他目睹一名和尚当众自焚，后者脸上的笑容一直停留在他脑海里，挥之不去。阿单加入革命组织，和一群自由战士试图推翻执政者。然而，当革命行动持续不断挑战他的道德底线、以及他对“自由”的概念时，阿单开始怀疑革命的初衷。

文本概要：

佛教僧侣陈金（Tran Kim）当众自焚，临死前脸上平静的笑容不断困扰阿单。为理解笑容背后的意义，他来到郑怀庙（Thing Hoai Pagoda）拜访施松大师（Superior Thi Tung）。阿单向施松大师阐述经过，认为僧侣陈金的自焚行为属于自杀，但遭施松否定。陈金的举动对施松而言，并非为了达到“Abhaya”——透过自我毁灭（self-destruction）以满足使其不存在（non-existence）的渴望，而是为了更广大的民族利益所做出的自我牺牲（self-sacrifice）。

阿单的父亲担心儿子参与的革命组织已被警方监视，然而阿单不予理会，持续和其他革命者会面。和其他来自工人阶级的组织成员不同的是，阿单家境富裕，曾在欧洲留学。阿单在组织结识、并爱上了18岁的老师——美（My）。

为躲避追捕，阿单等革命伙伴转为地下活动，并迁往郊区的一座共产主义军队的营地。阿单开始军事训练，也伏击敌军载满补给品的车队，然在歼灭第一个敌人后，他便开始质疑动用武力的必要性。曾在报社担任记者的战友邝士严(Quang Tuyen)告诉阿单，凡事过于认真、狂热将置自己于险境。士严也向他保证，感到困惑是人之常情，反之若他拥有“上帝般的确性”（godlike certainty）则将导致他盲目地相信过分激情的领军者，其结果必定是毁灭性的。

小说接近尾声时，一场空袭摧毁了营地，幸存者被迫返回城市，各自执行任务。阿单接获组织的指示，在元旦这一天袭击越南国家主席府（Presidential Palace）。这高风险的任务使他感到迷失、陷入困境。他恳求美在他前往执行任务前一起逃跑。美无情地拒绝请求，阿单也决定离开她。

阿单从主席府侥幸逃脱，在街上遇见一位病危的老先生——蓝（Old Lam）。阿单意识到全城实施宵禁，两人一起享用晚餐后沉沉睡去。夜晚，阿单在梦中见到僧侣陈金临死前安详的笑容，他从噩梦中惊醒，发现蓝已在睡梦中离世。

重点与备注：

《自焚事件》（The Immolation）向读者揭示了革命者所面对的道德挑战。

在一次争执中，阿单和他的父亲展开辩论——面对贪污腐败的政府，我们应该挺身而出，为正义而战，或选择接受体制的运作，明哲保身？阿单和父亲之间的讨论恰恰表明，“对”与“错”的问题并不像表面上看起来那么直接和明确，毕竟每个人的行为不能用同一道德标准来衡量。对阿单而言，他并没有盲目听从上级的命令，偶尔也会质疑自己参与革命的理由。阿单也因为亲眼目的冲突而带来的暴力血腥事件，而有所动摇。因此，《自焚事件》对固定的身份认同概念提出挑战，并向读者展示，自身经验和创伤如何改变我们一开始看似不容置疑的想法和观念。

《自焚事件》促使读者思考对事业（目标）感到忠诚和感到狂热之间的，微妙的二元对立。就如僧侣陈金在街上的自焚行为一样，他个人为改善社会而采取的行动，可以被视为一种利他、勇敢的行为，但也可被视为过于极端的自我毁灭。

潜在的比较文学分析：

暴力、战争、创伤、共产主义、社会评论、宗教、文化、亚洲与西方价值观、家庭

画室 ART STUDIO

Primary Language: Mandarin
Secondary Language: No
Translation Available: Art Studio
Number of Pages: 496
Author: Yeng Pway Ngon
Year of Publication: 2011
Publisher: Tonsan Publications Inc.

Characterisation Notes:

A victim of political repression, the Chinese-educated male protagonist Yan Pei loses his job and dedicates his life to art, running his own studio. He is impoverished in his old age, even as his ex-wife, Wan Zhen returns to offer palliative care in his remaining days after he is diagnosed with prostate cancer. Si Xian and Ning Fang learn painting from Yan Pei. Si Xian has a crush on Ning Fang, and was emotionally affected when he was unable to stop Ning Fang from leaving Singapore with her Indian vocal tutor Ananda. Si Xian could not get over Ning Fang after her departure, and even after 30 years, he had not given up on her.

Text Synopsis:

The novel juxtaposes various experiences of life in 1970s Singapore—academics, career, marriage—through the experiences of the main characters Yan Pei and Si Xian, and the minor characters Jian Xiong, Ning Fang, Su Lan, Ji Zong and Ye Chao Qun in an art studio. The novel is divided into two parts. The first part, titled "Distant Songs" depicts the struggles of an artist: Yan Pei is detained by the Internal Security Department and loses his job as a teacher; his marriage with Wan Zhen hits rock bottom as their differences in worldview become increasingly obvious and irreconcilable. Meanwhile, the devastated Si Xian decides to carve a career for himself in Taiwan after his childhood sweetheart Ning Fang decides to leave Singapore for Chennai, with Ananda. After 5 years of hard work, Si Xian finally holds his solo exhibition, to great acclaim. Moving on, the second part of the novel, titled "Coming Home," highlights the achievements of the protagonists in contrast to the drearier first part which chronicles their low points in life: Si Xian curates a memorial exhibition for his late teacher Yan Pei, whose works posthumously earn effusive praise and accolades from the region. In the hopes of holding more art exhibitions for Yan Pei, Si Xian visits Paris, where he is reunited with Ning Fang and has the chance to rekindle their relationship.

Significance and Remarks:

In 2008, Yeng Pway Ngon was diagnosed with prostate cancer; while receiving treatment, he worked on *Art Studio*, his epic full-length novel which took him around 4 years to complete and has a word count of nearly 250,000 words. *Art Studio* received international acclaim and was selected by Asia Weekly as one of the Top 10 Chinese Novels in 2011.

The 2 main themes explored in the novel are Death and Loneliness. Like many talented artists, Yan Pei has no choice but to resign to a life of loneliness and dejection: he is adamant in dedicating his life to art but his wife does not support his dreams. He is determined to paint but suffers from arthritis and faces terminal prostate cancer alone in his old age. To a certain extent, Yan Pei is fortunate as he eventually achieves regional recognition for his art, albeit posthumously: Si Xian curates and holds memorial exhibitions for him in Taipei and Hong Kong; however, this also has to be Yan Pei's greatest loneliness and regret as an artist—it is only after his death that the mainstream media in Singapore notices his artistic talent and considers him as a valuable member and contributor of the Singapore art community.

This novel also illustrates the common trope of the Chinese-educated student. The author chooses to exemplify the traits of the Chinese-educated characters by pairing each character with an English-educated character (Yan Pei and Wan Zhen, Si Xian and Ning Fang). The author accentuates the contrast between these characters through episodic challenges: for instance, due to lifestyle differences, Yan Pei fails to get the blessings of his English-educated in-laws, and is alienated by Wan Zhen's colleagues; Si Xian is out-of-place in a conversation with Ning Fang and Ananda due to his inferior grasp of English. In the novel, language transcends race to divide Singaporeans—the Chinese-educated are not only alienated by other races but also other English-speaking Chinese.

Interestingly, the English-educated characters in the novel are all female. These characters are independent, strong-willed and are not reliant on men. This shows that the educational differences between the Chinese and English-educated goes deeper than mere language and has profound influence on the social lives of the characters. Further, the novel also presents a nuanced portrayal of the Chinese-educated in Singapore. While Yan Pei lived in poverty and is disappointed in both his career and relationships, Si Xian succeeds in both. Due to his flexible and robust character, Si Xian becomes an established artist and even invites Yan Pei to exhibit together in Taiwan.

Spatial dispersion and cross-culture interaction

This novel stretches across a multitude of spaces: Singapore, Hong Kong, Taiwan, China, Malaysia, India, and France. The novel begins and ends in Singapore—the hub of dispersion of all its characters.

Yan Pei's story unfolds in Singapore: his relationship with Wan Zhen (marriage to divorce to reconciliation), his life as an art teacher, and his diagnosis of prostate cancer. Wan Zhen, after her divorce from Yan Pei, heads to Hong Kong, where she meets Liang, and has a brief romance with him. A substantive relationship fails to materialise and Wan Zhen, in her loneliness, grows to miss Singapore. She decides to return to Yan Pei after meeting with Si Xian to provide palliative care for his last days.

Yan Pei's mentor, Li Yun Shi, is Taiwanese. Li received his art education in France and is adept at developing the talents of his pupils. Yan Pei's student, Si Xian, heads back to Taiwan to improve his prospects as a portrait artist. It is also in Taiwan that Si Xian becomes recognized for his work on faceless female forms and achieves commercial success. Si Xian then invites Yan Pei to visit Taiwan and exhibit together. Yan Pei is thrilled by the prospect: he works non-stop despite his cancer. The Taiwan trip is also fulfilling for Yan Pei: he had never felt happier and finally understood what they meant by money can in fact buy some happiness after all. Ning Fang, formerly Yan Pei's student, goes to Chennai to learn ancient India songs with Ananda. There, she falls in love with Ganesan. The couple marry and settle down in Paris, France, where they have a daughter, Indranee. Many years later, Si Xian meets Ning Fang, his childhood crush, in Paris while preparing for an exhibition.

Potential areas of comparative analysis:

English vs Chinese Educated Students, Sex and Sexuality, Spatial Dispersion, Cross-Culture Interaction, Love, Interracial Marriage, Death, Loneliness

画室 ART STUDIO

主要语言： 繁体中文
次要语言： -
翻译版本： Art Studio
页数： 496
作者： 英培安
出版年份： 2011
出版社： 唐山出版社

人物简介：

主人翁颜沛是名华校生，因政治迫害失去教职工作后，决定献身艺术事业，以经营画室为生，一生穷困潦倒，郁郁不得志。当他晚年确诊患上前列腺癌后，与他分开多年的前妻婉贞回到他身边，陪他走完最后一段路。思贤和宁芳是颜沛的爱徒。思贤多年来暗恋宁芳，可宁芳和印度歌唱老师阿难达一起离开新加坡，思贤感到不是滋味，却无法阻止。宁芳离去后，思贤对她念念不忘，尽管分开30年，也放不下她。

文本概要：

故事从新加坡20世纪70年代的一间画室里开始，作者以颜沛及思贤为主、以健雄、宁芳、素兰、继宗和叶超群等为辅，呈现出一群艺术爱好者各自在学业、事业以及婚恋等的生命风景。小说分上下两部。第一部分"远方的歌声"描绘艺术工作者追求理想的坎坷：颜沛被内安局拘留、被学校革职，和妻子婉贞的婚姻触礁。他的徒弟宁芳和阿难达远赴印度，深爱宁芳的思贤感情受挫决心到台湾发展。经过5年的努力后，终于在台北举办了个人画展，并深受好评。在第二部分"回家"中，他们在磕磕碰碰后，终于苦尽甘来：思贤为过世的老师举办纪念展，颜沛的艺术造诣终于收受到肯定，守得云开见月明。感情方面，思贤和宁芳终于在巴黎重逢，得以再续前缘。

重点与备注：

2008年，英培安确诊患上前列腺癌，近25万字的《画室》便是他在接受治疗期间耗时4年完成的长篇著作，气势磅礴，作品于2011年问世后备受肯定，同年入选《亚洲周刊》年度十大中文小说。

《画室》的两大主题莫过于死亡和孤独。正如所有有天赋的艺术创作者，颜沛是孤独且寂寞的——他坚持对艺术的追求，却得不到妻子婉贞的谅解和支持。他不放弃创作，却先后饱受风湿关节炎和前列腺癌的折腾，生命受到威胁，独自面对死亡的降临。某种程度上，颜沛是幸运的：他的徒弟思贤在台北和香港为他举办纪念展，他的艺术成就终究获得高度的肯定。但这也是颜沛身为艺术家最大的孤独和悲哀一他在死后才成了新加坡主流媒体口中新加坡画坛的损失。

在人物塑造方面，作者主要描写华校生的形象。身为华校生的颜沛，一生穷困潦倒，在事业和感情的道路上郁郁不得志。有趣的是，在《画室》中，作者有意将华校生和英校生凑成一对，如颜沛与婉贞，以及思贤与宁芳。这种做法凸现了他们之间的差别，强调他们所面对的挑战——颜沛不仅无法得到婉贞父母的祝福，也无法融入婉贞和她的同事，生活水平的差距越来越明显。当思贤、宁芳和印度老师阿难达在交谈时，思贤因为英语程度不佳，明显无法融入。因语言隔阂，华校生不只被异族排挤，也被华人排挤在外。《画室》里的英校生都是由女性角色为代表。她们在小说里呈现出独立、坚强自主的个性，展现了英校生与华校生接受的教育有所不同。在《画室》中，并非所有华校生都是失败潦倒的形象，例如：思贤成功的关键在于他的灵活和变通，他靠绘画谋生，改变生活品质，在台湾成功后不忘饮水思源，邀请老师一起办画展。

小说涉及的空间众多，包括：新加坡、香港、台湾、中国、马来西亚、印度和法国。小说以新加坡为起始和结束，是人物离散的中心地。以颜沛为例，他和婉贞的恋爱、结婚与离婚，包括在学校教书，发现并治疗前列腺癌，都发生在新加坡。婉贞与颜沛离婚后去了香港，同时又与梁生发生了一段无疾而终的感情。只身一人在香港的孤独感，使婉贞思念新加坡。在香港，婉贞偶遇颜沛的弟子思贤后，与前夫颜沛再续前缘，返回新加坡陪他走完人生最后的旅程。

颜沛的老师——李韵士是台湾人，留学法国，善于因材施教，对颜沛的影响深远。颜沛的学生思贤因为感情受伤，到台湾通过替商人画肖像画赚钱维生。两年后，思贤开始画没有脸孔的冷艳女体，深获好评、收入不菲，并在台北开了个展。成名后，思贤不忘饮水思源，邀请老师前往台湾旅游。颜沛在台湾最大的两项收获是：一、思贤想和他在台北联展画作。颜沛感到很兴奋，虽然罹患癌症却依旧笔耕不辍。二、颜沛非常享受台湾之行，并深刻体会到金钱的确可以买到某种程度的快乐。

思贤单恋着宁芳，后者因为要学印度古曲而追随阿难达前去印度马德拉斯（又称钦奈），学艺未成，却爱上了另一印度男子伽内山，并和他赴法国巴黎定居，两人育有一女——英德拉妮（Indranee）。多年后，思贤前往欧洲准备画展，和自己暗恋多年的宁芳在巴黎重新相遇。

潜在的比较文学研究分析：

华校生与英校生、性/情欲书写、空间离散、跨文化交际、异国恋情、死亡、孤独

誓鸟 THE PROMISE BIRD

Primary Language: Mandarin
Secondary Language: No
Translation Available: The Promise Bird
Number of Pages: 312
Author: Zhang Yue Ran
Year of Publication: 2006
Publisher: Guangming Daily Press

Characterisation Notes:

Chun Chi is a visually impaired woman. She travels between China and the South Seas on a boat, returning every few months with wooden chests filled with seashells. Chun deliberately distances herself from her adopted son, Xiao Xing, but the latter grows increasingly affectionate towards her as he matures. When Chun Chi succumbs to old age, Xiao Xing sets off to unravel her mysterious past and the memories sealed in the seashells.

Text Synopsis:

The novel begins with Xiao Xing's recollection of his childhood with Chun Chi. Chun had attempted to abandon him at a bustling lantern festival celebration one night. However, Xiao Xing believed that he was bonded to Chun by a bond stronger than kinship (they were not related by blood).

Chun Chi only receives one visitor: Master Zhong Qian, a eunuch who polishes seashells for her. On his deathbed, Zhong tells Xiao Xing that Chun Chi cares only for the past. Hua Hua, Master Zhong's adopted daughter, moves in with Xiao Xing and becomes his wife later. When Chun Chi's health deteriorates and she becomes too weak to go out to sea again, Xiao Xing goes on her behalf.

The narrative then flashes back to a younger Chun Chi, who lives in a refugee shelter on Lian Yan Island after surviving a tsunami (she had been saved by Tsong Tsong, a Dutch-Chinese "song-girl," who spotted her comatose body on the beach). At the shelter, she meets and has a brief romance with Camel, a tribal chief from Lombok Island. Upon realising that Chun Chi has lost her memories in the tsunami, Camel passes her a small knife and instructs her to return it to him once she recalls the past.

At the same time, Chun Chi encounters a mysterious silver-haired hump-backed woman. The woman shows Chun Chi the path to regain her past by rubbing and circling her fingers on seashells. Since the incident, Chun Chi becomes obsessed with spirals and conches.

In the following chapters, a complex romantic relationship between Chun Chi, Tsong Tsong, Camel and Zhong Qian begins to unfold. It is also revealed that Tsong Tsong and Camel are Xiao Xing's biological parents, and that Chun Chi had been entrusted to take care of the newborn before Tsong Tsong's death. Along with Zhong Qian, Chun Chi returns to China to raise Xiao Xing.

Chun Chi's origins finally come to light as the novel draws to a close. Born in the Ming Dynasty, she is the daughter of a high-ranking military governor who was appointed by the emperor to explore the unmapped islands. A disastrous storm wrecked her father's fleet and washes him up an unknown island located in the South Seas. The natives save his life, and he plans an arranged marriage for Chun Chi. Chun Chi had subsequently set off to reunite with her father but had encountered a tsunami which obliterated her memories.

Significance and Remarks:

The Promise Bird is set in China and the islands of the South Seas in the early 15th century (during the reign of Ming dynasty emperor Yongle). The novel tells the story of a morbid and uncompromising obsession.

The protagonist Chun Chi is characterized by morbid determination. In the pursuit of her lost memories, she blinds herself intentionally, using needles to minimize disruption from the light, and removes her fingernails with a knife and pliers to prevent them from making unnecessary sounds when she is stroking her conches.

Memories shape and represent the temporal entirety of one's lives and hence each piece of memory is integral to one's identity. In Chun Chi's own words, "troubled memories are tearing her body apart" but she must persist because every recollection—complete or fragmentary—is essential to her identity.

Chun Chi's baffling past compels Xiao Xing to journey to the islands of the South Seas (modern day Indonesia). Over the course of his journey, he uncovers the mystery of his birth and the entangled fates of his biological parents, Zhong Qian and Chun Chi. As he retraces Chun Chi's footsteps, he enters her sealed, labyrinthine memory palace and fulfils his desire to reconnect with his adoptive mother.

The title of the book is derived from *Classic of Mountains and Seas*, a compilation of Chinese mythologies. The "Promise Bird" is known as Jingwei (精卫), a bird with a white beak and red feet, in one story of the collection. The bird had been a reincarnation of Nuwa (女娃), who perished while swimming across the Eastern Sea and had been magically transformed into a bird after her death. The bird will drop pebbles and twigs to the sea every day to fill it and prevent further deaths from drowning. The Chinese idiom, "Jingwei Tries to Fill the Sea" (精卫填海) derived from the story illustrates an unwavering dedication to accomplish the seemingly impossible. Chun Chi, whose blood-red feet bear partial resemblance to Jingwei, acts in accordance with the myth in her unflinching dedication to a seemingly futile pursuit.

As the Chinese aphorism goes, a tree may grow high and tall, but its leaves will always return to their origins. Chun Chi's lifelong, undying search for her lost memories is not just a quest to uncover her history, but also a search for her sense of identity and belonging in an unfathomably vast universe.

Potential areas of comparative analysis:

Historiography, Multiculturalism, New Migrants, Diaspora, Sense of Identity/ Belonging, Sense of Loss/Displacement, Obession/Desire

誓鸟 THE PROMISE BIRD

主要语言：中文

次要语言：-

翻译版本：The Promise Bird

页数：312

作者：张悦然

出版年份：2006

出版社：光明日报出版社

人物简介：

盲女春迟大部分的时间都在往返于中国和南洋的轮船上度过，每隔数月，才会带着装满贝壳的木箱子回家。春迟刻意地和养子宵行保持距离，但随着年岁增长，后者对养母的感情愈加深厚。春迟老去后，宵行前往南洋，揭开养母神秘的过往以及封存在贝壳中的记忆。

文本概要：

小说从宵行的童年说起。在一个热闹的花灯节晚会上，春迟试图趁乱抛弃宵行，但宵行平安无事回到家中。他相信有一种比亲情(他们没有血缘关系)更亲密的关系将他和春迟紧紧地联系在一起。

宦官钟潜(钟师傅)每月一次上门为春迟打磨贝壳，是春迟唯一接待的客人。临终之际，他告诉宵行，春迟此生唯一执着的只有她的过去。钟潜死后，她的养女婳婳搬进宵行家中，后成为他的妻子。当春迟的身体逐渐衰弱，无法出海时，宵行代替她前往南洋揭开过去神秘的面纱。

一场海啸将春迟冲上潋滟岛，所幸荷兰中国裔歌女淙淙在海滩上发现了她，使她幸免于难。春迟在潋滟岛上的难民营里和龙目岛（Lombok Islands）的部落首领骆驼（Camel）发生一段短暂的恋情。骆驼意识到海啸已夺走了春迟的记忆，他将一把小刀递给春迟，并嘱咐她，一旦恢复记忆，便将小刀交还于他。与此同时，她也在岛上撞见一名银发弓身老妇。老妇用手指搓揉着贝壳，并在贝壳上划圈，引导春迟找回遗失的记忆——春迟从此迷恋上各式各样的贝壳。

春迟、淙淙、骆驼和钟潜陷入一场复杂的四角关系中——淙淙和骆驼是宵行的亲身父母。淙淙在临终前将宵行托付给春迟；春迟以及钟潜一同回到中国，一起抚养小宵行长大。小说尾声，春迟的身世之谜终于浮出水面。春迟是明代将帅之女，她的父亲奉旨展开航海生涯，探索、发现未知的岛屿。有一次，她父亲的舰队在海上遭遇风暴，流落南洋一座不知名的荒岛，当地的土著首领救了他一命，以示诚意，他答应将春迟许配给首领的儿子。春迟接受父亲的提议，动身前往南洋和父亲团聚，却在路上遭一场海啸吞噬了她的记忆。

重点与备注：

《誓鸟》以15世纪初（明永乐年间）的中国和南洋群岛为年代背景，叙述一段关于病态和执念的故事。

女主人翁春迟的毅力坚定得令人毛骨悚然。为寻找遗失的记忆，春迟无所不用其极：她先刻意用针戳瞎双眼，减少光线干扰，提升触觉和听觉的敏感度。第二，她用刀和镊子将指甲从手指头剥离下来，避免手指在划过贝壳时发出不必要的声音。

记忆形塑、象征生命的整体，因此每一段记忆都是建构身份至关紧要的部分。用春迟自己的话说，记忆不断就缠着她，像是要把她撕裂一般，但她必须坚持寻找记忆，因为每一个片段，或完整或零碎，都是拼凑身份必不可少的部分。春迟神秘的过去驱使宵行前往南洋群岛（今印度尼西亚），他在旅途中揭开他的身世之谜，以及他的亲身父母、春迟和钟师傅的错综复杂的情感纠葛。当他沿着春迟的脚步时，他进入了春迟密封、犹如迷宫般的记忆宫殿，满足了他渴望和春迟拉近距离的心愿。

小说名字《誓鸟》源自收录古代神话传说的古籍《山海经》，传说中女娃不幸溺毙于东海，死后化身成为一只白嘴红脚的鸟，名为“誓鸟”(别称“精卫”)。为了不让东海再次夺去无辜的生命，精卫鸟日复一日地向大海投掷石头和树枝，望有一日能填满大海；成语“精卫填海”便是由此而来，后人用以比喻坚定不移、锲而不舍，完成艰巨任务的精神。在小说中，春迟血红的双脚，以及她终其一生、对一件徒劳无功的事的坚持都体现了精卫鸟般无所畏惧、永不退缩的执念。俗语说得好：树高千丈，叶落归根，春迟终生不渝地寻找散落的记忆，不仅是为了要挖掘过去，更重要的是，在苍茫浩瀚的宇宙之间，确立自己的身份认同和归属感。

潜在的比较文学分析：

史学、多元文化主义、新移民、离散经验、身份认同、归属感、位移感、执念、欲望

SOY SAUCE FOR BEGINNERS

Primary Language: English

Secondary Language: A little Mandarin, dialects and local slangs.

Translation Available: No

Number of Pages: 250

Author: Kirstin Chen

Year of Publication: 2014

Publisher: Houghton Mifflin Harcourt

Characterisation Notes:

The protagonist Gretchen Lin is a thirty-year-old woman. She walks out on her failed marriage and postgraduate studies in San Francisco to return to Singapore and work for her family's soy sauce business.

Text Synopsis:

Packed with familial intrigue and romantic drama, *Soy Sauce for Beginners* is a story about a woman's journey of self-discovery, as she learns more about and finds joy in the brewing of artisanal soy sauce. The protagonist Gretchen Lin returns to Singapore to escape from her failed marriage and post-graduate studies in San Francisco, only to realise that the tropical paradise of her childhood is gone. Her mother is an alcoholic and her father's soy sauce company is facing public backlash after Gretchen's cousin Calvin pushed for a cheaper line of soy sauce and other ready-to-cook condiments that caused food poisoning amongst their customers. Gretchen decides to work at the family business as a temporary staff while she picks up the broken pieces of her marriage. She is joined by Frankie Shepherd, her old college roommate, who was hired to work as a consultant at Lin's Soy Sauce on Gretchen's recommendation. At the same time, Gretchen pursues a romantic relationship with James Santoso, the son of one of the company's clients. As the company struggles to restore its reputation and expand its distribution to the US, the family unwittingly turns to Gretchen, the only other person who can take over the business. Consequently, Gretchen finds herself torn between her personal desire to return to San Francisco and her filial duty to uphold her family's artisanal soy sauce legacy.

Significance and Remarks:

Soya Sauce for Beginners focuses primarily on the female protagonist, Gretchen Lin, and her struggle to reconcile with her diasporic identity as a Singaporean living in the US. When she decides to leave behind her unfaithful husband and an uncompleted Master's thesis to travel to Singapore, she is confronted with a dilemma: to remain permanently in Singapore and oversee Lin's Soy Sauce as requested by her father or to return to the US and complete her studies as her mother had proposed.

The novel presents the process of brewing soya sauce as a metaphor for how Singapore identity is becoming more transnational. It also presents the condiment soy sauce as a metaphor for the conflictual hybridity of Singaporean society and the clash between Chinese traditions and Western liberalization.

The conflict between Eastern traditions and Western modernisation is especially apparent in the bitter family feud involving Gretchen, her father, Calvin and Calvin's father, which threatens to upend the business. Calvin, who argues that customers want a cheaper alternative to their premium line of soya sauce, introduces a line of fibreglass-container-aged soy sauce, which has a reduced fermentation period and lower production cost. This invites the ire of Gretchen and her father as the fiberglass tanks are incapable of replicating the soy sauce's signature earthiness. In the end, Gretchen rises to the challenge and resolves to safeguard her family's traditional method of brewing artisanal soya sauce, at the cost of pursuing her postgraduate studies.

Potential areas of comparative analysis:

Diasporic Identity, Feminism, Singapore Literature, Modernity, Tradition, Diaspora, Home, Liberalism, Hybridity, Metaphor

SOY SAUCE FOR BEGINNERS

主要语言： 英文

次要语言： 少许中文、方言和地方用语

翻译版本： -

页数： 250

作者： Kirstin Chen

出版年份： 2014

出版社： Houghton Mifflin Harcourt

人物简介：

30岁的格雷琴（Gretchen Lin）走出失败的婚姻、舍弃未完成的学业，从美国回到新加坡继承家族的酱油厂生意。

文本概要：

充斥着家族斗争的紧张关系和戏剧性的浪漫，小说描述女主人翁格雷琴在学习酿造手工酱油的过程中，寻找、并发现自我的故事。为逃离失败的婚姻和研究生课业，她从旧金山回到新加坡，但很快意识到，她童年的热带天堂早已不复存在。她必须同时面对母亲酗酒的问题，以及挽救林氏酱油厂的生意。较早前，格雷琴的堂弟凯尔文（Calvin）急功近利，推出新的生产线，为客户供应更廉价的酱油以及其他的即煮酱料，不料消费者食用后却投诉食物中毒，林氏酱油厂随即遭公众强烈抵制。

格雷琴一边暂时地在酱油厂工作，一边修复破碎的婚姻。经格雷琴的推荐，她的大学好友弗兰奇（Frankie）也加入公司，成为酱油厂的顾问。与此同时，格雷琴结识客户的儿子詹姆斯（James），和他展开一段浪漫的关系。酱油厂的声誉遭受重挫。此时，格雷琴的父亲将希望全部寄托在她身上，认为她是唯一能继承家族生意的接班人，希望她能挽回酱油厂的名声，并将市场拓展到美国。格雷琴顿时陷入两难——她应该遵从自己的新意回到旧金山，抑或留在新加坡继承家族生意并将之发扬光大？

重点与备注：

小说聚焦在格雷琴以及身为在美国生活的新加坡人的她，面对离散者身份（diasporic identity）的挣扎。当她放下未完成的硕士课程，离开对她不忠的丈夫回到新加坡时，她陷入一个两难境地——是按照父亲的要求定居新加坡，并将家族生意拓展到美国，或是接受母亲的提议，反其道而行？

小说的题材——酿造酱油象征在跨国（Transnational）的互动当中所产生的对身份认同的变化。它同时也揭示因新加坡的混杂文化所产生的冲突，以及传统文化和西方自由主义文化之间的碰撞。

我们可以从格雷琴如何卷入一场涉及她、凯尔文以及凯尔文的父亲的激烈家族纠纷可见一斑。凯尔文主张现代客户更倾向经济实惠的替代品，因此推出新的生产线，改用玻璃纤维缸酿造酱油，减少发酵时间的同时也能降低成本，此举引起格雷琴的不悦，毕竟玻璃纤维缸无法赋予酱油其天然的风味。格雷琴迎难而上，决心守护传统酿造酱油的工艺，当然这当中免不了牺牲她未完成的硕士课程。

潜在的比较文学分析：

离散身份、女性主义、新加坡文学、传统与现代性、离散、家、自由主义、糅杂/混杂、隐喻

A BIT OF EARTH

Primary Language: English

Secondary Language: A few Singlish and Malay words

Translation Available: No

Number of Pages: 423

Author: Suchen Christine Lim

Year of Publication: 2001

Publisher: Times Books International

Characterisation Notes:

The protagonist, Wong Tuck Heng, is a tenacious young teenager who escapes from his native village Sum Hor in China following the murder of his entire family at the hands of the 'Manchu devils'. He travels by sea to a rural mining settlement on the coast of the Bandong River in Malaya, where he is adopted by Wong-soh, the second wife of the well-respected leader of the Cantonese White Cranes, Tai-kor Wong. Tuck Heng is initially rejected by his adoptive extended family—the Wees—but soon makes a name for himself by becoming an influential Chinese trader operating under British colonial rule. Tuck Heng's stepbrother and the eldest son of Tai-kor Wong's first wife, Wong Boon Leong, is a Cambridge educated lawyer who becomes the bane of Tuck Heng's existence in the later half of the novel.

Text Synopsis:

The novel weaves together the lives of three different families—the China-born Wongs, the Straits-born Wees and the Malaya-born Mahmuds. The novel is separated into four parts and predominantly follows the life and growth of Wong Tuck Heng. Although initially rejected by his adoptive extended family, Tuck Heng is eventually accepted by the Wee family after he saves Baba Wee—Tai-kor Wong's father-in-law—during a riot between the Cantonese White Cranes and the Hakka Black Flags in Penang.

In addition, the novel describes the colonisation of Malaya at the hands of the British and the antagonistic relationship between the Malaya-born datuks and the European invaders. Prior to the signing of the Pangkor Treaty, the well-respected menteri of Bandong, Datuk Long Mahmud, owned lands and other properties. He was forward-thinking and had even planned to send his eldest son Ibrahim to an English school in Penang so that his son would be well-informed about the socio-political changes in his country. Subsequently, Datuk Mahmud was killed for his role in the assassination of a British official, James Birch, and his family was stripped of their wealth and properties. Ibrahim takes over as the head of the family and attempts to recover the lands and titles that his family had lost.

After the untimely death of his adoptive father, Tuck Heng learns to speak English while working as a clerk at Baba Wee's shop and eventually becomes one of the most respected and wealthy Chinese tradesmen in the district. Tuck Heng's relationship with Boon Leong sours as he resents his stepbrother for the opportunities that he was never given due to his adoptive status.

Near the end of the novel, Tuck Heng is arrested for his role in the riots involving White Crane coolies (labourers). He is deported to China despite the efforts of Boon Leong who represents him in court. Tuck Heng finally realises that family unity is more important than personal reputation and willingly accepts his punishment. Before leaving the country, he tells his son Kok Seng not to worry and that he will be back under a new name and identity to reclaim "this bit of earth".

Significance and Remarks:

A Bit of Earth paints a vivid picture of the impact of colonialism on different ethnic groups in Malaya across multiple generations. The younger generation find themselves torn between their native traditions and the imported British practices that dominate the country's legal and political systems. In the course of the novel, the three families quickly realise that they cannot distance themselves from the British if they hope to survive and prosper in a rapidly changing environment. Furthermore, *A Bit of Earth* emphasizes the importance of familial ties over material gain by demonstrating how the desire for power and wealth will result in ever-shifting allegiances between individuals. The novel reminds us that we all share a bit of earth and that we must do all we can to protect it. Ultimately, the novel forces readers to reconsider their own definitions of home and their place within society.

Potential areas of comparative analysis:

Interracial Communication, Traditional vs. Modern values, Social Commentary, Languages in Malaya, Religion, Culture, Asian vs Western values, Eurasian Communities, Colonialism, Family

A BIT OF EARTH

主要语言：英文

次要语言：夹杂新加坡式英语以及马来语

翻译版本：-

页数：423

作者：Suchen Christine Lim

出版年份：2001

出版社：Times Book International

人物简介：

父亲王天庆（Wong Tin Keng）遭"满清鬼子"（Manchu Devils）杀害后，王德兴（Wong Tuck Heng）带着坚韧不拔的精神从中国乘船来到马来亚半岛。他在万隆河（Bandong River）河边落脚，并被当地著名的广东白鹤（Cantonese White Cranes）寨寨主、人称王大哥（Tai-Kor Wong）的第二任妻子收为养子。初来乍到，他不受养母延伸家庭成员所欢迎，但他很快地凭借自身的努力扬名立万，成为英殖民统治下，具有影响力的华裔商人。在文中，王德兴同父异母的哥哥王文良（Ong Boon Leong）是名毕业自剑桥的律师，同时也是王德兴生活中的克星。

文本概要：

整体而言，小说将三组家庭——来自中国的王德兴、海峡土生华人（王德兴的养父母）以及在马来亚半岛土著拿督马哈茂德（Datuk Mahmud）的家族交织在一起。小说分成四个部分，主要叙述男主人翁王德兴的人生以及成长经历。一开始，王德兴养母的原生家庭并不待见他，但在广东白鹤以及客家黑旗（Hakka Black Flags）之间爆发的一场起义中救了养母的父亲一命后，最终被接纳。

小说刻画了英殖民统治者与当地拿督之间紧张的对立关系。在签署《邦咯条约》（Pangkor Treaty）之前，拿督马哈茂德是万隆当地德高望重的部长领袖，家中拥有祖辈所遗留下来的田地和奴仆。他也具有远见，深谋远虑——他计划让他的长子伊布拉欣（Ibrahim）学习英语，以确保他能掌握社会的脉动。不幸的是，拿督马哈茂德因涉嫌参与谋杀英国官员詹姆斯（James Birch）葬送性命，其家族成员也被迫流亡。伊布拉欣取代父亲的位置，誓言收复家族失去的财产和头衔。

养父去世后，王德兴开始学习英语，成为富甲一方、极具影响力的华裔商人。与此同时，王德兴和哥哥王文良的关系开始恶化，他厌恶他的哥哥，毕竟身为养子的他，永远不可能和同父异母的哥哥有相同、同等的机遇。小说接近尾声时，王德兴因牵涉白鹤寨劳工的暴动而遭逮捕，尽管王文良担任他的代表律师，他最终还是被遣返中国。比起他的尊严，他认为家庭的凝聚力更为重要，因此愿意接受所有处分。离开前，他告诉儿子国盛（Kok Seng）千万不要害怕，因为他将以新的身份东山再起，重新夺回属于他的"一撮土地"(bit of earth)。

重点与备注：

《一撮土地》(A Bit of Earth) 栩栩如生 地描绘了帝国主义(imperialism)在马来亚半岛横跨三代人的影响——尤其是年轻一辈，他们往往在自己的出生地文化（birth culture）和外来文化（imported culture）之间徘徊不定；在《一撮土地》中，英殖民统治着主导、掌管国家的政治和法律制度，因此书中的三组家庭很快地便意识到，为了生存，他们必须和殖民地政府保持一定的关系。对权利和财富的欲望只会令我们摇摆不定，因此《一撮土地》强调，家庭（家人）相较于地产和财富的重要性。归根结底，《一撮土地》提醒着我们，我们都生活在这一撮土地上，因此我们必须竭尽全力地去守护它。小说也借机迫使读者重新思考"家"的意义，以及在社会上扮演的角色。

潜在的比较文学分析：

跨种族沟通、传统和现代价值观、社会评述、马来亚半岛的语言、宗教、文化、亚洲和西方价值观、欧亚族裔族群、殖民主义、家庭

SELENDANG SUKMA (SHAWL OF THE SPIRIT)

Primary Language: Malay

Secondary Language: No

Translation Available: No

Number of Pages: 378

Author: Isa Kamari

Year of Publication: 2014

Publisher: Institut Terjemahan & Buku Malaysia (ITBM)

Characterisation Notes:

Ilham is a Singaporean architect. During a work trip to Bali, he meets property developer Pak Lempad's secretary Dewi and they fall in love. Their relationship attract the ire of Ketut Raharja, the son of a Balinese witch doctor. Ketut Raharja has a longstanding crush on (and desire to possess) Dewi and loathes the presence of Ilham. Ilham is betrayed by his employees upon his return to Singapore and he loses his contract with the Indonesian property developer.

Text Synopsis:

The protagonist Ilham accepts an invitation to Bali from Pak Lempad, who offers Ilham a project to build a hotel on the island on the condition that Ilham also agrees to undertake the construction of an orphanage for free. He meets Pak Lempad's secretary Dewi and they fall in love, and this attracts the ire of Ketut Raharja. Ketut Raharja exploits Pak Riwayat's (Dewi's father) trust in witch doctors to convince him that his chronic feet ailment was caused by Ilham. It is revealed that many Balinese are superstitious, and Pak Riwayat sees witch doctors as superior to Western physicians and he even observes a series of rituals when meeting with the witch doctor.

Returning to Singapore, Ilham remains infatuated with Dewi, neglecting his family and career. His already frigid relationship with his brother Sulaiman and father deteriorates (Ilham will only come to regret his actions after his father passes away). Ilham also loses the trust of his manager Jennifer and employee Simon. They betray Ilham to side with his competitor Zaman in a corporate feud and Ilham's joint property venture ultimately fails. Meanwhile, Zaman orchestrates a car accident to injure one of his employees, Syamsiah, after she threatens to expose his shady business dealings. It is then revealed that Zaman is the illegitimate son of Pak Lempad.

The novel ends with a news of an explosion at the orphanage being built by Ilham. The news report hints at Ilham's death (there was a Singaporean among the 40 casualties) and implicates Ketut Raharja as the perpetrator (the explosion was orchestrated by local youths). Prior to the incident, Ketut Raharja had been mocked by other villagers for his failure to woo Dewi and had resolved to exact vengeance on Ilham.

Significance and Remarks:

The novel is primarily set in Bali and engages with Balinese culture, geography, and history. There are two intertwining narratives that intersect at different points in the novel's timeline: one of Ilham's experiences in life, and another of Ilham's soul revisiting his past. The temporal complexity of the storytelling makes the novel exciting.

The author skillfully weaves Balinese religious history into the conversations between Ilham and Dewi. The author raises several religious issues such as the difference between Balinese and Indian Hindus, the origin of Islam in Bali, and the history and beliefs of the Balinese aborigines. To heighten authenticity, he draws on several primary historical sources and also uses Balinese terms (explained in a glossary) to delineate its cultural and spiritual norms.

Next, the author emphasizes mutual respect and dialogue between different religions. Ilham is a faithless Muslim whereas Dewi is a Hindu who seeks a deeper understanding of Islam because of her love for Ilham. Dewi's enthusiasm for Islam spurs Ilham to be a more devout Muslim; their in-depth discussions of Islam also strengthens their relationship.

Extending the discussion on Islam, the author explores the topic of religious extremism. He questions the origins of violence in Islam and states that Islam has never encouraged violence in its history. In so doing, the author invites the reader to consider the socio-political circumstances that lead to a person's designation as a Muslim terrorist (such as in the case of the Jemaah Islamiyah extremist Mas Selamat).

Potential areas of comparative analysis:

Family Drama/Tension, Islam, (Balinese) Hinduism, Religious Extremism/Terrorism, Witchcraft, History/Historical Memories, Cross-cultural Relationships

SELENDANG SUKMA

主要语言： 马来文
次要语言： -
翻译版本： -
页数： 378
作者： 伊沙 · 卡马里（Isa Kamari）
出版年份： 2014
出版社： Institut Terjemahan & Buku Malaysia (ITBM)

人物简介：

男主人翁伊利哈姆（Ilham）是一名建筑师。他到巴厘岛出差时和发展商伦帕德(Pak Lempad)的私人助理德薇（Dewi）坠入情网，引起拉哈尔加（Ketut Raharja）的不悦。拉哈尔加是岛上巫医的儿子，他一向爱慕德薇，对她有强烈的占有欲，因此痛恨伊利哈姆的出现。回到新加坡后，伊利哈姆惨遭员工背叛，失去和发展商的合作项目。

文本概要：

伦帕德邀请伊利哈姆到巴厘岛参与酒店建设的新项目，条件是他同时必须无偿地在岛上兴建另一所孤儿院。伊力哈姆答应伦帕德的条件，前往巴厘岛并遇见了德薇，两人陷入爱河，引起拉哈尔加的反感。巴厘岛民迷信巫术：德薇的父亲利瓦亚特（Pak Riwayat）脚有顽疾却不相信西医，反而求助于巫师，认为巫师的医术比西医高明，面见巫师时更是讲究各种避讳。拉哈尔加借机对德薇的父亲使用巫术，让利瓦亚特误以为自己的慢性顽疾是因伊利哈姆而起，由于利瓦亚特对巫师深信不疑，因此对伊利哈姆产生负面观感。

回到新加坡后，伊利哈姆仍痴迷于德薇，对任何事都漠不关心，冷落了家庭也忽略了了事业。伊利哈姆和兄弟苏莱曼（Sulaiman）和父亲的关系本已疏离的关系开始恶化，一直到父亲去世后，他才后悔莫及。除此之外，他也失去公司经理珍妮佛（Jennifer）以及员工赛门（Simon）的信任，他们背叛他，跳槽到对手扎曼（Zaman）的公司，使伊利哈姆的联合房地产投资项目以失败告终。与此同时，为了组织员工赛亚西亚（Syamsiah）揭发他不可告人的生意勾当，扎曼精心策划了一场车祸，使赛亚细亚在事故中受伤。

小说尾声，由伊利哈姆负责兴建的孤儿院发生一场爆炸案。案发前，纠缠德薇失败的拉哈尔加遭到村民耻笑，因此对伊利哈姆产生报复之心。媒体在事后报道，爆炸案造成40人死亡，其中包括一名新加坡人，暗示伊利哈姆已遭遇不测。另外，新闻也透露，几名当地青年嫌疑犯被捕，暗示拉哈尔加可能是爆炸案的主谋。

重点与备注：

Selendang Sukma 以巴厘岛为主要场景，聚焦当地文化、地理与历史。小说采用双线叙事，预叙和倒叙夹杂：一方面按伊利哈姆生前的时间线叙述，一方面是按伊利哈姆死后的灵魂回忆过去，叙事结构的复杂使小说情节更加精彩。

作者透过伊利哈姆和德薇的对话，叙述巴厘岛的宗教历史，试图处理巴厘岛的宗教问题。例如：巴厘岛Hindu（兴都教）与印度兴都教之间的区别、伊斯兰教如何传入巴厘岛、巴厘岛原住民历史等。为贴近真实，作者运用大量史料和巴厘岛当地的语言来交代巴厘岛人民的生活、风俗和信仰。作者在书末附上词汇表，为专有名词作注解。

跨宗教、种族之间的互相尊重、互相学习是小说的一大主题。伊利哈姆并不是虔诚的伊斯兰教徒，德薇虽然是一名兴都徒，但出于爱屋及乌的心理，促使她想要更深入了解伊利哈姆的信仰。德薇热衷学习德态度一定程度上鼓舞了伊利哈姆，两人的爱情也就在不断地知性交流下逐渐建立起来。

延续伊斯兰教的主题，作者进一步探讨宗教极端主义。他表示，伊斯兰教从未主张、更不崇尚武力，因此对当今伊斯兰恐怖主义到底从何而来？因此，作者在此邀请读者重新思考导致穆斯林。例如：回教祈祷团头目马士沙拉末（Mas Selamat）等人投向恐怖主义的政治社会环境因素。

潜在的比较文学研究分析：

家庭矛盾、伊斯兰教宗教信仰、巴厘岛兴都教信仰、宗教极端组织（恐怖分子）、巫术、历史记忆、跨文化/跨国恋情

EYE ON THE WORLD

Primary Language: English
Secondary Language: Chinese, local dialects and Malay
Translation Available: No
Number of Pages: 211
Author: Tan Kok Seng
Year of Publication: 1975, republished in 2016
Publisher: Heinemann Asia (Singapore); Epigram Books

Characterisation Notes:

Eye on the World is the third and final autobiography of the author. The book also involves the writer and traveler Austin Coates and his friends.

Text Synopsis:

Tan's final autobiography *Eye on the World* comprises two parts. In the first, Tan narrates his life as a driver for Austin Coates in Hong Kong. In the second, Tan records his travels with Austin Coates in Cambodia, Malaysia, Sri Lanka, Europe and America, and his eventual return to Singapore.

Significance and Remarks:

Tan's last "grown up" autobiography differs from his previous two in his appreciation of self-identity. In *Eye on the World*, Tan Kok Seng travels through various countries with different cultures and languages. This experience heightens his consciousness of class, culture, ethnicity, and nationality. In Hong Kong, Tan apprehends his class identity through his realization that Coates and his friends belong to a privileged and wealthy class very different from himself. In a similar vein, Tan confidently affirms his identity when he describes various cultural encounters and conflicts during his travels. When Tan encounters other "overseas Chinese people" in America, he realizes that "I too am an Overseas Chinese" only to assert that he is a Singaporean and belongs to Singapore.

Potential areas of comparative analysis:

Interracial Communication, International Communication, Traditional vs. Modern values, Elderly Perspectives, Social Commentary, Travelling Writing, Singaporean Identity

EYE ON THE WORLD

主要语言： 英文

次要语言： 零星中文、本土方言、马来文以及外语

翻译版： -

页数： 211

作者： 陈国盛 Tan Kok Seng

出版年份： 1975

出版社： Heinemann Asia (Singapore)

人物简介：

Eye on the World 是陈国盛自传体小说三部曲的最终回，阐述作者于1968年携家带眷移居香港工作，期间和上司高志一起周游列国、放眼世界的宝贵经验。

文本概要：

Eye on the World 由两个部分组成：第一个部分讲述陈国盛再次接受高志的邀请，远赴香港担任他的司机；第二个部分则是陈国盛的游记：他喜获一张环游世界的机票，和高志一同前往柬埔寨、印度尼西亚、马来西亚、斯里兰卡、欧洲（意大利、英国、法国以及葡萄牙等）、美国和加拿大旅行，最后返回新加坡。

重点与备注：

Eye on the World 与作者前两部自传体作品 (Son of Singapore 以及 Man of Malaysia) 的最大不同在于, 在游历世界一圈后，作者对自我身份（self-identity）的认同。陈国盛横跨亚欧美三大洲的旅程使他对文化、阶级、国籍和种族等有了更加深刻地认识。刚抵达香港那阵子，他在上司高志主办的一场晚宴上观察穿着奢华，长得像百万富的社会名流，意识到他们并不来自同样的社会阶层——他是个司机，而对方来自上流社会。同样的，在他描述在欧美等地碰上的文化差异和冲突的同时，也在建立自己的身份认同。旅居美国多年的亚洲朋友说服他到美国工作，但他不以为然。他向朋友解释，国籍并不会改变种族或肤

色，因此在外国人眼中，他跟大多数到海外捞金的华人一样，只不过是华侨（Overseas Chinese），但他可以在新加坡立足，养家糊口。因此他坚定地告诉朋友，自己是新加坡人，属于新加坡，再一次确信地肯定自己的身份。

潜在的比较文学分析：

无产阶级文学、自传体小说研究、跨种族沟通、国际交流、跨国经验、传统与现代价值观、年长者视角、社会评述、旅行文学、新加坡人的身份认同

GENRE, EXPERIMENTAL AND SPECULATIVE FICTION

PONTI

Primary Language: English
Secondary Language: No
Translation Available: No
Number of Pages: 291
Author: Sharlene Teo
Year of Publication: 2018
Publisher: Picador

Characterisation Notes:

The chapters do not follow a chronological sequence. They shuffle between different perspectives of three female protagonists: Szu Min, a 16-year-old who is fatherless and friendless, Circe, a transfer student who later forges an unexpected friendship with Szu, and Amisa Tan Xiaofang, Szu's 45 year old mother who had a short-lived acting career playing the role of a Pontianak in a B-list horror trilogy in the 1970s.

Text Synopsis:

The story begins in the hazy and sweltering heat of Singapore in 2003. Szu finds herself in deep trouble: not only are her grades at the bottom of the bell curve, but her disruptive nature in class also makes her a constant target for public detention. Shunned by all her classmates, Szu does not look forward to school and prays that she will be able to escape unscathed. School becomes more bearable when Szu befriends the transfer student Circe. Their friendship is intense but ephemeral. Circe gradually distances herself from Szu after the latter becomes insufferable after her mother's death (Szu is weighted down by grief after Anisa's death from cancer and stops eating regularly).

The narrative flashes back to the 1970s. Amisa is scouted by Iskandar Wiryanto, an Indonesian visionary film-maker/director and she is invited to play the role of the "Pontianak" in a three-part horror movie. By 24, Amisa had three films (Ponti!, Ponti 2 and Ponti 3: Curse of the Bomoh) to her name. However, the films remain relatively unknown and Amisa is offered no further roles.

The narrative then fast forwards 17 years. Circe is a divorced social media consultant assigned to work on the publicity campaign of *Ponti 2020*—a contemporary remake of the trilogy. The project throws Circe into the past and forces her to confront her relationship with Szu during her agonizing formative years.

As the novel closes, Szu and her husband watch the trailer of *Ponti 2020* on the television, jokingly commenting on how the remake is hate-watch material. Szu then replies to a message from Circe, who writes suggesting that they should catch up with each other.

Significance and Remarks:

The opening sentence of the novel sets its tone: "Today marks my sixteenth year on this hot, horrible earth." In the novel, Szu negotiates forlornness and emotional deprivation both at home and in school.

Everything is out of control from the very start. At home, Szu's arrival was a "happy accident" to her parents, who "never needed or wanted a child." In school, classmates pretend she does not exist.

Underneath Szu's ostentatious behaviour (for instance, being talkative in class) lies an intense longing to be heard, felt and understood. In the novel, Szu invites Circe home as a substitute for her lack of familial love.

Much of the novel centers around the image of the Pontianak, a vengeful vampire which seduces hapless men according to South-East Asian Mythology. In her career, Amisa plays the role of Ponti, a congenitally deformed girl who makes a deal with a witch doctor for beauty in exchange for a constant desire for male blood.

The image of the Pontianak in *Ponti* is a metaphorical representation of the enervating presence of hurt, grief, unfulfilled dreams and regret. Failing to gain fame or fortune, Amisa, to some extent, becomes the "Pontianak" of her daughter's life. Even during her final days, Amisa continues to affect Szu "more than any of the taunting girls at school." Amisa's death also turns Szu into another Pontianak towards Circe, who describes the former as "sarin gas, leaked poison" that she cannot block out; it was as if Circe was "carrying around a heavy, sloshing bucket of water."

What is also notable about *Ponti* is Teo's palpable employment of descriptive and affective language, and her peculiar usage of literary devices.

In one scenario, the century egg which is served during her birthday meal is cured for 10 days till it "looks like an alien embryo preserved in rotten jelly." In another, Teo describes her classroom as one of "impulse deodorant and soiled sanitary pads"; in a third scenario, the perspiration resulting from a heat-up building makes their blouses "translucent as onion peels" The novel is also enveloped in an intolerable humidity in which "the past rises up like the heat pimples that itch along the scalloped neckline of my top." In all, Teo successfully creates a nauseating and suffocating atmosphere by overloading the reader with grotesque sensory experiences.

Set against the backdrop of a convent school, Teo's coming-of-age debut depicts the reality faced by less well-off students. The author juxtaposes the image of a "prim and proper" young lady with the violence inflicted upon teenage girls—the less well-off students often have to grapple with campus bullying and many end up chopped up and trampled upon like "minced meat."

The final chapter echoes the beginning of the novel as Szu laments, "so it's a hot, horrible earth we are stuck on and it's only getting worse." However, while the "dreadful" world remains the same, Szu's loving husband Ben and daughter Elizabeth more than make up for the lack of familial love in her childhood.

Potential areas of comparative analysis:

Female bildungsroman, Nostalgia, Grief, Intergenerational tension, Love/ Loss, Desire/Obsession, Female Friendship, Campus Violence/School Bullying

PONTI

主要语言： 英文
次要语言： -
翻译版本： -
页数： 291
作者： Sharlene Teo
出版年份： 2018
出版社： London: Picador

人物简介：

小说章节不按时间顺序排列，它们分别在3名女主角的视角之间转换，她们分别是：16岁、无父无友的的思敏（Szu Min），转校生瑟茜（Circe）（后和思敏成为意想不到的好友），以及思敏的45岁的母亲阿米萨（Amisa Tan Xiaofang）。她曾在1970年代的二流恐怖片三部曲当中扮演马来女鬼（Pontianak）一角，拥有过短暂的演艺生涯。

文本概要：

2003年，故事在烟雾弥漫、闷热的新加坡展开。思敏发现自己深陷巨大麻烦之中——不仅学习成绩差强人意，在钟形曲线（bell curve）的分布末端，她也喜欢在课堂上吵吵嚷嚷的捣乱个性也使她成为老师们的眼中钉，次次被罚留堂（public detention）。在学校，所有同学都躲避她。她不期待上学，并祈祷自己能安然无恙地度过校园生活。

思敏的生活在结识转校生瑟茜后开始有了转变，上学对她而言不再那么难受。然而她和瑟茜浓烈、真挚的友谊的寿命却十分短暂。思敏在母亲患癌过世后，不仅迟迟无法走出伤痛，也不再按时吃饭。瑟茜觉得思敏变得难以忍受 ，渐渐地疏远她。

小说回到1970年代，阿米萨被印尼电影制作人/导演伊斯坎达 (Iskandar Wiryanto) 看中，受邀扮演马来女鬼一角，参与惊悚恐怖片三部曲的拍摄。阿米萨在24岁时完成了电影三部曲("Ponti!"、"Ponti 2"以及"Ponti 3: Curse of the Bomoh")的拍摄，然而，她的作品并没有引起关注，而她再也没有接到新的角色，短暂的演艺生涯嘎然而止。

时间快转来到2020年，离异的瑟茜是名社交媒体顾问，负责电影“Ponti 2020”（即当年三部曲的现代改编版本）的宣传活动。她陷入深沉的回忆，迫使她面对、在青少年时期和思敏之间的关系。小说结尾，思敏和丈夫在电视机前看到电影的预告片，开玩笑地评论改编版的电影内容虽不值得一看，但他们还是会为了嘲笑或批评它忍不住观赏（hate-watch）。同时，思敏收到瑟茜的简讯，后者提出叙旧的建议，思敏也欣然接受。

重点与备注：

“今天是我生活在这个炎热、可怕的世界的第16个年头”，小说开头第一句话就为小说定调。思敏的人生从一开始就失去了控制：在家中，思敏是个“幸福的意外”(happy accident)，她的父母“从来不需要也不想要一个孩子”(“never needed or wanted a child”)。在学校，同学躲避她，假装她从来不存在。思敏是个长期情感匮乏的孩子，不论是在家中或者在学校，她都努力、设法地和孤苦无依相处。而在她那惹人注目的行为（例如：在上课时故意说话，影响同学）下，隐藏着一颗强烈渴望倾听、渴望爱、渴望被理解的心。瑟茜的出现，某种程度替代她的父母，弥补了她情感上的缺失。

马来女鬼（Pontianak）的影子在小说中挥之不去，根据东南亚传说，她是个怨气极重、专门勾引无助男性的吸血鬼。而在小说中，阿米萨在她的演艺生涯中扮演“Ponti”，这一角色先天畸形、有缺陷，她恳求巫医赐予她美貌，然而，美丽需要付出代价——她必须持续不断吸男性的鲜血以维持妖艳的面貌。

小说中马来女鬼的形象隐喻着那使人无力、绝望的伤痛、遗憾以及未完成的梦想。阿米萨的作品未能让她名利双收，在事业上郁郁不得志的她某种程度变成了思敏生命中的女鬼。一直到临终之际，她的存在给女儿造成的困扰远超过学校中任何一个、嘲讽思敏的女同学。随后，阿米萨的死将思敏变成另一个女鬼，不断地困扰瑟茜。后者形容她为无法阻挡的“沙林毒气、泄漏的毒药”，并认为和思敏的关系就像“随身携带一桶沉重、哗啦哗啦翻动的水”。

另一值得注意的是，作者强而有力的情感描述，以及她独特的文学手法（literary device）。例如，在为她庆生的桥段中，作者把餐桌上那腌制了10天的皮蛋比喻成“保存在腐烂果冻中的外星人胚胎”。另外，作者认为那炎热的教室就像“不小心喷了太多的除臭剂和肮脏的卫生棉”的结合，汗水使她们的校服像“洋葱皮一样半透明”。小说也笼罩在一股难以忍受的潮湿中，对瑟茜而言，往事像“因上火而沿着上衣领口扩散开来的痘痘，令人浑身发痒”。作者透过可怖的感官经验，成功营造了令人难以负荷的窒息氛围。

Ponti是作者的首部作品，以修道院女校为背景，反映经济条件较差的学生在成长过程中的现实处境。女校生理应循规蹈矩、表现得体，然而她们对条件较差的同学施加暴力，使她们成为校园霸凌的受害者，像砧板上的肉碎任人践踏。

小说前后呼应，在最后一章，思敏感叹："我们被困在这个炎热、可怕的世界，而且情况只会越来越糟"，然而，尽管世界依旧糟透，但不同的是，思敏拥有疼爱她的丈夫和女儿伊丽莎白，足以弥补她童年缺乏家庭关爱的遗憾。

潜在的比较文学分析：

女性成长小说、怀旧、悲伤、代际冲突、爱与失去、欲望与迷恋、女性友谊、校园欺凌和校园暴力

THE BLACK ISLE

Primary Language: English
Secondary Language: Some Malay and Mandarin
Translation Available: No
Number of Pages: 472
Author: Sandi Tan
Year of Publication: 2012
Publisher: New York: Grand Central Publishing

Characterisation Notes:

The protagonist, Cassandra, is a woman gifted with the ability to see ghosts (both figuratively and literally) everywhere she goes.

Text Synopsis:

The Black Isle tells the tale of a tragic heroine who struggles to make the right choices during tumultuous times in Singapore's history, in particular during the Japanese occupation and then the period of rapid urbanization cum industrialization following its attainment of independence. As the novel begins, a young Cassandra leaves her home in Shanghai with her father and twin brother in search of a better future. She arrives at the mysterious Black Isle and discovers that the island is home to many immigrants, both living and dead. Driven by loneliness and her desire for freedom, Cassandra bargains with the dead and attains political clout among the island inhabitants. With her power, Cassandra radically transforms the island from a jungle slum into an urbanized city. However, the ghosts of the past refuse to be silenced by modernization and come knocking on Cassandra's front door. Cassandra is forced to confront the horrors caused by her choices and faces the challenge of how she can put "living" ghosts to rest.

Significance and Remarks:

The Black Isle highlights the discrepancies between official Singaporean history and its alternate narratives. The novel presents an alternate perspective on historical events such as the communist threat during the 1950s and 1960s. However, the author immediately destabilizes the narrative: in the novel, the protagonist is the only source of history, but she is shown to be unreliable for she has a flawed personality and an imperfect memory. The novel also demonstrates that Singapore's successes come with sacrifices such as the loss of history and tradition. In the novel, the past come to live as roaming ghosts who actively assert their presence—just like how alternate, perhaps fictional, accounts of the Singapore story demand to be heard.

Potential areas of comparative analysis:

Singapore Story, History of Singapore, Traditional vs. Modern values, Elderly Perspectives, Kampong, Supernatural Elements, Family / Domestic Life, Second World War, Feminism, Alternate Narratives

THE BLACK ISLE

主要语言： 英文
次要语言： 少许马来文以及中文
翻译版本： -
页数： 472
作者： Sandi Tan
出版年份： 2012
出版社： New York: Grand Central Publishing

人物简介：

女主人翁卡珊德拉（Cassandra）天生拥有一双阴阳眼，不论走到哪里，她都能通灵、确实看到超自然现象的存在。另外，她的过去也像形象化（figuratively）的“鬼魂”不断纠缠着她。

文本概要：

卡珊德拉是个带有悲剧色彩的女主角：小说阐述她在日军占领新加坡、以及随后的快速现代化发展这两段历史上最为黑暗、动荡的时期，努力做出正确决定的经历。为追求更美好的未来，卡珊德拉随同父亲以及双胞胎弟弟一起离开上海，来到神秘的黑岛（The Black Isle）。不少移民聚集在此，但卡珊德拉同时也发现黑岛夺走了不少移民的性命。在内心的孤独以及对自由的渴望的驱使下，卡珊德拉借助天赋和岛上的灵魂交涉、谈判，并从岛上居民中收获了政治影响力。她凭借这股能量将杂乱、贫困的岛屿彻底转变成现代化的城市。然而，过去始终阴魂不散，卡珊德拉被迫正视、并战胜内心的恐惧。

重点与备注：

小说凸显了新加坡官方历史和另类叙事（alternate narrative）之间的落差，举例而言，作者从另一个角度阐述了新加坡于1950以及1960年代所经历的共产主义威胁等历史事件。卡珊德拉是小说中是历史的唯一叙述者，然她的记忆和性格充满缺陷，某种程度上动摇了叙事的可靠性。除此之外，文本也表明，为成功和进步，新加坡选择牺牲历史和放弃对传统的坚守。然过去和历史就像漫无目的游荡在外的幽灵，它们不间断地宣誓自己的存在，就如同新加坡的另类叙事（或许是虚构的）强烈地要求读者倾听他们的故事一样。

潜在的比较文学分析：

新加坡故事、新加坡历史、传统和现代价值观、年长者视角、甘榜故事、超自然元素、家庭/家庭生活、第二次世界大战、女性主义、另类叙事

孕鱼 (FISH BIRTH)

Primary Language: Mandarin

Secondary Language: None

Translation Available: No

Number of Pages: 187

Author: Sui Ting

Year of Publication: 2019

Publisher: City Book Room

Characterisation Notes:

Fish Birth is a collection of eight short stories. The stories collectively capture the pervasive ennui, loneliness and hardships of urban life and relationships. Except for the first story "*Lao Dian* (Old Shop)," all stories in the collection are mainly focalised through a female perspective: notably, five of the short stories feature female protagonists who are either unnamed or possess made-up names.

Text Synopsis:

Fish Birth is centered around the ineffable loneliness of urban life: old and forgotten shophouses, women who work far from home, depressed and overworked fathers, mothers who prostitute themselves for their children, the third wheel in a marriage, the feeling of emptiness after a breakup. The protagonists are lonely, anxious, indignant, and eager to find a way out of their loneliness.

"*Lao Dian*" (Old Shop)

Lao Xiao has been running his barber shop for 59 years. Unable to keep up with the times, Lao Xiao is forced to terminate his business. Right before he shutters his shop, however, Lao Xiao is afflicted by a strange illness which causes him to talk to himself as if he were a deceased person, such as his late wife. The neighbours believe Lao Xiao to be possessed, whereas the doctors diagnose him with dementia. Lao Xiao's son, Xiao Xiao, thinks otherwise: he believes that his father has the "sickness of being detached from reality" as a result of his nostalgia and his inability to keep up with modern life. At the end of the story, Xiao Xiao arranges an exorcism for his father to banish the "spirits of the past" but also acknowledges and engages with the past by way of inviting neighbours to bear witness to Lao Xiao's ramblings of days gone after and by keeping artefacts from the barber shop in their family home. At the sight of the artefacts in his room, Lao Xiao snaps back to reality and is freed from his strange illness. From then on, Lao Xiao no longer speaks gibberish.

"*Yun Yu*" (Fish Birth)

The protagonist Angel is shipwrecked while on vacation. To survive while adrift at sea, she eats a black fish whole on a whim and discovers herself mysteriously pregnant soon after. The androgynous foetus which Angel believes to be the black fish trashes violently in her womb and can only be pacified when Angel sits in a bathtub filled with water. As Angel's body starts to change over the course of her pregnancy, she grows increasingly alienated from her own body: the presence of the strange foetus takes up primacy in her experience of her body, her memory starts to fail, her eyes become pale like that of a fish, and she becomes mute. At the end, Angel gives birth to an unknown eldritch body and finds herself completely transformed into a fish.

"*Yan Kuang*" (Eye Socket)

The nameless protagonist is afflicted by a strange condition which renders her body exceedingly dry. She is unable to perspire, and also loses her ability to reach orgasm and her sexual desire wanes as a result. Drained of desire and a corresponding zeal for life, the men in the protagonist's life lose interest in her, the exception being the earnest driver of her daily shuttle to work who strikes up a shaky relationship with her. Despite the driver's attempts to court her, the protagonist remains dispassionate and listless due to her affliction until a chance encounter with a vigorously urinating male horse in a cemetery. Thereafter, the protagonist's bodily functions are restored—a soothing and unceasing pleasure spreads throughout her body, her eyes become filled with tears and it is as if her passionless heart had been cured in that instant. Later, when the protagonist once again meets with the driver, weeping with joy, she directs him to identify her eye sockets as the sexiest part of her body.

"*Liu Ying*" (Homeless Canaries—an euphemism for "streetwalker" prostitutes)

Shen Guifang is a single mother of two. After her husband's incarceration, Shen struggles to make ends meet and resorts to covert sexual services for money. Though tiring of her bleak life and the drudgery of her work as a sex worker, Shen soldiers on, drawing determination from her husband's pre-incarceration instruction for her to fulfil her maternal duty to raise her sons. Without a clear end to her maternal duties and confronted with her sons' increasingly unreasonable demands for money to fund their marriage and education, Shen is gradually driven to desperation and unbearable anguish.

Shen's agony ultimately reaches a peak when she is confronted with the threat of fines when the police conduct an unannounced sweep of brothel premises, leading her to demarcate an end to her duty by leaping out of a window.

"*Li Kai Ni*" (Leaving You)

The nameless protagonist is a romantic. She leaves her cheating boyfriend but is unable to live independently and away from the spectre of their relationship. Haunted by past memories of their time together as she goes about her life, the protagonist surrenders to her longing for companionship and contacts her ex-boyfriend again. They have sex, which distracts her momentarily from her loneliness and persistent sense of emptiness. However, upon waking some hours later, the protagonist finds that she is disgusted by her actions and by her inability to conclusively leave her ex-boyfriend.

"*Chan Xiu Qi Ri*" (Seven Days of Meditation)

The nameless protagonist is the third party in an affair with a married man. The unexpected appearance of the wife while the protagonist is abroad with him in Chiang Mai leaves her with time on her hand. She decides to enter a Zen Buddhist monastery to engage in seven days of meditation in a bid to find peace. The protagonist follows the instructions and lessons of the abbot and finds a degree of serenity in her life. However, at the close of the sixth day, the protagonist's sojourn is interrupted by a text from her lover, and she ultimately chooses to leave behind the promise of peace and meaning at the monastery in favour of returning to her lover's arms.

"*Gai Tou Huan Mian De Na Yi Tian*" (the day she reinvented herself)

As the curious and befuddled masses attempt to explain a politician's mysteriously vandalised official portrait, the protagonist Zhuang Zhuang, who is studying abroad, attempts to find renewed meaning in her life upon her realisation that her relationship with her boyfriend has grown cold while other aspects of her life appear to be equally insipid. During an attempt to revitalise her love life by going on a blind date, Zhuang Zhuang receives a call from her mother informing her of her father's death, which then spurs her to make immediate arrangements to return home. While at the airport awaiting her flight, Zhuang Zhuang's mother calls again to tell her that it was a false alarm and that her father is merely ill. Relieved of her immediate directive to return home, Zhuang Zhuang again feels lost and directionless. Desiring to find meaning, Zhuang Zhuang follows her impulse to re-route her flight to see the politician's vandalised portrait.

"*Qiu Chan*" (Autumn Cicadas)

A mysterious woman abducts Zhuang Dashu's son during a class gathering. Zhuang investigates his son's disappearance and realises that the mysterious woman is his ex-lover Shen Xinjing. Visiting Shen's ex-cellmate in prison, Zhuang learns of the tragic life of Shen following their breakup, including her forced marriage to a divorced policeman in Beijing who was abusive to her.

Significance and Remarks:

The author Sui Ting (a pseudonym for He Ying Shu) is a Chinese emigrant to Singapore. Born in Hunan, China, she traveled to Singapore at age fifteen to pursue her education. Yun Yu, her first collection, features two award-winning stories. The eponymous "*Yun Yu*" (Fish Birth) won first prize in the 2015 Golden Point Award competition. "*Lao Dian*" (Old Shop) won first prize in the 2015 Singapore Tertiary Chinese Literature award competition. In addition, *Fish Birth* was also shortlisted for the 2020 Singapore Literature Prize (Chinese Fiction Category).

The author has a vivid imagination: her speculative stories capture the fantastical elements of life and yet remain realistic and faithful to daily experience. For instance, in the titular "*Yun Yu*" (Fish Birth), the strangeness of the protagonist inexplicably becoming pregnant upon ingesting a fish is undergirded by the emotional realism of a woman negotiating a changing relationship with her own body during pregnancy. The author masterfully interweaves realistic and speculative storytelling to highlight the dissonance and alienation of life.

Sui Ting is especially adept in her characterization of women—her female characters can be seen as embodied fables that depict the varied (emotional) conditions of womanhood. In the story "*Yan Kuang* (Eye Socket)," the protagonist is afflicted by a condition (the condition is correlated with her emigration to a foreign country) that dries up all her orifices from her eye sockets to her vagina and has to rediscover her way to desire and pleasure. Her physical condition is representative of her arid love life; her encounter with the enormous phallus of a horse at a cemetery and the subsequent nourishment of her body symbolizes her immensely repressed desire for sex and love. In other stories such as "*Liu Ying*", motherhood and a woman's perceived duty to her children are explored.

Love is also a prominent focus across the stories. In "*Li Kai Ni* (Leaving You)," the author adopts a "stream of consciousness" style to explore the vacillations of the mind of a broken-hearted girl. The unnamed protagonist attempts to exercise her agency and rebuild an independent life after her breakup. However, she is unable to fully relinquish her desire for her ex-boyfriend and returns to him despite her self-loathing.

In contrast to the richness of the female characters, the novel's male characters appear one dimensional. The shopkeeper in "*Lao Dian*" (Old Shop) is an ardent traditionalist who is alienated by modernity and progress; Zhuang Dashu in "*Qiu Chan*" (Cicadas in Autumn) has low self-esteem and his failings in his career and relationships result in depression and self-harm. Both male characters live tragic, deterministic lives.

Collectively, the stories in the collection suggest that loneliness does not belong to any one person—the reader may find echoes of themselves in the author's nameless characters. The author observes and pens, with great sensitivity and detail, the helplessness and disappointment of people left behind and forgotten by urban modernity, and of those troubled by the ennui of modern life.

Potential areas of comparative analysis:

Gender Studies, Diaspora Studies, Sexuality and Sexual Desire, Feminism, Tradition vs Modernity, New Migrant Literature

孕鱼

主要语言： 中文
次要语言： -
翻译版： -
页数： 187
作者： 随庭（本名：何颖舒）
出版年份： 2019
出版社： 城市书房

人物简介：

《孕鱼》是一本短篇小说集，作者在8篇作品中共同捕捉了都市生活和人际关系中普遍存在的苦闷、孤寂和艰辛；作者也尤其关注女性：除《老店》外，其余7篇均从女性视角出发。值得注意的是，其中5篇的女主人翁以化名或匿名的形式出现。

文本概要：

《孕鱼》围绕城市人不可言传的孤寂展开：被时代抛弃的老店、在异国他乡打拼的女子、患有重度抑郁的全职奶爸、为两名儿子卖身的母亲、婚姻中的第三者、空虚的失恋女子。随庭笔下的主人翁孤独、彷徨与无奈，迷惘的心急需找到出口，终结苦闷。

〈老店〉

走过59年历史的理发店因墨守成规不得不结业，店主老萧在休业前突然得了一场怪病——他自言自语，仿佛在代替故人（比方说，他的妻子）说话。邻居看到这一幕后妄言他被附了身、医生诊断他患有老年痴呆症、儿子小萧则认为父亲眷恋过往，跟不上现代化城市的步伐，将他的情况归结为“与现实背道而驰的病”。最后，小萧为父亲办了一场驱魔仪式，为父亲驱走身上的故人：当天，他邀请街坊邻居见证理发店的过去和倾听老萧最后的念叨。仪式结束后，小萧将理发店的旧物品搬回家中。老萧自此不再疯言疯语。

〈孕鱼〉

安琪（Angel）在一次旅行中遭遇海难，她在海上漂流时慌乱地生食一尾黑鱼，不久后她发现自己神迷地怀孕了。那看不清性别的“胎儿”（她认为是那条她生吞地黑鱼）在安琪腹中不断翻腾，唯有当安琪将自己浸泡在浴缸内才能得到安抚。安琪的身体在孕期间开始发生变化，逐渐地失控：腹中怪异的“胎儿”将她的身体占为己有，安琪的记忆开始衰退、眼珠和鱼珠一样泛白、唇舌发不出声，安琪最后在浴缸产下一尾模糊、骇人的躯体，而安琪也仿佛异化成一尾鱼。

〈眼眶〉

匿名女主人翁“她”的身体异常般干燥，不仅无法排汗，也失去性欲、达不到性高潮。她失去欲望，也相应地对生活失去热忱，她身边的男人对她失去兴趣，唯有每天接送她上下班的老实司机尝试追求她，和她产生联系，但由于长期以来她的身体异常干燥，感受不到湿润，她对对方的热忱始终感到无动于衷。一直到她碰到一匹撒尿的公马，她的身体才发生巨大变化——汩汩不断的快感和愉悦散布全身，她枯竭的身体终于拥有湿润的眼眶，仿佛瞬间治愈了她干涸的心。当女主角再次和司机相遇时，她热泪盈眶告诉他，眼眶是她身上最性感的部位。

〈流莺〉

丈夫入狱后，为养大两名儿子，沈桂芳省吃俭用，甚至悄悄提供廉价的性服务。沈桂方厌倦了暗淡和乏味的性工作者生活，但每当想起丈夫在入狱对她的嘱咐，她还是坚持下来，父兼母职，履行抚养儿子长大成人的义务。可是，没有人告诉沈桂方，儿子要养到哪一天才算成人了，她的任务也就完成了。面对儿子为娶妻和升学伸手向她要钱，她逐渐陷入绝望、饱受煎熬。一日，警察突击扫黄，面对巨额罚款，她痛苦万分，爬上栏杆，一跃而下，结束身为人母的职责。

〈离开你〉

匿名的女主角是名多情女子。她以为分手后能忘记出轨的前男友，活得独立自主，却走不出失恋的阴影。和前男友过去的记忆不断折磨着她，她渴望他的陪伴，主动联系对方。两人发生关系，短暂地从孤寂和空虚中抽离开来。数小时过后，女主角醒来，发现自己无法离开前男友，为自己的行为感到厌恶。

〈禅修七日〉

匿名的她是婚姻中的第三者。她和情人原打算在清迈共度二人时光，却不想情人的太太也在当地。独自一人的“她”走进清迈的一间禅宗寺庙禅修七日，以寻求宁静。禅修期间，“她”聆听禅师讲课，遵照指示每日慢走和静坐修行，某种程度上给生活找回了宁静。然而，在禅修第六天时，情人的一封简讯打断了“她”的片刻宁静，而“她”也选择舍弃在寺庙寻找平静和意义，回到情人的怀里。

〈改头换面的那一天〉

国家领导人的官方照片一夜间遭恶意破坏，被换成了猴子，引起好奇、困惑的网民各种猜测和分析。与此同时，在国外念书的“壮壮”觉得生活和男友维持的远距离恋爱一样枯燥乏味，因此开始寻找新的生活意义。经由好友介绍，“壮壮”在国外相亲，试图使她的感情生活重获新生，却在此时接到母亲的紧急来电，告知她父亲离世的消息，“壮壮”立即安排回国。在机场等待班机起飞时，她再次接到母亲的来电，告知她父亲只是病了，刚刚不过是虚惊一场。“壮壮”放下沉重的心情，再一次感到迷失方向。渴望找寻意义的她，心血来潮地走向机场柜台更改机票，决定亲眼看一眼被恶意破坏的领导人头像。

〈秋蝉〉

庄大树的儿子庄明明在同学聚会上被面容可怖的神秘女子拐走。他独自一人追查线索，从大学门口、医院、监狱到公司，试图追踪儿子失踪的经过，发现拐走儿子的女子竟是他的初恋情人沈心经。庄大树到监狱找寻线索，从心经前狱友的口中得知，心经在他们两人分手后到了北京，被迫嫁给了一名离异警察，婚后惨遭家暴。

重点与备注：

随庭生于中国湖南，15岁到新加坡求学，《孕鱼》是她的第一本创作集结，其中同名短文〈孕鱼〉和〈老店〉在2015年分别荣获金笔奖中文小说组首奖和新加坡大专文学奖小说组首奖。小说集也入围2020年新加坡文学奖（中文小说组）。

作者丰富的想象力使作品贴近现实之余也同时洋溢超现实色彩，同名短文〈孕鱼〉是为一例：安琪吞下一尾鱼后腹部莫名隆起，身体承受着诡异的孕期反应和变化，而作者对安琪在孕期间、写实的情绪描写（Emotional Realism）也一同构成了安琪的奇幻色彩。在现实和虚幻之间交错，作者虚实相应的手法强调他乡女子脱缰失序的生活状态。

随庭尤其擅长塑造多面的女性形象，她以女性为中心，通过身体寓言展现其情欲的多元面貌。　在〈眼眶〉中，异乡生活榨干"她"体内的水分，导致她全身（从眼眶至阴道）异常干燥，以致于她必须重新寻找获得欲望和欢愉的方式。"她"干涸的身体是重要的意象，作者先借此表达"她"苍白、贫瘠的情感生活，再安排"她"目睹一匹在撒尿的公马的桥段，那巨大的生殖器瞬间唤醒并滋润"她"干枯的日子，揭示"她"对爱的强烈渴望和极度被压抑的情欲。在其他的故事，例如"流莺"当中，作者也探索了如身为人母激起母亲对子女的责任的主题。

爱情也是作者小说中的一个核心主题。在〈离开你〉中，作者以意识流的手法描绘失恋女子迂回的内心——"她"在分手后试图建构以自我为中心的生活、掌握生活的主导权，但她始终放不下对前男友的渴望，一边自我厌恶、一边主动回到他的怀抱。

相较之下，故事中男主人翁的形象建构单一：〈老店〉中的店主坚守传统手艺，在现代化发展中显得格格不入，不得不结业。而〈秋蝉〉中的庄大树事业不顺心，加上抗压能力弱，几度自残后重度忧郁，两人的生活无奈、充满悲情。

整体而言，小说集意味着，孤寂并不专属于谁，就像作者选择以匿名的"她"或"他"呈现人物的空虚一般，读者或许可以在书中找到自己的影子，产生共鸣。随庭细腻且敏感地观察和书写被时代淘汰，被城市遗忘在一隅的人，那些关于失落的、无助的，和对现代生活感到倦怠后的忧虑。

潜在的比较文学分析：

性别研究、离散文学研究、性和情欲、女性主义、传统与现代、新移民文学

MENARA THE TOWER

Primary Language: Malay

Secondary Language: No

Translation Available: The Tower

Number of Pages: 153

Author: Isa Kamari

Year of Publication: 2002

Publisher: Pustaka Nasional

Characterisation Notes:

The novel's protagonist, an ailing engineer, is unnamed throughout. Since young, the protagonist displays an uncanny talent in architecture as well as a rebellious spirit that manifests in his distrust of his teachers. He is also plagued by recurring nightmares that may have inspired his architectural vision and enabled his success. Ilham is the protagonist's secretary who doubles as a facilitator and moderator of the protagonist's views and recollections.

Text Synopsis:

The novel delineates a series of exchanges between Ilham and the protagonist as the two ascend a tower designed by the latter on the eve of the new millennium. The protagonist recalls and reflects upon his life as a spiritual journey as he struggles physically to reach the top of the tower. He is tormented by dark and fragmented memories which surface in the form of veiled fables. The dialogue covers among other things Ilham's and the protagonist's views on life, religion and spirituality.

Significance and Remarks:

Menara can be read as a fable which depicts the search for spirituality in a materialistic world. The title "Menara" can be read to mean any tall building, or more specifically as a religiously symbolic tower that sits atop a mosque.

The novel has a very complex structure. Like a tree, the novel is supported by a main narrative which then branches into smaller stories. These stories are often improvised and "localized" by their narrators. The protagonist alludes to contemporary problems, sometimes jokingly, in a manner that fuses reality and fiction.

The novel's main narrative traces the protagonist's physical journey upward, and the parallel development of his philosophical self-awareness and transcendence. The author interjects this vertical and linear narrative with fables that introduces new characters, environments, and moral dilemmas. While some of these fables directly expound upon the themes of the main narrative, others seem obscure and difficult to grasp. Nevertheless, these obscurities prompt the reader to reflect upon the author's intentions.

Interestingly, Isa Kamari uses the storytelling strategy of polyphony. The bulk of the novel comprises the thematically diverse dialogues between the protagonist and Ilham—they discuss philosophy, spirituality, and even the nature of creation. In addition, the narrative is interspersed with many obscure and yet highly allegorical poems and songs to create a unique reading experience.

While these poems disrupt the flow of the narrative, they represent the protagonist's post-enlightenment state of mind: the novel vacillates between a calm and a passionate tone to mimic the protagonist's fragmented mind. At the same time, the poems remind the reader that existence is varied, many-sided, and multifaceted.

Potential areas of comparative analysis:

Religion, Spirituality, Life Philosophy, Existentialism, Self-Knowledge, Self-Realization, Transcendence and Epiphany

MENARA

主要语言： 马来文

次要语言： -

翻译版本： The Tower

页数： 153

作者： 伊沙 · 卡马里（Isa Kamari）

出版年份： 2002

出版社： Pustaka Nasional

人物简介：

匿名的主角是名成功的建筑师。他自小展现建筑天赋，常挑战老师的权威，是大人眼中叛逆的异类。他常年被噩梦困扰，从梦境中，他得到创作、设计的灵感和启发，奠定他走向成功的基础。伊利哈姆（Ilham）作为建筑师的秘书，在小说中扮演倾听者的角色，陪同他一层层爬上摩天大楼顶端，也频频向建筑师发问。小说便从两人的对话打开。

文本概要：

在千禧年来临之际，身患重病的匿名建筑师和伊利哈姆挣扎着登上他的最新力作——一座高200层的摩天大楼。在向伊利哈姆叙述人生经历的同时，过去不堪的回忆不断折磨他。作者将他的记忆编织成一系列隐晦、深奥的寓言，反映破碎以及矛盾的精神状态，也以对话的形式探讨成功、宗教、心灵、生命价值等命题。

重点与备注：

"Menara"是部寓言故事，讲述人们在物欲横流的世界里对精神追求的渴望。马来语书名"Menara"可以泛指任何一座高大的建筑结构，也可以具体指向清真寺的尖塔。

表面上，它是个简单的寓言故事，可其结构却犹如大树一般异常复杂：小说除了一个主干故事外，中间穿插许多类似树枝的分支故事。叙述者在分支故事即兴创作，使人物和情境本土化，并开玩笑似的对当代社会问题提出疑问，叙事在现实与虚幻之间交织、转换。

小说由两条故事线构成：主角和伊利哈姆攀登大楼的过程为其一，两人以哲学的角度阐发不同层次的自我认识和自我超越的平行旅程为其二。在这条垂直向上的道路上，小说用各种寓言引入新的人物、环境和道德窘境。分支故事和主干故事的连接或显而易见或隐晦深远，然而，正式因为难以捉摸，才能迫使刺激读者反复阅读并深思作者的叙事意图。

有趣的是，作者使用复调（polyphony）的叙事策略。小说大部分由两人的对话形式展开，其中包括对哲学、灵性和创造力的本质等主题的探索。另外，作者在小说穿插大量晦涩难懂、充满隐喻的的诗歌，使读者不瞬间转换阅读模式。虽然这些诗歌的插入可能会打断叙述的流畅，但它们代表了作者顿悟后的状态。作者的声音，人物的声音，在平淡和抒情的音域之间转换，作者通过这些声音，成功地说明了主人公破碎的心理，同时提醒读者现实本身的偶然性和多样性。

潜在的比较文学分析：

宗教信仰、心灵哲学、人生哲学思考、生命价值与意义、存在主义、自我认识、自我超越

TRIVIALITIES ABOUT ME AND MYSELF

Primary Language: Mandarin

Secondary Language: No

Translation Available: Yes

Number of Pages: 248

Author: Yeng Pway Ngon

Year of Publication: 2006

Publisher: Tonsan Books

Characterisation Notes:

The protagonist Ah-hui is a journalist turned entrepreneur. He possesses two split personalities—"Me" and "Myself." "Me" and "Myself" are indistinguishable in Ah-hui's childhood, but their moral values diverge in his adulthood. "Myself" is satisfied with a simple and honest life whereas "Me" is obsessed with wealth and consumed by excessive sexual desires. "Me" jeopardizes Ah-hui's business, marriage and his relationship with his son. In his final days, "Me" regrets abandoning "Myself" and seeks forgiveness by writing him letters longing for his return.

Text Synopsis:

Trivialities About Me and Myself traces the life story of Ah-hui's split personalities—"Me" and "Myself"—in three different sections that span Ah-hui's childhood to his twilight days.

In the first section, Ah-hui narrates the clash of differing world-views between "Me" and "Myself" that eventually led to the banishment of the latter. In Ah-hui's childhood, his different personalities exist harmoniously in the same body. At the onset of puberty, however, the personalities start to have minor disagreements, and "Me" soon yearns for another person besides "Myself" to confide in.

The ideological conflict between "Me" and "Myself" escalates as Ah-hui decides (and later regrets) to major in Chinese studies at the university.

"Myself" is an idealistic and spiritual introvert with a holier-than-thou attitude. He yearns to devote himself completely to education and is oblivious to materialistic goals or profit. In contrast, "Me" is realistic and sees the university degree as an instrument to secure a well-paying job. "Me" had witnessed firsthand his parents' constant quarrels over money and is adamant that he must free himself of penury and experience the finer things in life. Both personalities achieve a compromise in the attainment of a job as a journalist in a Chinese newspaper.

In the workforce, conflicts between "Me" and "Myself" further intensifies. "Myself" believes that it is imperative for a journalist to have a mind of his own and to always speak nothing but the truth. In contrast, "Me" starts to curry favor with the wealthy and influential to advance his career. The self-righteous "Myself" suffocates "Me" with his impractical and tyrannical moral strictures and threatens to impede the latter's career. In response, "Me" confronts "Myself" and makes a clean break with him.

"Me" is released from moral strictures and is uninhibited in his pursuit of desire satisfaction. He climbs the corporate ladder and begins to mingle with upper-class elites. He later marries Jieyi, a rich man's daughter determined to establish her worth by starting her own advertising agency. Without a moral compass, "Me" leads an opulent life and embarks on dalliances with other women, including Jieyi's personal assistant Lily. As a result, his marriage ends in divorce.

Jieyi moves overseas and hands the agency over to Lily. "Me" quits his job as a journalist and joins her in expanding their agency. Obsessed with fame and reputation, he donates to numerous cultural and academic organizations, who in turn lionize him as a "confucian businessman".

"Me" diversifies his business empire and establishes franchises in the food and beverage industry and even opens a realty brokerage. However, cash flow issues resulting from the 1997 recession sends his business spiraling downwards. Ah-hui comes to a late realization that he is a victim of his materialistic "Me" and desires his personality to return.

In the final part of the novel, Ah-hui, plagued by loneliness and isolation, starts writing letters to "Myself." He is convinced that he will see "myself" again if he writes more, but the latter never responds. Beset by chronic illnesses, Ah-hui is put into a nursing home by his son. He starts to hear the voice of "Myself" again as the two personalities reconcile on their deathbed.

Significance and Remarks:

The author laments the marginalization of Chinese Language and the effects it has on Chinese-educated graduates. This is a recurring motif in Singapore sinophone literature.

"Me" constantly grumbles to "Myself" that it was a mistake to major in Chinese—not only does the decision hamper their career prospects, they are also relegated to the status of a second-class citizen upon graduation. With English being the dominant language, the study of Chinese is considered impractical and pointless, even for those who see it as their "mother" tongue. Many members of the English-educated intelligentsia accept this mindset and do not question it.

The heart of the novel lies in the philosophical search for personal identity amidst the perpetual antagonism between two entirely distinct personalities—the hedonistic "Me" and the moralistic/idealistic "Myself." The author adopts a Freudian mirror imagery in his representation of the struggle for dominance between Ah-hui's id and superego; in so doing, the author exhibits the psychoanalytic dimension of Ah-hui's search for his lost identity and moral values.

In the first part of the novel, Ah-hui engages in a heated argument with his reflection. This provides insight into the subconscious of the pragmatic "Me" and the moralistic "Myself". Later in the novel, "Me" realizes that "Myself" continues to haunt him by reappearing in his mirror whenever he cheats on his wife. The former, in a sign of guilt and evasion, will avoid standing for prolonged periods in front of a mirror. However, after his business fails, "Me" fills his flat with mirrors—in the living room, the bathroom, the kitchen and the bedroom and makes regular visits to the Chinese bookstore owned by his ex-colleague Zhiqiang. The mirrors and the visits to the bookstore suggest a subconscious longing for "Myself," who is an avid reader of the Chinese writer Lu Xun. At the bookstore, Zhiqiang assures Ah-hui that desires are not sins per se and are only evil when coupled with the hunger for power. If not blinded by greed or fame, an intellectual's self can remain intact.

The novel also invites further reflection on the value of existence. What are we if we are without selves? Who can we be if our superego is non-existent? With copious references to Kant, Heidegger, Nietzsche, and Sartre, *Trivialities About Me and Myself* serves as a timely reminder concerning the modern imperative to scrutinize one's own ethical system and existential conditions of being.

Potential areas of comparative analysis:

Traditional vs Modern Values, Singapore's History, Existentialism, Chinese Educated Singaporeans, Identity and Self, Id, Ego, Superego, Philosophy

我与我自己的二三事
TRIVIALITIES ABOUT ME AND MYSELF

主要语言： 中文

次要语言： -

翻译版本： Trivialities About Me and Myself

页数： 248

作者： 英培安

出版年份： 2006

出版社： 唐山出版社

人物简介：

阿辉拥有双重人格——"我"和"我自己"。小时候，"我"和"我自己"形影不离、和谐共处，但长大后，两者的价值观产生冲突，最后"我"选择遗弃"我自己"。"我"利欲熏心、贪恋女色，最后生意失败、妻离子散。"我"不断地写信给"我自己"忏悔，希望能得到对方的原谅，期盼"我自己"能回到"我"身旁。

文本概要：

《我与我自己的二三事》透过三个部分，讲述"我"和"自己"从童年到临终前的经历。

在第一个部分，阿辉阐述"我"和"自己"价值观上的冲突如何导致"自己"离"我"而去。尽管体内住着两种人格，"我"和"我自己"自小便能和谐共处，每件事都能达成协议，从不争吵。但当阿辉进入青春期时，他们开始闹变扭。不久，"我"便期待身边除了"我自己"，还能有另一个倾诉的对象。

阿辉后悔选择在大学修读中文系，他认为这是"我"与"我自己"之间意识形态产生对立的主要原因。内向、独来独往，自命清高的"我自己"是个活在精神世界、渴望献身教育的理想主义者。"我"是个现实主义者，期待凭一纸文凭脱离穷籍，因此坚决不当老师，拿一份微薄的薪水。"我"与"我自己"各退一步，"我"加入报社当华文报记者。

加入职场后，“我”与“我自己”的冲突进一步加剧。“我自己”喜欢离群索居，浑然不知自己活在一个利益至上的唯物主义社会，而“我”在亲眼目睹父母因钱而起争执后，下定决心要摆脱贫困，提升生活品质，品味生活中的美好事物。尽管“我自己”认为新闻从业员必须拥有自己的立场，必须报道事实真相，但考虑到事业发展，“我”选择攀附权贵。“我自己”强烈的正义感让“我”的日子并不好过，不切实际、专横霸道的道德标准也让“我”喘不过气来。在“我自己”成为事业的绊脚石前，“我”和“我自己”当面对质，分道扬镳。

事业上，“我”平步青云；生活中，“我”跻身上流，有了新的社交圈子，和富家女洁仪结婚。尽管家境富裕，洁仪选择创业、成立广告公司，靠自己努力闯出一番事业。“我”的生活阔绰、奢侈，肆无忌惮地满足“我”的欲望，违背道德标准，失去方向。“我”和洁仪的价值体系南辕北辙，加上“我”和洁仪的私人秘书莉莉等其他女性发生婚外情，“我”和洁仪最后以离婚收场。

洁仪把广告公司交给莉莉后离开新加坡，而“我”也辞掉工作和莉莉一起经营公司。为了名利，“我”开始向多个文化和学术组织捐赠款项，提升了知名度，也赢得“儒商”的封号。事业上，“我”在餐饮业建立特许经营权，也成立了房地产经纪公司，大幅拓展商业帝国。1997年，金融风暴给“我”沉重的一击，因缺乏流动资金，“我”的业务螺旋式下降，公司面临倒闭的命运。“我”终于意识到这一切都是因“我”的唯物主义而起，“我”想起“我自己”，“我”给“我自己”写信，相信写得越多，就能看见“我自己”回到“我”身边，但“我自己”从未回信。临终之际，“我”在病床上听见“我自己”的声音，彼此实现和解。

重点与备注：

作者在小说中对中文在新加坡的边缘化和其对华校毕业生的影响表示哀叹，这也是新华文学中一个常浮现的命题。“我”不断地对“我自己”埋怨，选择中文系是错误的决定。它不仅阻碍就业发展，也在毕业后沦为二等公民。虽然华人说母语原本就是再理所当然不过的事，但英语仍是新加坡的主要用语。直至今时今日，国家的精英分子仍对中文抱有根深蒂固的误解，认为学习中文不切实际且毫无意义。

小说的核心在于，在现实主义的“我”和理想主义的“我自己”长期的纠缠中，主人翁阿辉如何透过哲学性的思考寻找自我的身份认同。贯穿小说的镜子是“我自己”(阿辉的“超我”)的隐喻表征。作者巧妙的利用镜子刻画“我”和“我自己”争夺主导权的斗争，并从精神分析的维度（psychoanalytic dimension）展现“我”寻找“我自己”的过程。小说的第一部分，“我”和“我自己”对质，使读者了解“我”和“我自己”的潜意识。当“我”出轨时，“我”发现“我自己”阴魂不散出现在“我”镜子里。愧疚的“我”为了避开“我自己”试图缩短站在镜子前的时间。生意失败后，“我”在家里的客厅、厨房、房间和厕所等角落放置镜子，期待“我自己”某一天会从镜子里走出来。

无独有偶，“我”的前同事志强所经营的中文书店和镜子有着异曲同工的功能。“我自己”钟爱鲁迅，“我”希望可以在书店和“我自己”重逢。志强向“我”保证，欲望本身并不是“恶”，唯有当“权利”伴随“欲望”时，“欲望”才会变质，成为万恶的根源。因此，智者不会失去自我，因为他们从不被贪婪和名利蒙蔽双眼。如果我们失去自我，那我们要如何定义我们自己？如果我们的“超我”不存在，那我们是谁？《我与我自己的二三事》大量引用西方哲学家的理论，如康德、海德格尔、尼采、萨特等思想，提醒我们内省，检验引导我们的道德体系，以及存在的本质。

潜在的比较文学分析：

传统价值观、新加坡历史、语言政策、存在主义、新加坡华校生、自我与认同、本我、自我、超我、哲学

TAWASSUL (INTERCESSION)

Primary Language: Malay

Secondary Language: No

Translation Available: Intercession

Number of Pages: 160

Author: Isa Kamari

Year of Publication: 2002

Publisher: Pustaka Nasional

Characterisation Notes:

The female protagonist Syan is a botanist. Like her grandfather Hasyr, Syan is an ardent empiricist and is undecided on matters of religion and faith. Hasyr is an anthropologist most notable for his book *Native World*, in which he analyses the lives of the Imorot people of the Tuwau Valley.

Text Synopsis:

Hasyr is treated as an apostate by his family as his anthropological research leads him away from Islamic teachings. He is forced to divorce his pregnant wife and he moves to live permanently with the Imorot people in the valley. Hasyr is introduced to Anisa and Hira by the chieftain of the tribe. Anisa gives birth to seven female babies in a row, and is considered to be cursed. She receives in-vitro fertilization treatment despite her tribe's protests and gives birth to Hira. Hira, known as the prophet Muhammad's clone, will rise to become the next spiritual leader of the Imorot people. In the interim, Hasyr marries Nutaib's young sister and they have a son Hijaz. On his deathbed, Hasyr tasks Hijaz to find his granddaughter Syan, who happens to be investigating Hasyr's whereabouts. She takes a helicopter to the Tuwau Valley and unravels Hasyr's mysterious past.

Significance and Remarks:

Tawassul is narrated in first person and takes the perspectives of Syan, Hijaz, Anisa, Hasyr, Nutaib, and Hira.

As the novel opens, Syan reads Hasyr's book and learns about the faith of the Imorot people. The Imorot people do not believe in science or religion (Islam); instead, they worship the 300 wooden and stone sculptures housed within a 10-meter-wide cube within the Valley. They pray to the sculptures for good health, peace and prosperity. Next, the author narrates, at great length, the birth and ascendance of Hira to the leadership of the Imorot people through the perspectives of Hasyr, Anisa and the previous chieftain Nutaib. Initially a non-believer in religion, Hasyr converts upon witnessing Hira's feats and even pens a hagiography/ biography of Hira—*Intercession*—at the invitation of Anisa. Hasyr sees the book as a sequel to his earlier work *Native World.*

This novel invites controversy in its portrayal of Hira as the cloned prophet Muhammad. Many Muslims, in history as well as in the present, hope that the prophet Muhammad will come before them and give them true guidance. Realistically, such a wish cannot be met (since the prophet passed away a long time ago) but the modern technology of genetic cloning allows one to imagine a situation where he is resurrected. Through a work of literature, the author explores question deeply significant to modern Islam: is Hira the historical figure prophet Muhammad if both are biologically identical? If we directly transpose the prophet to modern society, how would he react to modern challenges? Would it be appropriate for believers to completely submit to the direction of the prophet under such circumstances?

Potential areas of comparative analysis:

Islam, Muslim, Guidance, Cloning, Sense of Identity, Religion, Superstition, Science, Empiricism,

TAWASSUL (INTERCESSION)

主要语言： 马来文

次要语言： -

翻译版本： Intercession

页数： 160

作者： 伊沙 · 卡马里（Isa Kamari）

出版年份： 2002

出版社： Pustaka Nasional

人物简介：

女主角茜妍（Syan）是一名植物学家，她和祖父哈希尔（Hasyr）一样信仰科学，认为一切知识都得通过经验而获得，并在经验中得到验证，因此两人都对宗教迷信思想持保留态度。哈希尔是一名人类学家，著有《土著的世界》(马来原文：Peribumi Alam，英文原文：Native World）一书，是他常年研究住在图瓦山谷（Tuwau Valley）的原住民依莫洛特（Imorot）一族的成果结晶。

文本概要：

哈希尔因为研究人类学，渐渐偏离伊斯兰教的教诲，因此被家族视为叛教之人。在被迫与身怀六甲的妻子离婚后，哈希尔来到山谷研究原住民族群依莫洛特的生活，并在首领努太伊布（Nutaib）的介绍下认识了阿妮莎（Anisa）和希拉（Hira）。阿妮莎的家族连续7代受诅咒般似的只生下被族人唾弃的女婴，为光宗耀祖，阿妮莎不顾反对到国外接受胚胎移植手术，成功生下西拉，即先知默罕默德的克隆体和依莫洛特族人的精神领袖。哈希尔在山谷里娶了努太伊布的妹妹为妻，婚后生下儿子西亚兹（Hijaz）。临终前，哈希尔嘱咐儿子，一定要找到他的孙女茜妍。与此同时，为找寻祖父的足迹，茜妍不顾父母的强烈反对，独自一人乘直升机来到山谷，一步步解开祖父神秘的过往。

重点与备注：

Tawassul以第一人称的叙事，从茜妍、西亚兹以及依莫洛特族人的视角逐步揭开故事的面纱。小说开篇，茜妍从祖父的著作中初步了解依莫洛特族人的信仰：他们即不信宗教也不相信科学，在山谷中间用石头筑造一座高10米的方形大楼，供奉300多尊木雕、石雕神像，向祂们祈求健康、平安以及财富。作者花了大篇幅从哈希尔、阿妮莎和努太伊布的视角描述希拉的诞生、如何来到山谷并取代努太伊布领袖的位置，成为族人精神领袖的过程。作为非信徒，哈希尔对宗教信仰一直抱有怀疑态度，但在亲眼看见希拉后，无法无视他的存在，甚至接受阿妮莎的邀请，为希拉书写自传——Intercession。哈西尔更把自传视为他第一本著作的续集，进一步神话希拉的身份。

小说最具争议的莫过于作者所创造的克隆版先知穆罕默德——希拉。长久以来，穆斯林一直希望能在先知穆罕默德的教导下得到真正的指引。严格来说，这绝对不可能，毕竟先知穆罕默德已去世超过1400多年，然而克隆技术的发展使复制人成为可能。顺水推舟，作者利用克隆技术为一种文学手段探讨一个重要的命题：从生物学上来看，希拉或许具有先知穆罕默德的所有特征，但历史上的人物被克隆重生以后是否和本体相同？如果把先知放置在现今社会，祂又会如何应对当代的挑战，而对伊斯兰教的信徒而言，全盘接受先知的教诲又否契合时宜？

潜在的比较文学研究分析：

伊斯兰教、穆斯林、指引、克隆技术、身份认同、宗教、迷信、科学、经验主义

INDEX